The Soul of Mbira

Perspectives on Southern Africa

The Soul of Mbira

Music and Traditions

of the Shona People of Zimbabwe

PAUL BERLINER

University of California Press
Berkeley   Los Angeles   London

University of California Press
Berkeley and Los Angeles, California

University of California Press, Ltd.
London, England

ISBN 0-520-03315-9
Library of Congress Catalog Card Number: 76-24578
Printed in the United States of America

Designed by Theo Jung

1 2 3 4 5 6 7 8 9

To my parents, Ann and Joseph,
my brother and sister, Carl and Nancy,
and to the people of Zimbabwe

Contents

List of Figures and Tables

List of Musical Examples

Note on Orthography

The orthography used for writing Shona words in this work is that adopted by the Shona Language Committee in 1967 and outlined by Fortune (*Standard Guide to Shona Spelling*).

vh	as English v	b	implosive when used initially
v	bilabial fricative		
n'	velar stop as in English "sung"	dh	as English d
		zvi	sibilant voiced fricative
d	implosive when used initially	r	rolled

In addition, the vowels of the Shona words are pronounced approximately as follows:

a	as in English "father"	o	as in English "no"
e	as in English "make"	u	as in English "smooth"
i	as in English "meet"		

Preface

The purpose of this book is to draw attention to the mbira, a uniquely African contribution to the world of music. Although it is one of the most well-established and popular melodic instruments in black Africa, the mbira has rarely received the attention in the West that it deserves. Many Westerners have the limited view that African music consists entirely of drumming. They are unaware that the melodic traditions of African music are rich and varied, having as important a history and as profound a meaning in certain cultures as the magnificent drumming ensembles have in others.

The Shona people of Zimbabwe (Rhodesia) are among those people in Africa who place a special significance and value on the mbira. Their mbira players have developed an intricate polyphonic music which epitomizes the beauty and subtlety of the music of African melodic instruments. An ancient instrument, the mbira has had an important function in Shona culture for hundreds of years. It continues today, as it has in the past, to play a central role in the traditional religious experience of the people. For these reasons the study of Shona mbira music can contribute a great deal to the Westerner's understanding of sophisticated melodic African music.

Along with the recent growth of interest in the United States in African culture in general, there has been a particular increase of interest in the mbira. Westernized versions of the mbira are widely available in music stores. Popular groups have released recordings in which they have adapted these mbira-like instruments to their own music. Interest in the mbira, however, has failed to create a body of information readily available to people interested in the traditional instruments. While Americans appreciate what exposure they have had to the Westernized mbira through popular recordings, they have little knowledge of the authentic African instruments from which the commercial items are derived. Little information is conveniently acces- xiii sible even on the most basic questions concerning the instrument's background and cultural context. By providing readers with an introduction to Shona mbira, this book represents an attempt to fill this gap.

The present work stems from research conducted over the past seven years, during which I have been a student of mbira music working with African musicians both in the United States and in Zimbabwe. I first heard and succumbed to the beauty of Shona mbira music in 1969, when in the course of graduate studies in ethnomusicology at Wesleyan University I heard a performance by Dumisani Maraire, a Shona lecturer in African music, then at the University of Washington, Seattle. I was overwhelmed by the experience of the music and approached Maraire, who, sensing the way in which his music had affected me, kindly offered to take me on as an mbira student. After two years of periodic study and performance of the type of mbira Maraire played, I decided, with his encouragement, to travel to Zimbabwe for a year, where I would be able to study the advanced performance of the music in its cultural context.

When I arrived in Zimbabwe in 1971 I had the good fortune to meet Erick Mandizha of the Rhodesia Broadcasting Corporation. He was supportive of my interest and invited me to give an mbira performance on a weekly mbira music program that he produced. The broadcast proved to be significant by providing me with important feedback from the Shona community. Many listeners called the station and expressed pleasure that someone from so far away would take a serious interest in their music. In addition, some skeptics actually challenged the radio announcer, insisting that the performance they had heard had really been given by a Shona musician. These comments from listeners reflected Dumisani Maraire's great skill as a teacher as much as they encouraged me as a student of the music. The broadcast also served as an important introduction for me in the townships and villages. When I later travelled through the country, many people remembered having heard me on the radio. This opened doors which might otherwise have remained closed for me during 1971/72, when the European and African communities were bitterly polarized in Zimbabwe.

Shortly after the broadcast, through my association with Maraire and with Mandizha I met Hakurotwi Mude, the featured singer and leader of the famed mbira ensemble, *Mhuri yekwaRwizi*, a group I greatly admired. Mude was sympathetic to my interest in studying the large *mbira dzavadzimu* performed by his ensemble, and he warmly adopted me as part of his family of musicians. I became close friends with his mbira players, Cosmas Magaya and Luken Pasipamire, and soon I began taking mbira lessons and performing with them daily. Throughout the year, I travelled with the members of *Mhuri yekwaRwizi*, staying at their villages, visiting the homes of other great mbira players, and attending religious rituals at which their group or others performed.

After many months of study and practice, when I had developed enough strength and proficiency as a performer of the *mbira dzavadzimu*, I had one of the most exciting and rewarding experiences of my research in Zimbabwe: I was invited to perform with *Mhuri yekwaRwizi* at spirit possession ceremonies. Seated among the members of the group, I had the opportunity of experiencing directly the tremendous intensity of the music that accompanied such events. I came away with a lasting impression of the profound nature of the traditions associated with mbira music and the important role which the mbira has played in Shona culture.

Besides working with the members of *Mhuri yekwaRwizi* in Zimbabwe, I studied with a number of other mbira players. I learned a great deal from Ephat Mujuru, an outstanding player of the *mbira dzavadzimu* with a command of a great variety of playing styles. Although I concentrated my research on the *mbira dzavadzimu*, the main mbira of the Zezuru people, for comparative purposes I also studied the fundamentals of three other types of Shona mbira: the *ndimba* and the *njari* with Simon Mashoko, and the *matepe* with Garage Nyamudya. Cosmas Magaya and Luken Pasipamire assisted me in this research.

My interest in developing proficiency as an mbira player in Zimbabwe was connected with the broader goal of carrying out an ethnomusicological study of the mbira. This multidisciplinary endeavor involved research on related cultural aspects of the music such as its history, its folklore, the poetry which accompanied the music, the process of learning the mbira, the meaning of the mbira in the lives of its musicians, the role the music played in Shona culture, and analysis of the music itself.

I returned to Zimbabwe during the summers of 1974 and 1975. These trips were useful for a number of reasons. They provided me with an opportunity to crosscheck my earlier findings and to probe further into questions that had arisen during xv the interim. Since I had completed a rough draft of this work based on my earlier research, I sought to subject the manuscript to the scrutiny of the musicians who had shown an interest in my writing and had contributed to my understanding of mbira music, to be sure that I had interpreted their remarks correctly and had not inadvertently misrepresented their views. I felt this was especially important since I had chosen in my presentation of the material to quote musicians frequently, allowing them to speak for themselves and acting as their interpreter. Except where indicated to the contrary, the source of all direct quotations from musicians given in this book is personal communication during the years 1971–1975.

The return trips also allowed me to observe the process of change within the community of musicians with whom I had worked during the first year. Finally, since I had continued to progress as an mbira student during the years I had been away, when I returned to Africa my teachers felt that I was ready to learn more advanced mbira pieces and variations, and these afforded me insight into some technical aspects of mbira music which had eluded me as a beginning student. Thus, my research during the summers of 1974 and 1975 provided me with the final material on which this work rests.

This book tries to analyze mbira music in its broad cultural context and to give the reader a feeling for the significance of the music among the Shona. Just as it would be difficult to gain insight into the meaning of any music divorced from its culture, it would be equally difficult to develop a real understanding and appreciation of the music itself without reference to recorded musical examples.

With this consideration in mind I coordinated the present work with two albums of mbira music that I produced for Nonesuch Records' World Explorer Series from field recordings made in Zimbabwe: *The Soul of Mbira* (H-72054) and *Shona Mbira Music* (H-72077). Footnote references to specific musical examples on the records appear throughout the book. The records illustrate mbira performances in a variety of contexts, including spirit possession ceremonies. They exemplify the performance styles of the musicians whose biographies appear in Chapter 9. The appendix contains complete song texts and translations of pieces on *The Soul of Mbira* album. These records used together with this work can help bridge the tremendous gap between

words about music and the experience of live music itself, and can provide the reader with an appreciation of the beauty and power of Shona mbira music.

Finally, throughout this work I have used the African name Zimbabwe instead of Rhodesia. This is appropriate because the book deals with a traditional African art pre-dating by hundreds of years the colonization of the area by Europeans and bearing little or no relationship to the European culture of the country. Furthermore, Zimbabwe is the name that reflects the nationalist aspirations of the country's Africans.

Acknowledgments

There are always many obstacles facing an investigator doing field research in an alien culture. For this reason I owe a great deal to my Shona mbira teachers who not only exposed me to the rigors of their art and passed the gift of mbira music on to me as their disciple, but in so doing put me in a position to collect data that might otherwise have been inaccessible to me. I am especially indebted to the following musicians with whom I studied the mbira directly: Dumisani Maraire, who first inspired and directed my interest in mbira music; Cosmas Magaya and Ephat Mujuru, who were not only excellent teachers but whose help as research assistants was invaluable during my field work in Zimbabwe; Hakurotwi Mude, who welcomed me as part of his family of musicians and invited me to travel with his outstanding ensemble, *Mhuri yekwaRwizi*; and John Kunaka, Luken Pasipamire, and Simon Mashoko.

I also owe gratitude to many other Shona people with whom I came in contact during my travels to Zimbabwe. They include the family members of mbira players who assisted me in translating Shona song texts, and a multitude of Shona people whom I met only in passing but who contributed in significant ways to my understanding of Shona music. Many took time off from their chores to discuss their reactions to an mbira broadcast or to relay a folktale about the mbira remembered from childhood. Because of the welcome assistance I received in the course of my field research, I regard this book as essentially the product of a collaboration rather than an individual effort. For the degree to which I have been successful in my goal of presenting a picture of Shona mbira music true to its own traditions, I am indebted to all those mentioned above.

Of all the people to whom I am indebted in the preparation of this manuscript for publication, there is one to whom I wish to call special attention. My friend and colleague, folklorist Linda Morley, not only encouraged me in my research from the earliest days of the study, but also contributed greatly to this work, bringing to it her keen and sensitive editorial pen. I warmly acknowledge her assistance.

Because of the multidisciplinary nature of this work, I was fortunate to have friends and colleagues in various fields who looked over portions of this manuscript from the perspective of their own disciplines and made valuable suggestions for the revision of this work. They are: in music, Lois Anderson, Peter Gena, Hewitt Pantaleoni, Klaus Wachsmann, and Jeanne Bamberger; in African languages, George Fortune and Aaron Hodza; in African history, David Beach and Oliver Pollak; and in anthropology, Marshall Murphree. In addition, I am very grateful to several ethnomusicologists who worked in the field of Shona music before me: Andrew Tracey, John Kaemmer, Olof Axelsson, and Robert Kauffman. At various stages of my research I benefited from conversations with each of them.

I am indebted to several members of the ethnomusicology faculty at Wesleyan University, Connecticut, for their guidance and assistance in the early research on Shona mbira music which culminated in my Ph.D. dissertation (1974) under their direction: Theodore Grame, David McAllester, Mark Slobin, Gen'ichi Tsuge, and Abraham Adzenyah.

I owe special thanks to Shona language expert Aaron Hodza and to musicians Cosmas and Simon Magaya and Ephat Mujuru, who read through the entire manuscript and offered their critical observations.

Over the years on which I have been working on this study I have greatly appreciated the encouragement I received from a number of personal friends and colleagues. They include my parents, my brother and sister, Martha Campbell, historian Stanlake Samkange, and folklorist Kenneth Goldstein.

I would like to express my gratitude to a number of institutions and foundations which at various times supported the research on which this work is based: the Martha Baird Rockefeller Fund for Music, the John Anson Kittredge Educational Fund, the SUNY Research Foundation, the SUC Faculty Research Fund, and the University Research Committees of the University of Rhodesia and of Northwestern University. I owe a special debt to the African Studies Program at Northwestern University, under the direction of Abraham Demoz, for financial and moral support during the final stages of the preparation of this book for publication.

I am grateful to a number of institutions which contributed photographs illustrating mbira outside of Zimbabwe: the National Archives of Rhodesia; the Smithsonian Institution, Washington, D.C.; the Museum für Völkerkunde, Berlin; Musée Royal de l'Afrique Centrale, Tervuren; the Horniman Museum, London; the Livingstone Museum, Livingstone; and the Royal Geographic Society, London. Several of these photographs appeared earlier in an article by Bertil Söderberg in *African Arts* (Summer 1972) and appear here with kind permission of the editor and Mr. Söderberg. In addition, I wish to express thanks to my friend, Thomas Stewart, whose photographs of Shona mbira, *hosho*, and a stitched resonator appear here, and to Paul Attwell, who photographed the sculpture of the mbira player which illustrates this work. I am grateful to the International Library of African Music for allowing me to photograph the *mbira dzavaNdau* in their collection, and to the Hauptstaatsarchiv Stuttgart, for providing me with a photograph of Carl Mauch's nineteenth-century drawing of an *mbira dzavadzimu* for reproduction in this work.

I would like to thank Harold Averill and Alexander Katz for their assistance in facilitating communication with Shona musicians during those periods when I was not in Zimbabwe.

Portions of Chapters 6 and 8 of this work were previously published as articles in *Ethnomusicology* (1976) and *African Music* (1975/76). The editors of these journals kindly gave permission to use that material here.

Finally, I owe gratitude to Barbara White for the preparation of the typescript.

1.
Introduction

*What is with an old man is not to be
asked for; he gives what he likes.*

Shona Proverb

When I first went to Zimbabwe in 1971, I was very excited
about the prospects of studying the mbira in its cultural setting. I wanted to learn as much as I could about mbira music:
its structure, its history, its powerful role in traditional Shona
culture. During the two previous years in which I had collected
background information about the mbira, I had become particularly intrigued by the apparent metaphoric relationship between the structure of mbira music and the structure of the
instrument itself. It was through investigating this relationship
that I learned one of the most important lessons of my field research in Africa.

I had come across two differing, though possibly related,
pieces of information that led me to this question. First, my
former mbira teacher, Dumisani Maraire, had described the
keys on his *karimba*-type mbira in terms personifying their relationship to each other and to the instrument as a whole. He
called the lowest pitch on the instrument the "father"; the pitch
an octave above that, the "mother"; and the pitch an octave
above that one, the "child." According to this conceptualization,
the rest of the keys comprised four similar "families" of keys,
each with a "mother" and "child" or "twin children" (two keys
with the same pitch). There was one key on the instrument that 1

did not belong to any of these "families": that one Maraire called the "black sheep" or "independent note." Maraire's system had direct application in teaching students about the structure of mbira music and the elaboration of a piece. He pointed out that many of the pieces were based on two phrases, one seeming to "ask a question," the other appearing to "answer the question." Within this framework the "father" pitch served as the tonic of the piece and the "black sheep" pitch reappeared in each cycle at the end of the answering phrase. This created a tension which was resolved in the next repetition of the "question." Furthermore, Maraire frequently regarded the substitution of one pitch for another in the same family as an acceptable variation in the development of a piece. Maraire's approach proved very effective as a device for teaching the mbira to Westerners. In carrying out research in Zimbabwe I wanted to learn whether this "family" approach applied to different types of Shona mbira and whether other mbira players viewed the instrument and its music in the same personified terms.

A second reason for my interest was that I had recently read a fascinating, though controversial, article claiming that there were many deep levels of symbolism associated with a particular type of mbira, the *mbila dzamadeza* played by the Lemba and Venda of South Africa, which was morphologically identical to the *mbira dzavadzimu*.[1] The study claimed that the features of the *mbila* symbolized the entire structure of a village as well as the cosmological teachings and "laws" associated with the initiation ceremony of the Venda. Because of evidence that the *mbila* originally derived from the Shona *mbira dzavadzimu*, that the Lemba use the *mbila* for ancestor worship as do the Shona, and that the Lemba had adopted part of the *mbira dzavadzimu's* repertory,[2] I was curious to know if the symbolism ascribed to the *mbila* would also be associated with the *mbira dzavadzimu*.

Whenever I met new performers in Zimbabwe I asked them about the names of various features of their instruments, hoping that this might lead either to some insight into the way in which the musicians viewed the structure of their music or, possibly, to broader symbolic associations reflecting other important aspects of Shona culture. During most of my first year in Zimbabwe the results of this line of inquiry were not very fruitful. Some of the younger musicians did not know of any names for different mbira keys, and although older performers used a few

2   different terms to describe the keys on their instruments they

only signified a general differentiation of groups of pitches according to register (high, low, and middle).

Toward the end of the year, however, after having attained some proficiency as a student of the *mbira dzavadzimu*, several of the musicians with whom I had been travelling suggested that I should meet a great virtuoso and "grand old man" of the mbira, Mubayiwa Bandambira (Plate 50), who was living in a village up in the hills of a remote section of Mondoro. I was excited about this prospect not only because Bandambira had been a revered figure to many of the mbira players I had met, but because as a member of the oldest living generation of mbira players Bandambira was likely to have a great knowledge of the history and oral traditions associated with the mbira.

After making prior arrangements for a visit, several mbira players and I travelled to Bandambira's village and received a formal welcome. Our mbira ensemble performed for Bandambira's village, and in return Bandambira and his son performed for us. With permission from Bandambira, I recorded his performance. Throughout the afternoon we listened together to the playback of the recordings and talked about a variety of subjects related to the mbira and Shona culture. As the day drew to an end, I casually asked Bandambira whether the keys of the mbira had any particular names. He thought for a while and then said simply, "No, I have never heard of such a thing." My question having been answered by the great master of mbira music, we exchanged ritual handshakes and polite goodbyes, and I headed back for Salisbury with my companions.

It was several years before I was able to return to Zimbabwe again. During this period, I carried on a one-way correspondence with Bandambira. *The Soul of Mbira* album produced from my field tapes featured a solo performance by Bandambira, and I sent him a copy of the record along with a royalty check. When in 1974 I finally returned to Zimbabwe for further research, I reestablished contacts with my former teachers and made arrangements to visit Bandambira once again. When I arrived at Bandambira's village with a few other mbira players, Bandambira greeted me and thanked me as a "man of my word" for having sent him the record and the check. We exchanged mbira performances, and before the day ended I chanced to ask him once again whether he had ever heard of the mbira keys having names. Again he thought for a while, then said, "Yes, four of them do." I hid my surprise, and as he played them and 3 announced their names, I recorded each of the four keys. Then we listened to recordings of mbira music together and I took photographs of his immediate family and the members of his village. As the sun began to set, I thanked Bandambira for his time and his information and we parted.

I returned to America shortly thereafter, eager to examine the information he had given me. If only four of the keys had names, I wondered, did this imply some hierarchy of importance among the pitches? Were these four keys more central to the structure of the music than others? I studied a large body of transcribed musical examples for the function of the particular keys that Bandambira had named and discovered to my disappointment that the situation was very ambiguous. It was not clear to me why Bandambira's four keys would necessarily be more important than the others. To check further, I listened to the original recording of my conversation with Bandambira and discovered, to my increased dismay, that as a result of background noise and the presence of a loud overtone which competed with the fundamental pitch of one of the keys, I could not be perfectly sure which key Bandambira had referred to on his instrument when he had announced its name. With this much uncertainty, I set the whole project aside and decided that it would be fruitless to proceed further without more information.

The following summer, I had the opportunity to try to obtain this information when I returned to Zimbabwe for a third research visit. While I had not corresponded with Bandambira directly about this matter, I had tried to continue our relationship by sending him prints of the photographs I had taken in his village, as well as a second copy of *The Soul of Mbira* record, since I had noticed that his original copy had become worn.

Because my summer research schedule was an extremely busy one, I asked another mbira teacher of mine, Ephat Mujuru, if he would see Bandambira on my behalf and help make arrangements for me to visit him before I left the country. Mujuru was happy to assist, because Bandambira was his former teacher and Mujuru considered him a good friend. I asked Mujuru to convey my apologies to Bandambira for having confused some of the information given me last year, and asked him to check with Bandambira about which of the keys on the *mbira dzavadzimu* had names. Mujuru returned the next evening, having made arrangements for me to meet Bandambira again, and to my astonishment he brought with him an entire sheet of paper filled

4

with the names of mbira keys. Very excited about this, I looked at the list carefully, and noticed that it was full of inconsistencies. Bandambira mentioned some keys more than once, assigning different names to them, and other keys he had not mentioned at all. It was clear that my only hope for working out this apparent confusion was to discuss the matter again with Bandambira.

As Mujuru and I travelled together once again to visit Bandambira, I began to feel awkward, recalling an old Shona proverb: "What is with an old man is not to be asked for; he gives what he likes." Perhaps it was rude, according to the mores of traditional Shona culture, for a younger person like myself to "ask of" an old man in the first place, and here I was returning to ask an old man the same question for a third time.

When we arrived at Bandambira's village the welcome given us was characteristically warm. There did not seem to be any undue notice of the purpose of my visit. The mbira players and I spent some time relaxing with the villagers. People thanked me for sending the photographs, and brought them out to show us. We performed for the village and Bandambira performed for us. When the time seemed appropriate, I apologized to Bandambira for having to ask him about the keys again, explaining that my Shona language skills were rudimentary and that I sometimes failed to understand things when they were first explained to me. He smiled kindly and said that he understood this and that it was quite all right for me to ask him again. With that, we sat down beside each other. I set up my tape recorder as the whole village gathered around us to listen.

When everyone was seated, I thanked Bandambira for the list of names of mbira keys that he had sent to me through Mujuru, but added that I was still somewhat confused about which name stood for which key and asked him if he would please go over this with me. Bandambira thought for a moment and then said that this would be possible. He pointed to each key on his instrument, stopping occasionally to think about a particular key's name before reciting it aloud. As he pointed to each key I wrote down its name and designated its position on a chart that I had sketched. After he had named each of the keys on the left side of the instrument and several on the right, I began to crosscheck a few keys at random, to make sure I had understood Bandambira correctly. At each attempt on my part, however, Bandambira invariably shook his head, saying "*Aiwa* [No]! That one

5

is called [such and such]." Therefore, as I checked each key, I crossed out its name on the sheet and began drawing arrows to the correct names in the margin. It was not long before my entire diagram was a practically illegible entangled web of arrows and crisscrossed words.

Beginning to feel discouraged again, I stopped writing and tore off the sheet of paper. Mustering up my courage, I apologized profusely to Bandambira, explaining that I had made many mistakes. "If it is not too much trouble for you," I asked, "could I please ask you about the keys once more?" Bandambira paused, and finally said, "If you like, you can ask me again." As the village looked on with keen interest, we proceeded across the keyboard of the mbira for a second time. Bandambira recited the names of individual mbira keys and I wrote them down on a clean sheet of paper. It was not long before familiar inconsistencies arose. This time around the names of some of the keys differed from those that Bandambira had given to the same keys during the previous recounting. As confusion mounted, I tried to crosscheck several keys, with the same result as before: my diagram became a web of contradictions and corrections.

Wrestling to reconcile my worry over the impropriety of repeated questioning and my intuitive feeling that there was important material here if I could only come to understand it, I apologized even more profusely than before for my lack of comprehension and managed to ask Bandambira if he would explain the names of the mbira keys to me again. Bandambira, whose patience I could not help but feel was beginning to wear rather thin, thought for what seemed a long time and finally declared that I could ask him one more time about this matter if I wished to. A third time, then, we proceeded across the keyboard of mbira dzavadzimu. I felt a little relieved about having one more chance to straighten out the problem. The feeling was short-lived, however, because the same thing happened all over again. Although I tried not to show my discouragement outwardly, I gave up inside. I could not face asking Bandambira to repeat himself another time. Furthermore, the sun was setting. The wind had picked up and sand was half-burying my recording equipment and making us all uncomfortable.

Resigning myself to the fact that there was no way I could figure out Bandambira's system at this time, I made a slight move to turn off my recorder in preparation for concluding my visit. Sensing my intention, Bandambira gestured for me to re-

6

main seated. He then smiled and announced to the village, "Well, it seems to me that this young man is serious after all. I suppose I can tell him the truth now." Then to my utter amazement and relief, Bandambira proceeded to lay out his entire system clearly and unambiguously. As several of the villagers sighed with approval, Bandambira named each key carefully for my benefit, revealing a totally consistent and precise set of classifications.[a]

After a warm parting from Bandambira's village, a final touch was added later that evening when Mujuru and I returned to Salisbury and listened to recordings of the day's deliberations. Although it was too subtle for me to have picked up at the time, the villagers themselves had figured in my interchange with Bandambira. At various points in the discussion, when Bandambira was considering whether or not to divulge to me the correct information, people were whispering in the background, "No, don't tell him; it's our secret!" or "Oh, tell him; he's our friend now," much like a Greek chorus trying to influence the protagonist.

I will long remember the lesson that Bandambira and the members of his village taught me about field research technique and about the nature of knowledge as privileged information. As implied by the Shona proverb, the elders who are the guardians of an oral tradition do not treat their knowledge lightly. Rather, "they give what they like." Moreover, they give only the amount of information they believe to be appropriate to the situation and to the persons involved. In my own relationship with Bandambira, for example, he decided that I was worthy of being entrusted with the single piece of information that I sought to collect from him only after six years of studying mbira music, three trips to Africa, and many rigorous tests.

[a] See Table 1 for a detailed description of Bandambira's system of naming mbira keys. See pages 56–59 for discussion of Bandambira's system and its relationship to other research on the subject.

7

2.
African Mbira and
the music of the Shona

An Introduction to African Mbira

At a lecture demonstration I once attended in Seattle, Washington, Dumisani Maraire, a visiting artist from Zimbabwe, walked onto the stage carrying a round-box resonator with a fifteen-key instrument inside. He turned toward the audience and raised the round-box over his head. "What is this?" he called out.

There was no response.

"All right," he said, "it is an mbira; M-B-I-R-A.[a] Now what did I say it was?"

A few people replied, "Mbira; it is an mbira." Most of the audience sat still in puzzlement.

"What is it?" Maraire repeated, as if slightly annoyed.

More people called out, "Mbira."

"Again," Maraire insisted.

"Mbira!" returned the audience.

"Again!" he shouted. When the auditorium echoed with "Mbira," Maraire laughed out loud. "All right," he said with good-natured sarcasm, "that is the way the Christian missionaries taught me to say 'piano.' "[1]

Dumisani Maraire was reacting to the fact that people from the same culture that supports missionary education in Africa continually referred to his instrument in ethnocentric terms as

8   [a] Pronounced: mm-bée-ra (r is rolled).

"finger piano," "thumb piano," or "hand piano," and showed little interest in learning its African name.

Throughout black Africa, however, where the mbira is one of the most popular traditional instruments, it has many regional names. Among the most common are *sanzhi, likembe, kalimba,* and mbira.[2] These and similar names often have interesting linguistic associations.[b] For example, it has been suggested that the literal meaning of *mbila* is "the aggregate of wooden slabs (or of metal tongues), and perhaps even the succession of sounds constituting the scale or mode to which the instrument is tuned."[3] It has likewise been conjectured that another name, *nsansi,* comes from the verb *-sansa,* to wipe with a quick movement, apparently referring to the playing technique of the instrument.[4]

The myriad forms in which mbira are found in Africa extend south to South Africa, north to Ethiopia and Niger, east to Mozambique, and west to The Gambia. Areas of concentration in-

[b] The word *sansa* also appears frequently in the literature on mbira music. Although *sansa* is still commonly used by some ethnomusicologists (as well as museum curators and others) to refer to the mbira, it apparently is not used by Africans themselves. Hugh Tracey ("A Case for the Name, Mbira," p. 17) suggests that the word *sansa* is an error dating back to an early publication by Charles and David Livingstone who, in their travels through Africa, originally misheard the word *sansi*. While Gerhard Kubik ("Generic Names," pp. 25–32) reports that several names for the instrument belong to a "*sanzhi*" stem group (for example, *isanzu, lisanzo, sanzu,* and *thandi*), there appears to be no reference in the literature on the subject to the existence of the specific term *sansa,* either as the name of a particular African instrument or as a generic African term.

In the earliest written account of the mbira, in 1586, missionary Father Dos Santos refers more accurately to the "ambira" of the present country of Mozambique (Theal, *Records,* p. 203). This name, actually spelled mbira, is still used today in southeastern Africa. Tracey ("A Case for the Name, Mbira," p. 21) argues that the term mbira should replace that of *sansa* as the generic name for the instrument because of the extent of its usage in Africa and because he believes that the greatest technological and musical development of the instrument has been attained under the name mbira.

In the Shona language, the word mbira is both singular and plural, and can be used to denote either one or more individual mbira keys, the instrument itself (that is, an aggregate of keys), or several instruments. In keeping with the Shona language the word mbira is used as the generic name for the instrument in both its singular and plural forms in this book.

clude Zaire, Zimbabwe, Mozambique, and parts of Angola.

In spite of the great variety of instruments, all mbira have four elements in common: a soundboard, a method of amplifying the sound, usually some device for producing the buzzing quality that characterizes mbira music, and, of course, a set of keys.

Many mbira have soundboards, carefully shaped by their makers, which can be used to distinguish one type from another. For example, mbira in southeastern Africa have been classified in terms of "board-shaped," "fan-shaped," "box-shaped," and "bell-shaped" soundboards.[5]

Additionally, mbira usually have a way of amplifying their sound. In some types of mbira the soundboard is hollowed out, providing a hardwood soundbox resonator. Mbira of the soundbox variety sometimes utilize other materials as well. For example, the soundboards of some instruments are mounted on large gasoline tins for additional resonance. In a similar fashion, mbira makers in certain parts of Africa attach a tortoise shell, a skull, or a bark trough beneath the soundboards of their instruments as resonating chambers.[6] Mbira with soundbox resonators range in size from small, high-pitched Ghanaian instruments built on sardine tins ($6\frac{1}{2}''$ x $3''$ x $1\frac{1}{2}''$) to large, deep-voiced Gambian instruments built on wooden boxes ($22''$ x $14''$ x $6''$).

Other types of mbira, particularly those with more than one manual of keys, use a bowl-shaped calabash resonator.[c] Mbira of this type with small soundboards are played over the mouth of a small, hollowed gourd four to five inches in diameter. Larger instruments are performed inside the half-shell of a gourd twelve to eighteen inches in diameter (Plate 1). In Zaire, certain mbira are attached to small gourd resonators in an unusual manner: a stick protruding at an angle from the end of the soundboard is attached to the top of a gourd, the opening of which is pressed against the stomach of the mbira player during the performance.[7]

There is great diversity in the overall design and ornamentation of African mbira (Plates 2–13).[d] Some soundboards and resonators of mbira are highly decorated and others not decorat-

[c] The term manual refers to a single row of keys mounted on the mbira's soundboard.

[d] Pictures of several of the mbira shown in Plates 3–13 appeared in a 1972 article by Söderberg in which he discusses the ornamentation of the mbira and its significance.

ed at all. Resonators may have decorations carved into them. In one example, the contrasting black and white designs were made by charring or rubbing chalk into lines engraved on the outside of the gourd. In addition, colored beads and shells were stitched around the rim (Plate 2). In some parts of Africa, musicians carve inscriptions onto their instruments. I knew performers in Zimbabwe, for example, who engraved their names on the backs of their gourd resonators so that viewers could read them. In other countries, mbira decorated with both painted designs and inscribed proverbs or slogans have been reported.[e] Finally, some mbira are works of graphic art as well as musical instruments. Two from Zaire, for example, consist of sculpted human figures, the chest cavities of which serve as resonating chambers (Plates 12 and 13).

There is usually some device on the mbira for producing the buzzing, vibrating quality considered to be an integral part of the music. This quality is appreciated by African musicians in the same way that Westerners appreciate the sound of the snares on a snare drum or the fuzz-tone on an electric guitar. It may be seen as analogous to the mist that partly obscures the mountains and small figures of certain Chinese silk-screen paintings: the mist is an integral part of such paintings, establishing mood and feeling, and the figures are not supposed to be seen more clearly. The same is true for the buzzing that accompanies the pure sound of the mbira. Once he or she has become accustomed to this quality, the listener or performer would miss it if it were absent; the music would seem naked without it. Thus it is rare to find an mbira which does not have some means of creating this effect. Metal beads placed around the instrument's keys, pebbles placed inside a soundbox resonator, or a membrane stretched over the surface of a hole drilled in the soundboard each produces an appropriate buzz.[f] The devices vibrate with the stroke of each key, producing a continuous, drone-like buzzing. Shona

[e] Kubik ("Generic Names," p. 34) has published the photograph of a large mbira from Nigeria with the inscription, "Pride is the forerunner of destruction." I have in my possession a morphologically similar instrument from The Gambia with the more contemporary slogan, "Faisons l'amour et non pas la guerre" (make love, not war) painted on it.

[f] Jones ("Kalimba of the Lala," p. 324) reports one such device consisting of a piece of the white opaque covering of the eggs of certain spiders stretched under a hole drilled into the soundboard. The membrane acts like tissue paper on a comb and buzzes whenever a key sets the soundboard vibrating.

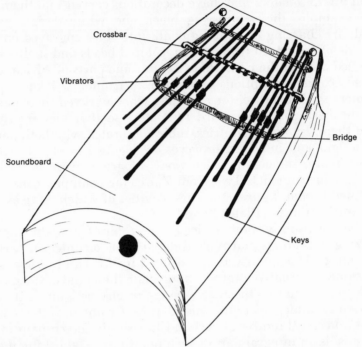

Figure 1. An Mbira.

mbira makers attach snail shells, sea shells, tortoise shells, or, more recently, bottle caps to a metal plate on the soundboard of the instrument. The buzzing produced on Shona mbira is louder and less constant than that produced by other devices.[8]

The layout of mbira keys and their tunings differ among mbira types just as mbira soundboards differ in style. In the most basic type of mbira, the keys are fastened to a plain hardwood soundboard. The keys are often slightly curved, resting over a bridge, so that they are raised from the soundboard in the direction of the performer (Figure 1). A crossbar holds the keys in place tightly enough so that they are fixed in position for playing, but loosely enough so that they can be moved forward and backward over the bridge for tuning. The soundboard is held with both hands by the musician and the keys are plucked with the thumbs and sometimes by the index fingers (Plate 14).

The keys for a given type of mbira are arranged in a prescribed geometric pattern on the soundboard (Figure 2) and

Figure 2. *Various Key Arrangements on Different Mbira.*

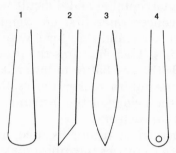

Figure 3. *Various Shapes of Mbira Keys.*

tuned in one or more prescribed ways. The number of keys is also generally prescribed for different types of mbira. This number ranges from as few as three on small mbira in southern Ethiopia to as many as fifty-two on some mbira in northern Zimbabwe.[g] Mbira keys can be made from iron, copper, steel, brass, maize stems, redwood strips, or pieces of bamboo. The shapes of the keys often differ from one type of instrument to another. For instance, some are narrow, pointed keys, one-eighth of an inch in width; others are large, spatulate keys almost one inch wide at their tips; and there are a variety of styles in between (Figure 3). The keys are usually flexible and responsive to the touch of the player, but some mbira have steel keys with especially heavy playing action. Such instruments are often played with metal rings, similar to banjo finger picks, protecting the musician's thumbs.

Formerly in Africa, mbira keys were often made of hand-forged iron.[h] However, in more recent times such materials as

[g] I have never seen Shona mbira with more than thirty-seven keys, but Ephat Mujuru has discovered some musicians in northern Zimbabwe whose instruments have from forty-eight to fifty-two keys.

[h] It was reported as recently as 1963 that in the Transvaal, an area where the mbira is associated with religious ritual, keys were still being made by blacksmiths according to the old methods (Roumeguère-Eberhardt, "Pensée," p. 76).

13

hard drawn wire, nails, or umbrella staves are used. In con-
structing keys the mbira maker is concerned with three factors
that affect their pitch: length, weight, and flexibility. Because
he must preserve a particular geometric pattern in the layout
of the keys, he cannot rely solely on changing the length of the
keys over the bridge for tuning. If tuning were accomplished
solely by this method, the result would be a jagged line of keys,
both esthetically unacceptable and difficult to play.[9] Typically,
an mbira maker concentrates first on weight and flexibility,
pounding the metal wide and thin for low pitches, narrow and
thick for high pitches. Then he trims the tip of the key to raise
the pitch or pounds the key flatter to lower it. For the fine tuning adjustments, the mbira maker moves the keys backward
and forward over the bridge of the instrument until he arrives
at the precise pitch for each one.

An alternate method of tuning is used in Angola and the
Cameroons. In these countries the mbira maker constructs all of
the keys with identical shape, length, and weight. By adding
variable amounts of wax or solder to the underside of each key,
he is able to create the variety of pitches that comprise the
sounds of each instrument.[10]

The many mbira tunings throughout Africa are frequently
based on melody and chord patterns prevalent within each culture.[i] For the most part they are comprised of five, six, or seven
different pitches, contained within one octave on small instruments and sometimes duplicated in as many as three octaves on
larger instruments. In some areas a single tuning is recognized
as the correct one and has prevailed unchanged over many
years.[11] This is not always the case, however. Today in central
Zimbabwe, for example, a number of tunings have been adopted by different players of the same type of mbira.[j]

The mbira is performed in a variety of musical contexts. It is
often played as a solo instrument accompanied by the voice of
the musician. In certain parts of Africa the mbira is played in
combination with other instruments. In the Central African

[i] There are many exceptions to this. For example, Blacking (*How Musical Is Man?*, p. 12) has reported that the tunes of the *kalimba* of the
Nsenga people of Zambia do not sound like other Nsenga music.

[j] An early European missionary, MacDonald (*Africana*, p. 272), also
reported a diversity of tunings in Mozambique in the late nineteenth
century: "The [African] musical scale is not the same as ours," he says,
"and although there is a certain method about the instruments, it is rare
to find two of them tuned exactly the same way."

Republic, for example, the mbira can be played together with the marimba.[k] In northern Mozambique, while one mbira player performs his instrument a second musician accompanies him by drumming with two sticks on the calabash resonator of the mbira.[12] Sketches by Thomas Baines, who travelled with David Livingstone in Mozambique in 1859, show the mbira played in consort with a marimba, rattles, and panpipes.[13] While ensembles of this precise combination of instruments are not reported in southern Africa today, others are common. One frequently finds groups consisting of like melodic instruments (mbira, marimba, or panpipes) accompanied by rattles and sometimes by drums. The organization of mbira ensembles varies from one part of Africa to the next. Among the Soga people of Uganda different types of mbira with different ranges ("bass," "tenor," and "soprano," for example) are played in the same ensemble.[1] In contrast, Shona mbira ensembles in Zimbabwe are comprised of several mbira of the same type; at special religious events, Shona ensembles sometimes include fifteen or more mbira players.

Mbira throughout Africa are diverse in type, in function, and in musical style. There are toy mbira for children, simple mbira on which beginners can learn, and more complex ones for advanced players. In some cultures mbira are used exclusively for entertainment; in others they are used also for religious ceremonies. Even within a single culture, different mbira types with individualized functions frequently coexist. Certain instruments are performed by professionals at formal social events. Simpler instruments function less formally, as, for example, the instrument played by a watchman accompanying himself on guard duty through an evening.

While some types of mbira are regarded solely for their value in music-making and can be played by anyone with an interest in them, others have a broader significance and may symbolize the owner's position within the culture. The right to possess such mbira can be exclusively reserved for chiefs, diviners, or doctors. Furthermore, the right to play the instruments may be restricted to special occasions.[14]

[k] Side 1, band 1 of *Musique Centrafricaine*, Ocora Records 43, illustrates an mbira and marimba duet.
[1] For an illustration of a Ugandan ensemble of six mbira, refer to Hugh Tracey's *The Music of Africa Series; Musical Instruments 2. Reeds (Mbira)*, Kaleidophone Records KM2, side 1, band 5.

15

Mbira also sometimes differ in musical style within a culture.[m] Among the Nsenga of Zambia, for example, the *kalimba* is frequently played by young people for their pleasure when they are on a journey, and its music is based on "harmonic figurations and rhythmic variation." In contrast, the *ndimba* is played by semi-professionals for public performances and its music is characterized by the "melodic basis of its tunes."[15]

In some parts of Africa where small mbira are used primarily to accompany the voice of the singer, the instrument often repeats a basic ostinato figure throughout the performance of a piece. In other parts of Africa larger mbira are appreciated as solo and as accompanying instruments. In such places, mbira music consists of a complex of different melodic, rhythmic, and harmonic parts interacting with each other throughout a performance.

As an important complementary aspect of musical style, tone color can also be a distinguishing factor among various kinds of mbira. Although the tones of mbira are generally full-bodied in resonance and rich in sonority, the overall timbres differ considerably because of the materials used in their construction.[n]

The mbira, an ancient instrument in Mozambique and Zimbabwe, appears to have been of more recent origin in other countries such as Uganda.[16] Its origin in some parts of Africa is grounded in mythology. In accounts given by musicians among the Dan, the instrument is associated with themes of magic and the spirit world, the power of the mbira to improve a person's fortune in life, and the ability of the mbira to comfort one's loneliness. Frequently, spirits or gods appear in these stories and teach an unhappy or unfortunate man to build an mbira.

[m] For reference to a variety of styles of mbira music on commercial recordings, see Merriam, *African Music on LP*, p. 163, and Hugh Tracey, *The Sound of Africa Series, Vol. 1*, pp. 80–83.

[n] The tone color of some mbira can be compared to the tone color of various other African instruments such as the marimba. A similarity between the mbira and other African instruments in certain parts of Africa has been noted in nomenclature as well. For example, Kubik ("Generic Names," pp. 30, 33) has reported a similarity between the names of mbira and harps and lyres in certain African cultures, and other ethnomusicologists have discussed the relationship between mbira and marimba (for example, Kirby, "Note on Hornbostel," p. 109; H. Tracey, "Case for the Name," p. 24; Jones, *Africa and Indonesia*, p. 53). In fact, Jones has gone so far as to consider the mbira to be essentially a "miniature" (ibid., p. 111), and "portable xylophone" (ibid., p. 153).

Thereafter the lonely man finds himself in the company of many people and his life becomes filled with good fortune.[17] These stories share certain similarities with those told by the Shona people of Zimbabwe. In the Shona stories the mbira is a highly personal instrument having the power to comfort and to protect its players, with deep associations with ancestral spirits.

Thus while different types of mbira in Africa have elements of sound production in common, their history and social function, as well as morphological and musical style, can be very dissimilar. These differences are great enough that a musician who has mastered one type of mbira is not likely to be able to play another type, even one from within his own culture, unless he has been schooled in the performance of the second instrument as well.°

Outside of Africa, the mbira has enjoyed periods of popularity in several parts of the world where it was introduced by African slaves: for example, in the French Antilles, Brazil, the Dominican Republic, Cuba, Haiti, Jamaica, Puerto Rico, and the United States. In a description of the early musical practices of Afro-Americans in Congo Square, New Orleans, novelist George Cable described a popular instrument called the *marimba brett*:

> A single strand of wire ran lengthwise of a bit of wooden board, sometimes a shallow box of thin wood, some eight inches long by four or five in width, across which, under the wire, were several joints of reed about a quarter of an inch in diameter and of graduated lengths. The performer, sitting cross-legged, held the board in both hands and plucked the ends of the reeds with his thumbnails.[18]

The *marimba brett* appeared at large, colorful nineteenth century festivals featuring a multitude of musical instruments, dance, and song.

Although mbira died out in the United States and Brazil in the nineteenth century, they are still played in parts of the Car-

° Although women who play the mbira are reported in certain parts of Africa, such as Zaire (Laurenty, *Les Sanzu du Congo*, p. 218), and Ethiopia (Astair Gebremariam, personal communication, 1977), I chose to use the masculine pronoun throughout this work because in my research on Shona mbira music I have found that the players, with few exceptions, are men. One noted exception to this rule is a popular recording artist, Antonia Diogo (Bula). She is the featured singer and one of several mbira players with her ensemble, *Mhuri yekwaAntonia Diogo*.

ibbean (Cuba and the Dominican Republic, for example), where they are commonly known as *marimbulas*.[19] They are usually deep-voiced mbira with wide metal keys attached to a large wooden box resonator, "two feet or more high [or long]." Smaller versions have also been reported (Plate 5 illustrates the African prototype of these instruments).[20] Such instruments, as vestiges of an African heritage, together with the great variety of mbira found throughout black Africa, represent a unique contribution to the world's music.[P]

The Shona People and Their Music

The name "Shona" refers to a group of Bantu-speaking peoples who live between the Zambezi and Limpopo Rivers in Zimbabwe and in parts of Mozambique and Zambia (Figure 4). Their population is over four million, and their basic dialects include Karanga, Zezuru, Korekore, Manyika, Ndau, and Kalanga. As a people the Shona are culturally and linguistically distinct from their fellow Bantu-speaking neighbors both north of the Zambezi and south of the Limpopo.

It is thought that the Shona settled in the south of Zimbabwe by the tenth century and in the north by the twelfth century. It was one of the southern groups that a few centuries after arrival developed the awesome Zimbabwe state south of the present-day city of Fort Victoria. By the sixteenth century, however, this area had ceased to be a major site. Today, ruins of a great complex of stone walls, towers, and rounded gateways stand as monuments to the early Zimbabwe state.

This Zimbabwe state had two immediate successors: the Khami state in the west and the Mutapa state in the north. At the end of the seventeenth century the Rozvi gained control as the dominant Shona rulers of the Khami state and established two capitals, Manyanga and Dhlo Dhlo. During the following

---

[P] Kirby ("Musicologist") and Jones ("Indonesia" and *Africa and Indonesia*) have pointed out similarities among various aspects of Indonesian and African music and culture and have speculated upon a possible Indonesian influence on the development of the African marimba, and, by extension, the mbira. This is conjectural, however; similarities between two different musics do not in themselves indicate that one music developed from another, and possible historical influence resulting from early contact between Africans and Indonesians can be argued both ways, as Jeffreys ("Negro Influences") points out.

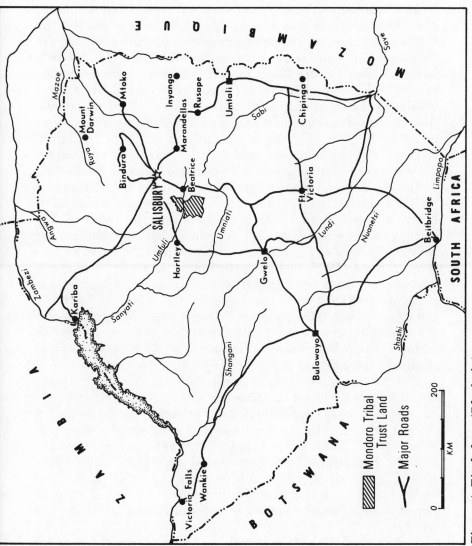

Figure 4. Zimbabwe (Rhodesia).

century the Rozvi served as the leaders of the loosely united southern Shona groups.

In the early nineteenth century the Shona fell victim to a series of three invasions by the Nguni warriors from the south. The third invasion was led by Mzilikazi, whose people, the Ndebele, were seeking independence from the rule of Shaka, the Napoleon-like Zulu warlord in southern Africa. The Ndebele were defeated by the Boers in South Africa and were forced across the Limpopo River into the southern part of Zimbabwe. While the Ndebele did not actually conquer all of the Shona, they exercised a sometimes oppressive authority over many of them, raiding Shona villages for cattle, women, and children. It is the Ndebele who are said to have given the appellation "Shona" to the native peoples they encountered in Zimbabwe.

Toward the end of the nineteenth century the Europeans, lured by prospects of gold and fertile farmland, invaded Zimbabwe and subjugated both the Shona and the Ndebele. For many years afterward, Zimbabwe, which the Europeans named Rhodesia, was a self-governing colony within the British Commonwealth. In 1965 the local government, fearing the country's movement toward political parity for Africans and whites, illegally declared unilateral independence. The political control of the country then fell into the hands of a white oligarchy under the leadership of prime minister Ian Smith. In the seventies, the world's attention focuses on Zimbabwe as African nationalists challenge the political order of the Smith government.

The current Shona music world, in which the mbira plays an important part, is a complex one. It encompasses a great variety of music-making activities in various contexts, including formal social or religious events as well as others of a more personal nature. Shona musical practices range from the most ancient to the most modern, from sacred traditional mbira music played in the villages to secular dance music of the nightclubs in the cities, the latter strongly influenced by musical styles of pop and rock bands from other parts of Africa and from the West.

The Shona have been primarily an agrarian people for whom music has been an integral part of the culture.[21] Even in a changing society, as the Shona child grows up he or she is exposed to music accompanying most community events. Music is a part of children's games and storytelling sessions. Herdboys play musical instruments. Laborers accompany agricultural chores with work songs. Workers sing beer songs at the parties that frequently follow communal labor in the fields.

Court musicians were prominent figures in the past history of the Shona. At one time, war songs and signal drumming were of great importance. Traditionally, singing and dancing have been central to weddings, funerals, and religious events.[22] Within many of the contexts enumerated above, the Shona play several kinds of musical instruments, the general types of which have been reported in other parts of Africa as well.[23] These instruments are classified here according to the major categories of the Sachs-Hornbostel system.[24]

Within the category of chordophones (string instruments), the most popular traditional instruments among the Shona have been various types of musical bows, usually accompanied in performance by the player's singing or whistling. The most widespread type of these instruments is the mouth bow, which is a string attached to two ends of a stave. It is plucked with both hands, and the mouth controls the overtones. Musical bows were formerly favored as solo instruments by herdboys tending their cattle. In recent years, however, the popularity of these instruments has diminished and they have been replaced by homemade or storebought guitars and banjos.

Traditional Shona aerophones (wind instruments) include a variety of flutes, pipes, and horns. Among flutes reported in the past are two side-blown reed instruments—one of which is a double flute with the bass at one end and the treble at the other —an end-blown flute constructed from a dried fruit pod and bamboo, and hand-flutes.[25] Hand-flutes were once popular among herdboys. Both hand-flutes and end-blown flutes were sometimes played in ensembles of like instruments.

Traditional Shona pipes range from the single hunting pipe to panpipes consisting of as many as eight different lengths of bamboo held together with string and wax.[26] In an ensemble, panpipes require a remarkable coordination of different musical skills on the part of the player. Musicians wearing leg rattles dance with synchronized movements in a circle, repeating a steady, often complex, rhythmic pattern. Simultaneously they interlock their panpipe phrases, sing vocables on the off-beats of their respective parts, and accompany themselves with hand rattles. Drumming and singing by other villagers integrates with the ensemble's performance. The panpipes, which are more commonly played today than the flutes mentioned above, 21 are used both for entertainment and in connection with special occasions such as the all-night dancing which precedes certain ceremonies.[27]

The Shona play animal horns for signalling, and occasionally for music in performances at traditional religious ceremonies.[q] In some instances Shona independent Christian churches have carried over this instrument and its function into their contemporary services.[28]

Various kinds of membranophones are (instruments with stretched membranes) used by the Shona people. These are frequently played in ensembles of two or more drums, accompanied by rattles, and they range in size from eight inches to four feet in height. Different drums often have different playing techniques associated with them as well as separate functions within the ensemble.[29] For example, in a common ensemble in the Madziwa area, the smallest drum, which is played with sticks, provides the "regulative, steady rhythm," while the medium drum, played with either sticks or hands, has the greatest freedom of variation, changing accents and producing cross patterns. As in the case of special royal drums or ritual drums, some Shona instruments are reserved for specific ceremonies or specific types of dance. Other drums are not formally associated with particular events or dances and any available instrument can be used. In a similarly flexible fashion, handclapping is sometimes substituted for drumming. Singing can take place with or without a drum accompaniment.[30]

In the category of idiophones (literally, self-sounding; an instrument in which "the substance of the instrument itself, owing to its solidity and elasticity, yields the sounds, without requiring stretched membranes or strings")[31] there is a wide variety of Shona traditional instruments, many of which are still played today. One of the most popular is the *hosho*, a gourd rattle or, more recently, a tin can with seeds inside it, which is used, usually in pairs, to accompany almost every Shona ensemble. A

---

[q] At one village where I carried out research, there was an old man who used to imitate the sound of the animal horn (*nyanga*) with his voice during religious ceremonies. Whenever he sang, he occasionally punctuated the spaces between his lines of poetry with very rhythmic phrases: "te-te-te te-te-te-te.$_{wo}$. Te-te-te te-te-te te-te-te te-te-te te-te-te-te.$_{wo}$." He had heard such patterns performed by horn players at ceremonies when he was a child. Since that time, however, the instrument had disappeared from the village.

variation on this idea consists of kernels of rice or maize placed in an enamel pan and tossed rhythmically from side to side. Additionally, several types of leg rattle are sometimes worn by Shona dancers to bring out the rhythm of their steps. Woodblock clappers are occasionally used to reinforce the sound of the handclapping patterns.

Among the most common of other Shona idiophones are the marimba and the mbira. Although the marimba was at one time a popular instrument among certain Shona groups (for example, Father Dos Santos describes the popularity of the marimba among the Shona who lived in present-day Mozambique in the sixteenth century), it has not been a part of traditional Shona musical life in recent history.[32] Since 1960, however, the marimba has become a popular instrument for entertainment in some of Zimbabwe's African secondary schools, urban centers, and resort areas. This has principally been due to the introduction and dissemination of the instrument by the Kwanongoma College of Music, established in Bulawayo in 1960 as a professional school teaching European and African music. A number of Shona students have been educated there in the performance of the marimba. It is possible that the instrument will become a more important part of an "ever changing Shona music scene."[33]

Foremost among instruments in the musical traditions of the Shona people has been the mbira, which over the centuries has played a fundamental role in ancestor worship at a Shona religious ceremony called the *bira*. In addition to acknowledging the mbira's important association with religion in their culture, the Shona often praise the instrument for its complexity ("It sounds like many instruments being played at once") and comment on its relationship to other types of Shona music. For example, one man informed me that the mbira of the *matepe* type was originally invented so that a single performer could play all the different parts of a *ngororombe* panpipe ensemble. Another person expressed the opinion that mbira music could not be fully understood without first learning the way in which the patterns of the drumming ensemble fit together. He implied that mbira players sometimes imitate the sound of different drums being played together.[r] One line of traditional Shona

[r] The act of playing the mbira itself can be viewed as similar to drumming "as if a person were playing two drum parts together, with the

23

poetry explains that when the mbira is well played, it sounds like a flute.[s]

Other comments point to the similarity of the structure of mbira music to that of Shona singing. Musicians sometimes represent the three parts of their mbira keyboards, each of which produces a different layer of mbira music's texture, as "old men's voices," "young men's voices," and "women's and children's voices." Moreover, mbira music itself can serve in Shona culture as a "basis of conceptualization involved in singing."[34] These observations imply both that mbira music shares basic elements of style and structure with other forms of Shona music and that, as a single instrument, the mbira creates the complex effect of a larger ensemble or chorus. It is not surprising, then that mbira players are considered by the Shona to be their most accomplished musicians.[35]

In addition to performance of the instruments mentioned above, singing continues to play a fundamental role in the musical life of Shona communities. Shona song types range from traditional songs related to the social activities with which they have been associated in the past—for example, work songs, recreational songs, and ritual songs—to modern songs influenced by European music and associated with institutions such as churches and schools.

Traditional Shona songs have taken a number of different forms. There are those based on call and response patterns, in which parts are alternated between the leader and the chorus. Others are based on simultaneous singing. In songs of the latter type, similar in structure to mbira compositions, one part outlines common "harmonic pillar tones" and other parts provide simultaneous cross patterns, increasing the richness of the texture.[36] Besides verbal singing, Shona vocal practices include such non-verbal singing styles as humming and yodelling.

Traditional Shona dances are as diverse as Shona vocal and instrumental styles and are similarly subject to regional variations. The basic dance types include circle dances, line dances, exhibition dances, and dances built around a sequence of dance

---

thumbs instead of the hands" (Blacking, "Nsenga Kalimba Music," p. 29). Conversely, the interest in producing different timbres on the drums can be viewed as being similar to that of playing different pitches on the mbira (Kauffman, "Multi-Part Relationships," p. 103).

[s] Line 12 of Hakurotwi Mude's performance of "Nyamaropa," the translated text of which is provided in the Appendix, p. 260.

forms.[37] Shona ritual dancing, in contrast to the above types, is not based on prescribed formations. At the religious ceremonies accompanied by mbira music, ritual dancing tends to be highly individualistic in expression. It encompasses basic stomping patterns and more elaborate performances, including, at times, miming such events of the past as hunting.

Shona music has embraced a wide range of music-making practices. Over the years it has generated its own changes from within and has absorbed changes imposed from the outside. Changes from within the system took the form of shifting centers of popularity with respect to particular traditions of music, crossfertilization among musical idioms, and composition within the repertories associated with different instruments. The centers of popularity for particular musical activities have shifted within Zimbabwe over the years. The *njari*, for example, is now the type of mbira associated with the Karanga people in southern Zimbabwe who one hundred years ago commonly played the *mbira dzavadzimu*.[38] Crossfertilization among musical idioms is reflected in variations on mbira pieces, in which mbira players have imitated the styles of different types of mbira, and in the repertories for musical bows and panpipes, which have largely been taken from other Shona musical idioms.[39] Compositions of individual Shona musicians who are acknowledged in the titles of certain pieces have become a standard part of the traditional repertory of mbira players. Thus, change and innovation were certainly not new to traditional Shona musicians, although such processes were undoubtedly speeded up with the European occupation of Zimbabwe in the late nineteenth century and the subsequent development of urbanization and mass communication.

Dramatic changes were imposed upon Shona music as a consequence of European colonization of Zimbabwe. Early church groups of many denominations developed missions throughout the tribal trust lands and took on responsibility for the administration of African education. They imposed European religious and esthetic values on Africans and condemned traditional forms of expressive culture, including music. Thus as masses of Africans were converted to Christianity the traditional call and response singing styles accompanied by drums and other percussion instruments gave way to European four-part *a cappella* hymn singing. In more recent years, however, the pressures of African nationalism on European-dominated institutions of religion and education have led to an increased tolerance of traditional African forms of expression within many of these institutions. As a result, some Christian religious associations have introduced such African instruments as the mbira and drums into their services and have encouraged the performance of religious works by Shona composers who utilize traditional elements of Shona musical style in their compositions.[t]

Increased urbanization and mass communication have also had a powerful impact on Zimbabwe's music. With the advent of nightclubs and concert halls in the cities, Shona musicians and audiences were exposed to a wide range of musical idioms, from jazz bands from Zaire and South Africa to European and American rock groups. These styles were popularized further by programs of the Rhodesia Broadcasting Corporation and by the development of a local record industry, the products of which found their way throughout the townships and into the villages. Inspired by these new styles, musically-inclined individuals in the tribal trust lands began experimenting with homemade guitars and banjos. In the cities, professional Shona performers adopted electric guitars and Western drums as the basis for new ensembles oriented toward nightclub audiences. In contemporary urban music one finds bands combining the use of Western instruments with traditional Shona musical elements. At one end of the spectrum there are African groups who perform in English, imitating Western rock bands so well that it is very difficult to distinguish their sound from that of their Western models. At the other end of the spectrum are groups who perform traditional Shona compositions, including mbira pieces, which have been reorchestrated for Western instruments. Many Shona groups perform pieces representing the full spectrum described above, including their own compositions featuring original Shona texts and a unique amalgamation of musical styles.[u]

That modern Shona musical trends have made their impact in the villages as well as in the cities is illustrated by such popular hybrid African-Western styles as *makwaya*, syncopated choral pieces developed by black South African composers, and *jez* (jazz) or *jiti*, dance music, especially popular among the young

---

[t] Axelsson, "Neo-African Church Music," gives an historical outline of the development of neo-African church music in southern Africa.

[u] For further discussion of contemporary Shona music, see Kauffman, "Shona Urban Music."

people, which combines European harmony with fast African drumming and call and response patterns.[40]

In addition to changes brought about by the direct imposition of Western music in Zimbabwe, more subtle changes have taken place as well. These have been the result of the demise of those African institutions with which particular traditional songs were formerly associated, for example, the decline of the performance of children's story-songs and certain work songs. Traditionally, story-songs were used by the elders as a means of teaching their grandchildren the traditional values of Shona culture, preparing them for life as adults. Today the world of schoolchildren is substantially different from that of their elders, so much so that the former educational content of the songs no longer meets the needs of the younger generation. In the case of the work songs, the introduction of modern mechanized techniques of plowing and the proliferation of grinding mills have eliminated the kind of work that used to provide occasion for their performance.[41] Other traditional songs have survived because the Shona people have found new contexts with which to associate them; for example, former war songs are today commonly sung at boxing matches and also play an important role at African political rallies.[v]

Finally, some traditional musical activities have in recent years actually begun to thrive once again in Zimbabwe because of a revival of interest in the traditional institutions with which they were associated in the past and because of a renewed feeling of black pride and African nationalism. Music associations have been formed in many African townships for the purpose of perpetuating traditional practices such as panpipe playing and drumming. Developments of this nature in contemporary Shona music are epitomized by the recent trend among young musicians toward abandoning their homemade guitars in favor of learning to play the mbira. With the changes in political, social, and religious values among the Shona, the mbira stands today in Zimbabwe as a powerful symbol of traditional African culture and the ways of the ancestors.

[v] For further discussion of the political functions of songs among the Shona, see Berliner, "Political Sentiment in Shona Song."

3.
An Overview of Shona Mbira

The Instruments

Archeological and historical evidence points to the fact that the mbira was an ancient instrument among the Shona people. Archeologists have discovered several examples of mbira parts at the ruins of Inyanga and the nearby Niekerk ruins in northeastern Zimbabwe (see Figure 4). An estimate of the date of such finds is 1500–1800 A.D.[1] I have also seen mbira that were found at the old Karanga sites close to the better known Zimbabwe Ruins near Fort Victoria in the southern part of the country. For several reasons, however, a comprehensive history of the mbira cannot be based on archeological evidence alone. First, before archeologists reached some of the sites described above, adventurers had looted them in search of gold artifacts.[2] Second, Africans with a knowledge of iron smithing may also have utilized iron implements found earlier at these sites for their own purposes.[3] Third, it is difficult to ascertain the identity of badly corroded iron objects such as mbira keys.[4] For these reasons, substantiation of the mbira's antiquity must be supplemented by historical evidence, which in some cases even predates the available archeological evidence.

In 1589 Father Dos Santos, a missionary in what is now Mozambique, made the first written reference to the mbira:

> [Africans] have another musical instrument, also called an *ambira*, very similar to that just described [the resonated xylophone], but it was all made of iron instead of gourds, being composed of narrow flat rods of iron about a palm in length, tempered in the fire so that each has a different sound. There

are only nine of these rods, placed in a row close together, with the ends nailed to a piece of wood like the bridge of a violin, from which they hang over a hollow in the wood, which is shaped like a bowl, about which the other ends of the rods are suspended in the air.[5]

In 1865 Charles and David Livingstone published the first drawing of an mbira.[6] The artist, Thomas Baines, who accompanied David Livingstone through Africa, portrayed both a large twenty-two key mbira propped inside a beautifully decorated gourd resonator and a smaller nine key mbira; the large mbira (Plate 2), drawn by Baines in Tete, Mozambique, is very similar to the *matepe* (Plate 15), a type of Shona mbira which musicians report was originally imported into Zimbabwe from northern countries such as Mozambique. Like those on related Shona mbira, the keys of the instruments depicted were made of metal. Long before steel and scrap metal came to be commonly used as the raw material for making mbira keys, expert Shona blacksmiths used iron smelted from mined ore. Regarding the skill of Shona blacksmiths, in 1887 the explorer Wood commented that in the experience of his European guide "a Mashona knife for general use was superior to his own [European] knife. . . . The tempering was better and it would always keep an edge." Wood went on to say that "this was confirmed by another hunter. The Mashona are undoubtedly clever mechanics . . . although they are without files or tools of any kind except of their own manufacture; as a rule the only hammer used is a piece of granite and the anvil a granite rock. They smelt their own iron. . . ."[7]

The diaries of the first European missionaries and adventurers in southern Africa clearly indicate that the Shona were highly skilled blacksmiths and that the mbira was a well-established musical instrument among the Shona at least by the sixteenth century. Moreover, it is most likely that the mbira was an important instrument among the Shona long before its first printed documentation. The Shona are believed to have settled in Zimbabwe as early as the tenth century, and the Early Iron Age itself dates back to the third century in Zimbabwe.[8]

The Shona people play a variety of different types of mbira that reflect the great wealth of mbira found throughout black Africa. There are five general types of Shona mbira: the *matepe* (varieties of which in northern Zimbabwe include the *hera* and *munyonga*), the *karimba*, the *mbira dzavadzimu*, the *njari*, and   29 the *mbira dzavaNdau* (Plates 15–19).[a] Within these types there are variations which reflect a combination of the instrument-maker's style, the performer's esthetic, and the part of the country in which the instrument is played. There is enough agreement among the variations of the same type of mbira that an expert player can adapt his playing technique from one instrument to another. Because various types of mbira have frequently been concentrated in particular parts of Zimbabwe and because of the differences among them in key arrangement, repertory, and the like, most Shona mbira players specialize in the performance of one type of mbira.

The geographic distribution of these general types of mbira and their centers of popularity have in some instances remained fairly stable, but in others they have varied a great deal. For example, the center of concentration of *matepe* playing has always been northern Zimbabwe (Bindura, Mt. Darwin, Mtoko, etc.), and the *mbira dzavaNdau* remains, as its name implies, the instrument of the Ndau people in eastern Zimbabwe near the Mozambique border (Chipinga, for example). In contrast, the center of popularity for the *mbira dzavadzimu* has moved over the past hundred years. In the latter part of the nineteenth century the instrument was commonly played by the Karanga people in the southern part of Zimbabwe (for example, Ft. Victoria), until the arrival of the *njari* challenged its popularity.[b] Today, the *mbira dzavadzimu* is associated most closely with the Zezuru people of central Zimbabwe (for example, Salisbury, Beatrice, and Marandellas). Although the Ft. Victoria area and the Salisbury area remain centers of popularity for the *njari* and *mbira dzavadzimu* respectively, these instruments are found in many other parts of the country as well. Similarly, the *karimba* type of mbira can be found sporadically from Bindura to Wankie and from Salisbury to Bulawayo (at the Kwanongoma College of Music) and Ft. Victoria. The overlapping of areas of concentration of different mbira types is due in part to

[a] Performance examples using all these types of mbira are found among the recordings listed in the discography.

[b] Tracey ("The Mbira Class," p. 87) reported that in 1932 the *njari* was the most common mbira found throughout Zimbabwe, "in many places having completely ousted the [*mbira dzavadzimu*]." This trend may have been the result of the growth of popularity of the *njari's* musical style, or possibly of its association with the rituals of the *mashave* spirit cults, which, according to one source, became dominant in Shona religion in the 1920s (Burbridge, "In Spirit Bound Rhodesia," p. 25).

the increased transience of Africans in recent years; this is epitomized in the Bindura area, where I met players of the *mbira
dzavadzimu, njari, karimba,* and *matepe.*

The types of Shona mbira can be distinguished from one another on the basis of physical characteristics, musical style, and
function within the culture. In physical characteristics, the
Shona mbira range from the most basic type of *karimba* with
eight keys arranged on one manual to a variety of the *matepe*
which can have as many as fifty-two keys distributed on three
or more manuals.[c]

The shape of the keys and their layout on the soundboards of
the instruments also differ from one mbira type to another: the
keys of the *matepe* are thin, narrow, and long, curving gracefully upward from the soundboard (Plate 15); the keys of the
karimba tend to be shorter and lie somewhat flatter across the
bridge of the instrument (Plate 16). The keys of the contemporary *mbira dzavadzimu* are thicker, wider, and more spatulate
than those of the other Shona mbira (Plate 17). While many
Shona mbira have two rows of keys across their soundboards,
the *mbira dzavadzimu* has two on the left side and only one on
the right side.

The soundboards of the several mbira types also have distinguishing features. The *njari's* soundboard is tray-shaped with
its bottom wall removed (Plate 18). On the soundboard of the
mbira dzavadzimu, however, the bottom wall remains in place.
The *mbira dzavadzimu* can also be distinguished by the finger
hole in the lower right corner of the soundboard. Differing from
both the *njari* and *mbira dzavadzimu* is the *matepe's* soundboard, which is hollowed out. Furthermore, the vibrators on the
matepe consist of metal beads mounted on a thin rod inside the
hollowed soundboard, in contrast to the other mbira types in
which the vibrators are attached to a plate on the surface of
the soundboards.[d]

[c] I am indebted to Ephat Mujuru for bringing this instrument to my
attention. The description given here is based on a drawing of the mbira
made by Mujuru at the home of one of its makers and players. I had
hoped to photograph the instrument for reproduction in this work, but
as a result of the increased guerrilla activity in 1972 the army blocked
access to the Mt. Darwin area of northern Zimbabwe, and I was unable
to see the instrument for myself. The largest Shona mbira that I have
personally examined was a variety of the *matepe* with thirty-seven keys.

[d] For a more complete description of the distinguishing features among
Shona mbira, see Hugh Tracey, "Mbira Class of African Instruments." 31

In spite of morphological differences, Shona mbira have a number of basic characteristics in common, including aspects of their tuning plans, playing techniques, and musical style.[9] With the exception of the *mbira dzavaNdau* and certain small varieties of the *karimba* based on six pitches, all Shona mbira utilize seven distinct pitches duplicated in as many as three octaves.[e] Shona mbira often have duplicate pitches on opposite sides of their keyboards to facilitate the production of a tremolo effect, a common feature of Shona mbira music, in which keys of the same pitch on opposite sides of the keyboard are played alternately in rapid succession. This feature varies in degree from one mbira type to another: on the *njari* the left upper manual mirrors the pitches of the right upper manual precisely, but on the contemporary *mbira dzavadzimu* there is usually only one pair of identical pitches.

On most Shona mbira the bass keys are located in the center of the keyboard and scales ascend outward; an exception to this rule is found in the *mbira dzavaNdau*, on which bass keys are arranged on the left and its scale ascends to the right (Plate 19). Adjacent keys on each manual of the mbira often produce adjacent pitches of the scale. Additionally, pitches on one manual are frequently arranged in adjacent positions to their octaves in a lower manual so that they can be played either simultaneously for emphasis or consecutively for wide melodic leaps. Shona mbira also utilize similar playing techniques: outside keys on both sides of the mbira play with an upward stroke of the index fingers and keys in the center of the instruments play with a downward stroke of the thumbs. On the *karimba* and *mbira dzavaNdau*, however, some keys on the upper right manual can be stroked downward with the right index finger.

Finally, while individual types of mbira can be distinguished from one another on the basis of such general factors as tone color, range, and to some extent, repertory and certain individual stylistic features, there are overriding similarities in their musical styles. This is recognized by mbira players, who point out that a particular piece performed on one type of mbira is the "same as" another piece associated with a different type of

[e] Andrew Tracey, "Original African Mbira?" and "Family of the Mbira," shows the similarity of the tuning plans of different Shona mbira types and makes a case for the *karimba* as the basic instrument from which the others developed.

mbira.[10] Additionally, most musicians can, with little difficulty, adapt to their own instrument pieces they originally heard performed on another type of mbira.

Major differences in the function of particular types of mbira exist in Shona culture. For example, the *mbira dzavaNdau* and the small varieties of the *karimba* are played largely for entertainment. The small *karimba*'s repertory is oriented largely toward accompanying the *shangara* exhibition dances performed for relaxation at beer parties following a long day's work in the fields. Although these *karimba* are smaller than the more typical Shona mbira, they have attracted a number of outstanding Shona mbira players.[f] There are larger types of *karimba*, some with twenty or more keys, played in northeastern Zimbabwe. These are not limited to the somewhat restrictive musical structure of the smaller instruments (see p. 82) and are used for playing the important ritual pieces associated with the ancestral spirits.[11]

In contrast to the small *karimba*, the *mbira dzavadzimu* and, to some extent, the *matepe* are the only Shona mbira associated almost exclusively with religious worship.[12] While the *mbira dzavadzimu* can be played for entertainment outside of religious ceremonies, its players report that, unlike other mbira, the *mbira dzavadzimu* is not "for playing in the beer halls."[13] The *njari* and *matepe*, however, can be played in the beer halls or for spirit possession.

The distinctive nature of the *mbira dzavadzimu* is reflected in its traditional repertory, all of which is said to be for the spirits, and in its name, "the mbira of the ancestral spirits." While the name *mbira dzavadzimu* is commonly found in the literature on Shona mbira music, performers often refer to their instruments simply as "mbira" (as distinct from the *njari, matepe*, etc.). The term *mbira huru*, "big" or "great" mbira, is also used by performers of *mbira dzavadzimu*. Finally, the great mbira virtuoso Mubayiwa Bandambira reported that the proper

---

[f] Such musicians as Jege A. Tapera and Stephen R. Gumbo have distinguished themselves as great virtuosi with this type of *karimba*. Tapera's outstanding student, Dumisani Maraire, can be heard performing an mbira of this type on the recordings, *Mbira Music of Rhodesia*, University of Washington Press, and *The African Mbira*, Nonesuch Records H-72043. Stephen Gumbo's performance on the *karimba* can be heard on Kaleidophone Records KMA-8.

full name of the instrument is actually *mbira huru dzavadzimu*, "the great mbira of the ancestors," thus combining all of the names given above.

The *mbira dzavadzimu* has a unique standing among Shona mbira because it is regarded by musicians as the only Shona mbira to have originated in Zimbabwe itself.[g] Musicians indicate that the other Shona mbira were originally imported from Mozambique or from other countries to the north of Zimbabwe, such as Zambia. Because of its seemingly unique position among Shona mbira, the *mbira dzavadzimu* has been chosen as the central focus of this study.

Today the *mbira dzavadzimu* usually consists of twenty-two spatulate keys, wider and thicker than the keys of other Shona mbira. The keys are mounted on three manuals, two on the left and one on the right, on a tray-shaped soundboard with a finger hole in the lower right corner. The little finger of the right hand is inserted into the hole from the front of the mbira and helps to support the instrument while playing. In general, each of the mbira's three manuals encompasses a different range of pitches. The left bottom manual is the lowest register, the left upper manual contains pitches of a middle range, and the highest are played on the right manual. The lower pitches of each manual are in the center of the keyboard and there is typically only one pair of identical pitches on the instrument; it is not uncommon, however, for advanced players to add an extra key to the outer end of the upper left manual of their instruments, increasing the number of pairs of identical pitches to two. The playing technique of modern *mbira dzavadzimu* differs from the other large Shona mbira in that only three fingers are used;

---

[g] In fact, the *mbira dzavadzimu* has had a strong impact on the musical practices of groups outside of Zimbabwe. For example, the *mbila dzamadeza* played by the Venda and the Lemba in Zoutpansberg, South Africa, is morphologically identical to the Shona *mbira dzavadzimu* and is acknowledged by the Venda to have come from Zimbabwe. Moreover, the Lemba use the *mbila dzamadeza*, just as the Shona do, for ancestor worship and for performing some of the same traditional compositions (John Blacking, personal communication, 1975).

It is possible that the Shona people themselves introduced the *mbira dzavadzimu* to the Transvaal. Historical evidence indicates that Shona-speaking people immigrated to Venda-speaking areas as early as the seventeenth century, and later the Rozvi, in particular, exerted considerable influence over the Venda as their rulers (David Beach, personal communication, 1976).

34

the left thumb plays both manuals of keys on the left side of the mbira, while the right thumb plays the first inside three keys and the right index finger plays the outer six on the right manual (Plate 14). In a fashion characteristic of Shona mbira playing technique, the thumbs pluck downward from above and the index finger plucks upward from underneath the keys.

There is some evidence that the morphology and playing technique of the *mbira dzavadzimu* have undergone several changes over the past hundred years. For example, observations and drawings made by early Europeans in Zimbabwe in the mid to late nineteenth century indicate that the traditional versions of the *mbira dzavadzimu* had a greater number of keys, sometimes as many as "twenty-nine" (Plate 20) or "thirty or more."[14] These keys, thinner and less spatulate than those of the modern version, were more like those of other Shona mbira. The soundboards of *mbira dzavadzimu* have also changed. While soundboards of the modern instruments are unornamented and flat, there are older instruments in existence that have smaller soundboards with gracefully curved backs and chevron designs carved on them.

The mechanisms for holding the keys of the *mbira dzavadzimu* to the soundboard and for producing the buzzing quality that accompanies the music have also been modified over the years. On antique instruments as well as some contemporary ones, the crossbar that holds the mbira keys in place over the instrument's bridge is bound to the soundboard with wire. Today eyebolts are often used for this (compare Plates 17 and 21). This recent innovation facilitates the tuning of mbira keys, for one can now tighten a small section of the keyboard with a ratchet where previously one might have had to rebind the entire keyboard with wire. In the old days, the buzzing mechanism on the instrument consisted of thin strips of metal wound loosely like beads around a raised wire bar that extended across the lower face of the soundboard. In more recent times this mechanism has been replaced by shells or bottle tops attached loosely to a tin plate fastened to the soundboard.

While the general layout of the keys on the *mbira dzavadzimu* has remained the same,[h] the playing technique of the more modern instruments has been modified, apparently in connec-

[h] The only exception to this that I have discovered occurs on particular antique mbira played by Muchatera Mujuru (Plate 21), on which the

tion with the decreased number of mbira keys on the newer instruments. The technique used for the older instruments employs two index fingers and both thumbs in a manner typical of the other large Shona mbira. The playing techniques of musicians who possess antique instruments evidence this. For example, Muchatera Mujuru owns several twenty-five key *mbira dzavadzimu* with metal-bead buzzing mechanisms and curved soundboards (Plate 21). These instruments, blackened with age, are said to have been played at the nineteenth century court of Chitungwiza for Chaminuka, a principal spirit of the Shona. The three extra keys which distinguish Muchatera's instruments from the modern twenty-two key versions are located on the left side of the soundboard and are plucked upward with the left index finger. These keys duplicate other pitches on the right side of the instrument (Figure 5, keys R1, R2, and R3), thereby raising the *mbira dzavadzimu*'s number of pairs of identical pitches from one to three. It is interesting to note that a number of the features which today distinguish the *mbira dzavadzimu* from other Shona mbira (wider keys, fewer duplicated pitches, and disuse of the left index finger) appear to have been the result of changes in the instrument introduced within the past century.

Among all Shona mbira players a resonator, usually a large gourd resonator (*deze*), is considered an essential part of the musician's equipment.[1] At times, musicians prefer the light and soft unamplified sound of their instruments, when practicing by themselves or playing informally with other mbira players. However, when they perform before an audience they always use resonators. With the addition of the calabash the tone of the mbira comes alive, full-bodied, mellow, and rich.

Many farmers cultivate crops of gourds and market them in townships where they are always in demand not only for reso-

---

positions of the keys B1 and B2 appear to be reversed in relation to the corresponding keys on the ancient mbira sketched by Mauch (Plate 20) and on typical modern instruments (Plate 17).

[1] The association of the mbira and the gourd resonator is so strong in Shona culture that a colorful figure of speech in the Shona language plays upon it. The expression "*mateze kunge mbira*" ("calabash resonators without mbira") is used in reference to someone who speaks with "empty words." For example, "*Nyamba ari mateze kunge mbira*" ("thoughts that seem profound but are really empty deceits") (Hannan, *Standard Shona Dictionary*, p. 120, entry for *deze*).

nating mbira but also for carrying water and for use as storage containers (Plate 22). Depending on the quality of the harvest from season to season and on the part of Zimbabwe in which they live, however, mbira players sometimes find gourd resonators difficult to acquire. For this reason the staff at the Kwanongoma College of Music has experimented with the use of plywood, round-box resonators, and, more recently, with gourd-like fiberglass resonators as a substitute for the traditional calabash resonators. In addition, one Shona mbira, the *mbira dzavaNdau*, is sometimes played inside a large oil tin for resonance.

To prepare gourds for use as resonators involves a number of steps. When the plants have grown to full size, the farmer cuts them from the vine and leaves them in the field until their color has turned from green to white. The calabashes are then processed to facilitate their drying and to strengthen their walls. John Kunaka described this process, which is either carried out by the farmer or, in many cases, by the mbira player who purchases the gourd. According to Kunaka, the processor cuts a small section from the top and removes the seeds and pulp. Then he fills the gourd with water and leaves it inside a drum of boiling water for a few hours. Next, he peels off an outer layer of transparent skin. He then cuts the top further open, scrapes out more pulp, and sets the gourd to dry in the sun. After it has dried thoroughly, its preparation is usually handled by the mbira player, who scrapes the inside wall as clean as possible and carves the opening of the gourd's mouth to the appropriate dimensions. The quality of resonance of each gourd depends on its size and shape, the thickness of its shell, and the skill of the musician who prepares it. If the gourd is cut down too much or if the opening is left too small, the mbira will not sound well inside it.

Once the gourd has been cut to the musician's satisfaction, small holes are made along its outer edge and vibrators are strung in a row around the mouth of the resonator. These vibrators, traditionally made of snail, tortoise, or sea shells, are today frequently supplemented with or replaced by bottle tops. I once asked an old musician why these changes were taking place. He winked at me and replied, "Well, you see, in the old days our ancestors used shells because they couldn't get any bottle tops." Appreciating the humor in his statement, he went on seriously to explain that the bottle tops vibrated as well, if not better, than the shells, and were more durable; they didn't break and   37 fall off the gourd resonators. Moreover, with the growing popularity of bottled drinks both in the towns and in the reserves, bottle tops were becoming increasingly more accessible than shells.

After vibrators have been added to a new gourd, the calabash is often stored in a kitchen for some time. The heat and smoke dry out the gourd thoroughly and add to its surface a shiny finish appreciated for its appearance (reportedly, the body of the calabash can also be polished with graphite to simulate this).[15] As revealed in sketches and paintings made by Thomas Baines in Tete, Mozambique, in 1865 (Plate 2), gourd resonators were at one time beautifully carved and colorfully decorated. In contemporary Zimbabwe, however, the gourds are usually left their natural color.

Since the gourds are brittle and very easily broken, care is taken to store them in safe places. Musicians also learn techniques for repairing damaged gourds with needle and thread. It is rare to see a well-used resonator without at least one stitched crack (Plate 23). Unless a musician is very wealthy he usually keeps the same gourd until it has been stitched in so many places that it no longer resonates the mbira well.

When musicians are preparing to perform with a resonator, they use one or two sticks called *mutsigo* to prop their mbira inside their gourds at an angle (Plate 24), leaving room for their hands to fit around the sides of the mbira's soundboard and support it from behind. Players often find one position within the gourd that provides the best resonance for their mbira, and regularly stabilize their instruments there when performing. One of the favored materials for a *mutsigo* is *tsanga*, a reed that grows on river banks. Mbira players cut the reeds carefully to suit the dimensions of the gourd, for an oversized *mutsigo* forced inside is capable of breaking the resonator. For this reason musicians also prefer somewhat flexible reeds. In preparing a *mutsigo*, mbira players may round off one end of the reed to fit against the roof of the resonator and notch the other end so that it slips over the crossbar which holds the keys in place on the mbira, or they may position the reed against the "tails" of the keys just above the crossbar. Some players stitch a wooden hoop around the outside of the gourd's mouth to strengthen the walls of the calabash so that it can withstand the pressure of the *mutsigo*.

In addition to amplifying the mbira and transforming its 38 tone, the gourd resonator adds its own substantial buzzing sound to that produced by the vibrators on the soundboard. Some musicians have told me that this buzzing serves a purpose. Ephat Mujuru once described to me the importance of the emotional effect the vibrators produced: he said that when he played the mbira the buzzing from his instrument produced "tensions" and created a sense of drama for him, as he thought deeply of his ancestors and their images crystallized before him. Cosmas Magaya reported that the buzzing sometimes assists in preventing "bad music" by "covering" the sound of keys that became slightly out of tune during a performance and could not be readjusted immediately. Most musicians, however, shun any elaborate explanation for the presence of the vibrators: they "belong with the mbira because they were given to us this way by our forefathers."[16]

It should be added that not all buzzing is appreciated by mbira players. There is a certain type of buzzing emitted from an mbira key which is not being held tightly enough between the bridge and the crossbar. When this occurs, the key is jiggled slightly from side to side or removed from the instrument and reshaped to fit tightly when wedged back onto the soundboard. Such buzzing is considered extraneous.

To facilitate the techniques of playing, musicians usually develop calloused thumbs and finger tips or grow long finger nails. Some musicians use a combination of methods, striking the keys with calloused fingers and using their finger nails for support. In the case of players of *mbira dzavadzimu*, however, metal "rings" like picks or thimble-like covers are sometimes used as additional protection (Plate 25). These devices can be made of wire, corrugated iron, or hard leather. Several factors unique to *mbira dzavadzimu* warrant their use. The playing action of the keys of the *mbira dzavadzimu* is heavier than that of other types of mbira. Furthermore, its playing technique places a disproportionately large burden on the left thumb, which plays all the keys on the left side of the instrument. Finally, it has wide spatulate keys that can accommodate the use of finger guards.

The use of protective devices such as rings depends on the context in which the music is performed. When musicians play informally for their friends or for themselves, the music is relaxed and guards are not really necessary. However, when they accompany religious ceremonies mbira players are called upon to perform with a great deal of power for long stretches of time; some mbira players have played with such force at these events 39 that they have actually broken keys on their instruments. In religious rituals, therefore, these devices can be very helpful aids for musicians, not only protecting their thumbs but also allowing the mbira players to perform with greater power.

In such performance situations, musicians who use rings protect at least the left thumb. Some players use rings on their right thumb and index finger as well. The corrugated iron and heavy leather guards fit around the thumb as one solid piece, but the wire rings sometimes bend out of shape or loosen while playing, and it is not uncommon at a religious ceremony to see mbira players, during breaks between pieces, raise their hands to their mouths to bite down on the rings to tighten them around their thumbs. As an alternative to the use of guards, some musicians apply petroleum jelly or a similar substance to the tips of their fingers to cut down the friction on the keys. Before the musical event they store a small quantity of the lubricant in the indentation on the back of their gourd resonators and occasionally dip into their supply when their finger tips become too dry.

Mbira players usually play seated, with their instruments resting on their laps. Typically, they sit either on a stool or a bench with their backs against a wall, or on the ground (sometimes on a reed mat or a goatskin rug) with their legs stretched out before them and their backs straight (Plate 1). Certain mannerisms are common among performers of mbira music. An mbira player may turn his head to the side as if trying to capture the intensity of the mbira's sound through one ear. He sometimes temporarily rests his ear on the resonator in order to hear the sound directly from the instrument.

Some musicians say that physical movement is important while playing. Frequently players, particularly the older musicians, tilt their heads slightly and nod them subtly up and down to the main beat of the *hosho* accompaniment; others occasionally sway to the music. Moving one's body while playing mbira is said to increase the player's interest in the music. How a musician expresses this movement, however, is a matter of personal style.

Mbira players among the Shona can be regarded as professionals or semi-professionals depending on the nature of their commitment to their art and on the strength of their identification as performers. Although I have heard of musicians who managed to make their living solely by playing mbira, most mbira players derive a substantial part of their income from unrelated fields: mbira players I met during my research in Zimbabwe held such diverse positions as general store manager, messenger servant, upholsterer, carpenter, teacher, blacksmith, salesman, catechist, and farmer. Shona mbira players are almost exclusively men, but there are a few players in Zimbabwe today who are women.

The Depiction of Shona Mbira in Historical Literature and Shona Folklore

In journals and diaries documenting their travels, many of the early European explorers and missionaries in southeastern Africa discuss such aspects of mbira music as the quality of its sound and its importance in Shona culture. Several early European travellers commented that mbira music reminded them of their own popular musical traditions. According to Father Dos Santos (1589):

> [The Africans] play upon this instrument by striking the loose ends of the rods with their thumb-nails, which they allow to grow long for this purpose, and they strike the keys as lightly as a good player strikes those of a harpsichord. Thus the iron rods being shaken and the blows resounding after the fashion of a jew's harp, they produce altogether a sweet and gentle harmony of accordant sounds.[17]

Traveller and geologist Carl Mauch reported that the mbira reminded him "of homely sounds, not foreign to one's ear. The tone is fairly soft and the only real difference is the rhythm. . . . The sound of the mbira approaches closest to that of the zither."[18] In a diary entry typical of those of early Europeans, Theodore Bent wrote, "[The mbira] is decidedly melodious and recalls a spinet."[19] The historical literature contains many such examples of early Europeans in Africa praising the beauty of mbira music and comparing it to their own European musical instruments.[j]

[j] The first Europeans travelling through Africa indicated certain similarities between African and European music pre-dating European colonization of Africa. The overwhelmingly favorable impression that mbira music made on these travellers must be attributed to the fact that they heard in mbira music "homely sounds, not foreign to one's ear." That is, one has only to glance through the diaries of such writers as Mauch to realize how uncharitable and disdainful they were toward those aspects of African culture that were foreign to them. Mauch's 1872 descriptions of Shona mbira music (including his own   41

The historical literature on the mbira also emphasizes its importance in Shona life. Mbira music was prevalent in the sixteenth century Shona courts. Of the ruler Kiteve, a son of the great emperor Monomotapa, Father Dos Santos writes:

> Quiteve [*sic*] also makes use of another class of [Africans], great musicians and dancers, who have no other office than to sit in the first room of the king's palace, at the outer door, and round his dwelling, playing many different musical instruments, and singing to them a great variety of songs and discourses in praise of the king, in very high and sonorous voices. . . . [The mbira] is much more musical than the [marimba] but it is not so loud and is generally played in the king's palace, for it is very soft and makes but a little noise.[20]

Oral sources indicate that the mbira once had an important function in Shona military life. In discussing the meanings of the titles of these traditional mbira compositions, John Kunaka says:

> "Nhemamusasa" is a song for war. When we [the Shona] were marching to war to stop soldiers coming to kill us, we would cut branches and make a place [tent shelter] called a *musasa*. "Shumba huru" means to fight like a lion. "Muka tiende" means to wake up, let's go; it was played when soldiers wake up the next morning in their *musasa* and begin their march again.

Another well-known mbira musician, Ephat Mujuru, spoke to me of two others:

> "Mandarendare" implies arguing without compromise ending in a fight. It is a war song used to raise the soldiers' emotions. "Nyamaropa" means "blood and flesh" and is a war song used to raise emotions before a battle.

These interpretations suggest that some mbira pieces originated in Zimbabwe at a time when the Shona were a powerful military people, long before the coming of the Ndebele in the early nineteenth century.

---

transcriptions) reveal basic similarities with mbira music today in Zimbabwe (Kubik, "Carl Mauch's Mbira Transcriptions," p. 75). It would appear, then, that the aspects of mbira music which seemed familiar to the early Europeans would have included the "harmonic" foundation around which mbira music is built, certain of its melodic patterns, and a tuning system which may have sounded to them like a Western major scale. See Chapter 4 for an elaboration of these characteristics of Shona mbira music.

Mauch writes that mbira music was popularly used to accompany the chores of farming, such as when "girls and boys thresh corn together," and mentions the performance of the mbira by a blind beggar.[21] The literature also mentions the important association of the mbira with Shona professionals involved with medicine and religion. An account exists of the use of a "medicine drum . . . and . . . three or four [mbira]" to bring about the possession of a man by the spirit of his departed father, a physician, who thereby appoints him as his successor.[22] In another account, the medium of Chaminuka, a principal Shona spirit, was said to have "lived in a state of . . . pomp, surrounded by his retainers and musicians who followed him, singing and dancing, with the melodious airs of the 'mbira.' "[23]

In the past, as today, the mbira has been used in traditional Shona religious ceremonies to create the essential link between the world of the living and the world of the spirits. The mbira is believed to have the power of projecting its sound into the heavens and attracting the attention of the ancestors, who are the spiritual owners and keepers of the land and the benefactors of the people's welfare. In formal ceremonies (described in detail in Chapter 8) mbira music culminates in the possession of mediums who then serve as counselors to the villagers.

The mbira has played such an important role in different aspects of Shona culture that the instrument is said to have become a focal point for the identity of particular Shona groups. According to one account, in the eighteenth century the Rozvi, who had taken over the leadership of the Shona peoples at Khami, separated themselves from the other Shona groups and gave each group a name. They distinguished themselves from the VaMbire because of the latter group's skills and close identity with the mbira. The VaMbire are said to have identified themselves as the "people of the mbira."[24] The clan name of another people, the "Njanja," is said to have been a nickname derived from the sound of their mbira, the *njari*.[25]

As one would expect, then, given the importance of the mbira among the Shona people, mbira players have been afforded high status and an honored position in traditional Shona culture. This is reflected in the following account from Shona oral history:

About two centuries ago, five sons of a chief named Umsana [*sic*] whose tribe resides to the present day in the Abercorn District, are supposed to have quarreled with their father. These

43

five were named Chiseno, Mabgwasha [sic], Nyamashakwi, M'Neekwa [sic], and N'Danga [sic]. Chiseno, the eldest, was supposed to have struck his father, hence the quarrel. The five sons then fled; they were all [mbira players] and on arrival at Nyashana's they played for the Chief and pleased him so much that they were each given a wife, and Nyashana, being a powerful chief, placed each of these men as head of a sub-district. [Correct spellings are Musana, Munyikwa, Mabwazhe, and Ndanga.][26]

Examples of mbira players having sought or having been given political or social privilege on the basis of their skill can be found in modern Zimbabwe as well. One renowned mbira player was involved in a divorce case that was under the jurisdiction of a district chief. The mbira player went regularly to the chief's court, playing mbira with his group and buying beer for the chief in an attempt to elicit a favorable decision from him. In another village in Chihota, a visiting mbira player's performance was so well appreciated that the people built a house for him so that he would stay with them and play for their religious ceremonies. Several mbira players reported that they were allowed to ride the African buses without charge. The drivers made an exception for them: "You are the ones playing for our *svikiro* (spirit medium) and for our forefathers who are keeping us."

Reflecting both the appreciation of the art of mbira players by many lovers of tradition and the strong association in the culture of mbira players with their instruments is the not uncommon identification of musicians by nicknames related to the mbira. These include such names as Bandambira, Maridzambira, and Gwenyambira. "Bandambira," from the verb *kubanda*, to crush, suggests the image of a musician who plays with tremendous force, enough, perhaps, to crush the mbira keys. When such a musician plays, the sound of the mbira "explodes" from the gourd resonator. "Maridzambira," from the verb *kuridza*, to play, means "you [who] play the mbira," or simply "the mbira player." "Gwenyambira," from the verb *kukwenya*, to scratch, applies to a musician who "scratches" the mbira's keys with great finesse. Such names are also used as terms of affection for young musicians by relatives who recognize their serious interest in the mbira. The nicknames of established musicians can either augment or supplement their surnames. For example, John Kunaka, a skilled mbira player and mbira maker, can be

44

addressed as "Maridzambira," "VaMaridzambira" ("Mr. Mbira Player"), or, to distinguish him from others with that nickname, "Mr. John Kunaka Maridzambira." In some instances mbira players choose their own nicknames. Simon Mashoko told me that although he was first called "Maridzambira" for his skill, he let it be known to everyone that he preferred to be known as "Gwenyambira."

Many stories from Shona oral history and folklore reveal deep associations of the mbira with other aspects of Shona culture and reflect the mystique surrounding the instrument. These range in content from historical accounts of the origin of the mbira and its role in the nineteenth century court of Chaminuka to children's tales and story-songs in which the mbira has a central role.

One account of the origin of the mbira is given by Muchatera Mujuru (Plate 43), whose following in eastern Zimbabwe believe him to be the medium for the ancient Shona spirit Chaminuka.[27] According to Mujuru, the mbira first came from a place white men have never seen, called "Zimba Risina Musuwo" ("Houses Without Doors"), located north of Rusape in the direction of Mt. Darwin. At first the mbira mysteriously sounded from inside a large rock near a circular stone house with no door. People gathered whenever they heard the mbira's music emanating from the rock. A disembodied voice told the people the name of each song as it was played. The people believed that the voice was that of Chaminuka, the principal Shona spirit and great rainmaker. Later, Chaminuka took possession of a man named Nyadate, through whom he told the people to make mbira. Nyadate showed the people how to make mbira, which they learned to play by listening at the rock. Nyadate informed the people that mbira music was the favorite music of the spirits. He later disappeared into the sea, never to be seen again.

Simon Mashoko, a great *njari* player and singer from the southern part of the country, cautioned that he could not tell me "who was the first man to play mbira. I don't know," he said. "Our forefathers were making the irons from stones in order to build their mbira, but we don't know who started to do that because it is a mystery to us. We can't know the answer. If someone tells you that the mbira came first from Chaminuka, then he's just telling you. Really, it is just a mystery to us."

Several lines of poetry sung by Mashoko in the introduction to the traditional *njari* piece "Mbiriviri" portray this view of the   45 mbira in history. Mashoko offers the following translation and explanation of the elusive meanings of his words:

Literal Meaning	*Intended Meaning*
1. In this modern life, people aren't settled.	The lives of our ancestors were better and more settled.
2. My grandfather was a doctor who gave me a tattoo mark which will last forever.	My grandfather was not really a doctor. The tattoo stands for the mbira. The mbira has been given to us by our forefathers and with it come memories we cannot forget.
3. I was walking with a knobkerrie [cane] and saw a ditch ahead. I threw the knobkerrie to pass it over the ditch but it landed on this side of the ditch. I found honey with it. I don't know where it got the honey.	I took the soundboard of my mbira and threw it over the ditch, but it fell short, and landed on this side of the ditch. When it hit the ground I heard beautiful music. I don't know where it got the music. Then I took the music to the people.

In several respects, Mujuru's story and Mashoko's view represented in the song text above share basic themes. In both versions the people are at first passive recipients, rather than creators, of the music. In the first story the mbira music comes mysteriously from a rock, and in the second story the music comes equally mysteriously to the character whose mbira falls to the ground. In the first story the people are told specifically that the mbira is in effect the spirits' instrument, and that the spirits desire that the music be played for them. The people then accept their obligation and learn to make and to play the mbira. Similarly, the main character in the second story acknowledges the important associations of the mbira with the past and with his forefathers who are now spirits. Like a permanent tattoo, the mbira represents a tradition with responsibilities that he cannot neglect. Hearing the music from the mbira, the musician accepts his obligation to take the music to the people without requiring an explanation of the deeper mysteries. Few stories regarding the origin of the mbira contain as much metaphoric detail as Mujuru's. Most musicians would be inclined to express Mashoko's view that the origin of the mbira is, and perhaps is meant to be, a mystery.

46   Other stories describe the role the mbira played in the life of

Chaminuka, the great Shona spirit, prophet, and rainmaker.[k] These stories often center around one of the most dramatic events in Shona oral history, the confrontation between Chaminuka and the Ndebele under King Lobengula. In the latter part of the nineteenth century, when the Ndebele still enjoyed a certain domination over the Shona people, Pasipamire, who was the medium for Chaminuka, resided at his legendary headquarters of Chitungwiza (south of Salisbury, near Beatrice). Originally Lobengula was respectful to Pasipamire and his spirit Chaminuka, sending gifts and sparing Chitungwiza from the raids of his soldiers in return for promises of rainfall. Eventually, Lobengula, grown suspicious of Pasipamire, began to fear his influence among the Shona. Sometime in 1883, under pretense of convening a conciliatory meeting, Lobengula invited Pasipamire to visit him. When Pasipamire and a group of his followers travelled south to meet Lobengula, they were mercilessly attacked by his Ndebele soldiers. The Ndebele killed all of the followers and Pasipamire alone remained. It is said that the Ndebele tried time and again to murder him, but Pasipamire employed his powers as Chaminuka to thwart each attempt. Finally, in a gesture of self-sacrifice Pasipamire-Chaminuka advised the Ndebele that in order to kill him they would have to send a small boy with a spear. The Ndebele complied and a child who ventured onto the battlefield slew the great spirit.

Various versions of this event, differing slightly with respect to Pasipamire's actual involvement in mbira playing, stress the function of the mbira in the spiritual life of Chaminuka. According to one account, Chaminuka survived the Ndebele onslaught, in which all of his followers were killed, by playing the mbira.[28] According to accounts given by Pasipamire's descendants, however, Pasipamire never played the mbira himself, either in his own person or when possessed by Chaminuka. In-

---

[k] Chaminuka was a miracle worker and magician. He could read people's minds if he wished to, and in times of drought he would bring rain. If he clapped his hands before a barren tree, its branches would bear food for him to eat. He could turn himself into a child, a woman, or an old man; or he could change himself into a ball and spin on top of an ax. He had, moreover, an uncanny power of prophesy and is said to have predicted, among other things, the arrival of Europeans, the introduction of writing into Shona culture, the urbanization of Salisbury, and the advent of the railway (Woollacott, "Pasipamire").

stead he kept many great mbira players as permanent members of his court at Chitungwiza to perform in the service of Chaminuka.

Muchatera Mujuru agrees with the theory that Chaminuka was not an mbira player himself. According to Mujuru, in the court of Chitungwiza a man named Dandara was Pasipamire's acolyte (attendant to the possessed medium) and Zhanje, Mpawose, and Muchaonwa were among the most important mbira players. In the accounts of Mujuru and Pasipamire's descendants, a group of mbira players accompanied the great medium on his journey to meet Lobengula. In the confrontation with the Ndebele, Pasipamire's mbira players performed the music which enabled Pasipamire to become possessed by Chaminuka and thereby to elude his assailants. Mujuru reports that all the mbira players but one was killed in the slaughter that followed. Makunde, the survivor, recovered the mbira and returned with them to Chitungwiza.[1] (According to Mujuru, several of the original mbira from Chitungwiza are still played at his village in Dambatsoko, Rusape; see Plate 21. Another ancient mbira from this period is now kept in the household of Luken Pasipamire, a descendant of Chaminuka's medium. Luken says that the mbira was originally owned by a relative of Pasipamire named Kwari, who played for Chaminuka at Chitungwiza.)

The accounts provided above offer insight into the significance of the mbira in Shona culture. As in the case of Pasipamire, the mbira's music enables mediums to become possessed by spirits and to take on their personalities as well as talents and powers. In the first account the image of Chaminuka, whose mbira playing makes him invincible to the Ndebele, symbolizes the power of the mbira. It is as if Chaminuka were enveloped and sealed off in a protective world of sound.

Other stories from Shona oral tradition share a similar theme suggesting the strong effect of mbira music upon the performer. One tale connects the mbira with the origin of the name of Harare, an African township outside of Salisbury. Harare literally means "He does not sleep," which, according to the story teller, commemorates an old man's early settlement in that area when it was still inhabited by deadly snakes and lions. In the evenings the old man, fearful of the wild animals, was reluctant

---

[1] For a synthesis of oral and literary material concerning Chaminuka and his confrontation with the Ndebele, see Woollacott, "Pasipamire."

to sleep. In order to steady his nerves and to prevent himself from dropping his guard, he played the mbira all night long.[29] Reminiscent of this anecdote's message is the advice an mbira player once gave me. "If you find yourself in a terrible storm," he said, "with lightning and thunder crashing, and with people panicking around you, just play your mbira and you won't notice; you will just remain calm."[30]

One young, impassioned musician, prophesying with bravado the inevitable revolution of Zimbabwe's Africans against their European oppressors, envisioned that day: "When European soldiers come to surround my house, firing guns, I will play the ancient songs for the mbira and when the spirit comes to me, I will walk through their bullets without harm." In such stories mbira music is credited with power to strengthen the morale of the player and to protect the musician possessed by a spirit from antagonistic outside forces.

Several short children's stories describe the power of the mbira to affect the listener. In one tale a hare is persuaded by a sick lion to help him trap his dinner. Filled with sympathy for the plight of the ailing king of beasts, the hare digs a deep pit and covers it carefully with branches of trees and leaves. While the lion hides in the bushes nearby, the hare sits on one side of the pit and plays his mbira. Drawn by the beautiful sound of the mbira, many unsuspecting animals fall into the pit. The lion eats well that evening. In another story, a man walking through the forest is attacked by wild animals. He immediately reaches for his mbira, and before the beasts can catch him the music enchants them and they begin to dance. As the wild animals dance around and around, the mbira player escapes.

To conclude this discussion are the texts of two story-songs usually accompanied on the mbira. The first reveals the instrument's association with the spirit world.

A Man Who Was Staying in the River

(Muchatera Mujuru, singer; Ephat Mujuru, translator)

There was a man who lived in the pool, and in that pool there was a rock in the middle. This man was a great mbira player and travelled all over playing his mbira. He reached one of the villages where there was a very beautiful girl named Hazviemurwi which means "something which cannot be admired." This girl was so captivated with the music of the mbira player that she fell in love with him. Then she went to tell her father

49

that she wanted to go with the man who played mbira to see where he stayed. Her father agreed and she told some of her friends to prepare all the things she would need to carry and to accompany her. On the way the man played his mbira while the girl played the drum. These are the words of the mbira [that he sang]:

Waenda machekano	*Now this girl is*
wangu. Chirandu	*leaving with me.*
kugara zvedu pane	*We are not going*
zuva.	*to stay in the sun.*
nda-nda ndi-nde	*(The imitation of*
nda-nda ti-ndi	*the sound of*
nde	*the mbira.)*
Ndaenda Amai	*Then the girl*
Ndaenda Amai	*replied, beating the drum,*
	"I have gone, mother."
Kwindi kwindi	*(The imitation of the*
Kwindi kwindi	*sound of the drum.)*

The girl's friends and the villagers followed behind and when they reached the river bank they saw the two lovers going into the big river. The people accompanying the lovers were surprised and went back to tell the girl's parents. The parents returned with them to see the river where their daughter disappeared and then went back to tell the chief what had happened. The chief told them to gather together black, white, and red beads and a calf [as gifts for the spirit who played the mbira]. The parents then returned to the river with the villagers, playing the mbira and drum and singing the song which the lovers had played before entering the river. When the girl heard this song she came out of the river with a basket. She had become an herbalist.

Thus, lured by love of the mbira, the girl gained entry into the spirit world, and returned from the river a skilled doctor with the ability to cure illness in her parents' village.

The second story-song reveals two important cultural attitudes toward the mbira: the traditional status of those with the skill to master it and the importance of passing on the mbira from one generation to the next.

The Great Mbira Player Who Died Without a Son

(Magauri, singer; Ephat Mujuru, translator)

There was a man who was a great mbira player. He had one daughter but no son. One day he said to his daughter, "Look, you, my daughter, when I have died, you should be married by a man who can play my mbira!" When he died all the young people tried to play the musician's mbira, but they failed until there came another man who was poor, but said, "Let me try to play it!" The people then said, "You? You can't play this mbira!" Then he started:

Njenginje njenginje njenginje njerere.	*(Imitation of the sound of mbira.)*
Baba wangu wakafa, dendera.	*My father died, dendera (imitation of phrase of mbira music).*
Wafaka asina mwana komana.	*He died without a son.*
Akasiya deze rembira.	*He left his mbira behind him.*

All the people were surprised at the great performance of the poor youth, and the mbira player won the girl. They were married and lived happily ever after.

In this story the poor man triumphs over the other contestants for the daughter's hand in marriage. In spite of the fact that he was initially ridiculed for his poverty, his skill as an mbira player affords him such status that he is considered to be the most suitable prospect for marriage to the daughter of the deceased mbira master. Perhaps, also, the father's original request was partly because excellence in mbira playing was associated in his mind with other positive human qualities. He would rest in peace, it seems, if he thought that his daughter would marry such a man.

The stories about the mbira in Shona oral history and folklore complement those of early historical sources to suggest the depth of the mbira's association with all aspects of Shona culture, political, social, and religious. The theme of the mbira and the spirit world is a prevalent one, and mystery surrounds the origin of the mbira. Mbira music is the music of the ancestral spirits; few stories give an account of when the mbira was invented, by whom, or why. Finally, the stories reflect the mystique surrounding the mbira's powers: the mbira protects its players from fear and insulates them from danger. These recurring narrative themes will become more meaningful after the nature of mbira music itself and the unique relationship that exists between the mbira player and his instrument have been explored.

51

4.
The Nature of Mbira Music

The problem of describing Shona mbira music and illustrating the music with notation is a considerable one, for there is something unique about the quality and the effect of a live performance of mbira music that defies description. The mbira's sound has a special presence; one feels the music as much as one hears it. Its sound is penetrating and warm at the same time, immediately capturing the involvement of the listeners and drawing them into its mood. When the keys of the mbira are struck, they ring on in the gourd resonator with rich and sonorous tones "like bells,"[1] as one musician has suggested, or like flutes, as a line of classic poetry accompanying mbira music implies.[2] There is, in fact, no satisfactory analogy for conveying its quality to one who has not heard mbira music performed.

When an mbira player performs, he works his thumbs and fingers with agility over the mbira keys. As he plays interlocked polyrhythmic parts, the complexity of the mbira's music often gives the impression of more than one instrument being performed. Musicians explain this phenomenon in part by the fact that when they strike a sequence of keys, the keys' pitches are sustained in the gourd resonator, overlapping and intermixing. As several patterns are repeated in a cycle their beginnings and endings become ambiguous; new phrases appear in the music as one listens to the inner parts of the piece.[3]

An mbira piece itself is not a fixed musical structure with a specified beginning and end; it is a composition of certain characteristic cyclical patterns that provide a framework for elaboration and variation supporting the creative expression of the performer. As one would also expect, the length of a piece and the particular variations on it performed are largely subject to the mood of the musician. "If I feel like it, I will play one piece all night long," one performer, Ephat Mujuru, explains. "Listen to what I am playing and then come back in a half hour and I'll be playing altogether differently [on the same piece]."[a] Shona mbira music consists of a continuous stream of subtly changing musical ideas; its texture is like a fabric of tightly interwoven melodic/rhythmic lines that interact with each other throughout the performance of a piece.

Because of the elusive nature of mbira music, the visual representations provided in this chapter cannot portray the musical event in full, but only illustrate points about certain aspects of the music. The reader should not interpret the notations of mbira music narrowly; he or she must avoid the impression that the music itself is fixed and two-dimensional. In order to help to bridge the gap between the notated examples of mbira music and the experience of the music, specific illustrations in this chapter have been coordinated with musical examples on two records, *The Soul of Mbira* and *Shona Mbira Music*.[b] It is hoped that visual representations of the music used in conjunction with these recordings of the pieces will provide the reader with an understanding of the complexity of mbira music and an appreciation of its vitality.

In carrying out my research in Zimbabwe, I endeavored to allow the mbira players with whom I worked to guide me to an awareness of the music on its own terms. In an attempt to portray the music in a manner true to its own tradition I have, therefore, wherever possible employed concepts and categories taken from the Shona musicians themselves and from their repertories. In so doing I hope to have minimized the kinds of inadvertent distortions that can result when African music has imposed upon it Western concepts having little to do with the way in which Africans view their own art.

[a] Three recorded versions of "Taireva" demonstrate the degree to which renditions of the same mbira composition can differ. They are on *The Soul of Mbira*, side I, band 2, and *Shona Mbira Music*, side I, band 3, and side II, band 2.

[b] These albums were produced for Nonesuch Records by the author from field recordings made in Zimbabwe between the years 1971 and 1975. The first album, Nonesuch H-72054, illustrates a variety of Shona mbira, and the second, Nonesuch H-72077, features the *mbira dzavadzimu* and the famed mbira ensemble *Mhuri yekwaRwizi*.

Mbira Tunings

While there is a certain amount of variation among mbira of the same type constructed by different makers, the instruments' basic layout of keys and general tuning plan are essentially identical. For example, the *mbira dzavadzimu's* keyboard is comprised of three parts (Figure 5): a right-hand manual (henceforth, R manual, keys labeled R1–9), an upper left-hand manual (henceforth L manual, keys labeled L1–6), and a bottom left-hand manual (henceforth B manual, keys labeled B1–7). The three manuals correspond generally with the mbira's three registers, although there is a slight amount of overlapping among them (see keys B7, L1, and R1, and keys R2 and L6).

The R manual contains a basic scale, the pitches of which have octave and unison counterparts in the L and B manuals. The arrangement of keys on the R manual facilitates the performance of the eight-pitch stepwise descending melodic pattern that is characteristic in the upper voice of music for the *mbira dzadvadzimu*. Such patterns, as well as others involving larger melodic leaps, utilize two playing techniques. Musicians play the lowest three pitches on the R manual by striking the keys downward with the right thumb, and play the remaining pitches with an upward stroke of the index finger from underneath the key.

The pattern of pitches on the L manual conveniently places in adjacent positions several keys that produce melodic leaps of approximately a fifth (L1–L2) and a third (L3–L4). These occur frequently in the middle pitch strata of many mbira pieces. The B manual employs an equally efficient arrangement: several keys are placed next to one another for playing melodic leaps of a third (B1–B2 and B6–B7) which commonly appear in the lower voice of mbira music, and most of the keys are placed in positions adjacent to their octave counterparts on the L manual, facilitating the performance of octave leaps in the left-hand parts of mbira pieces. Keys on both the L and B manuals are played by striking downward with the left thumb. Altogether the range of the *mbira dzavadzimu* encompasses three octaves from its lowest pitch (key B1) to its highest pitch (key R9).

Musicians refer to the relationship among the pitches of the *mbira dzavadzimu* in various ways. It is common to hear the

54

pitches in ascending order

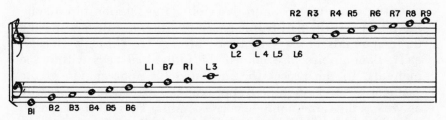

Figure 5. The Tuning Plan of Mbira DzaVadzimu. *This diagram illustrates the range of the* mbira dzavadzimu *and the relative relationship among the pitches of the instrument. However, as discussed further in this chapter, the precise intervals that comprise the tuning of* mbira dzavadzimu *can differ considerably from one instrument to another.*

pitches on each manual distinguished from those on the other manuals in terms of their register. For example, musicians often refer to the B manual, which contains the mbira's lowest register, as the "old men's voices," the L manual, the middle register, as the "young men's voices," and the R manual, or highest register, as the "women's voices." Other terms commonly used to make the same general distinctions include *nhetete* (that is, thin keys) for the R manual, *ngwena* (literally, crocodiles, symbolizing old age or old men) describing the B manual, and *nheverangwena* (literally, those who follow the crocodiles) for the L manual.

Mbira players sometimes make further differentiations within these general categories. The R manual can be divided into two parts: keys R1–3, *nhendure* (no literal meaning), and keys R4–9, *nhetete*, "thin keys." (Some mbira players include key R4 among the *nhendure*.) The *nhendure* are the first keys that beginners learn to use on the R manual. As described previously, they are played by striking downward with the right thumb. The *nhetete* are essential in the performances of advanced players and are played with the more challenging technique of striking upward from underneath the keys with the right index finger. Musicians use the terms *mhindimbi* or *whindingwi* to refer to pitches that are duplicated on opposite sides of the soundboard (for example, R2 and L6). These names appear to be onomatopoetic words, imitating the sound of the corresponding keys played in rapid succession.

While most performers today describe the relationship of the mbira keys in the general terms mentioned above, some older players like Mubayiwa Bandambira have a detailed system for classifying mbira keys and describing the relationship among the pitches on their instruments. In addition to categorizing the three manuals of keys in terms of register ("men's voices," etc.), Bandambira also named the individual keys within the manuals. In the process he indicated his appreciation of the "sameness" of keys tuned approximately an octave apart by assigning the same name to corresponding keys on the L and B manual. Additionally, he indicated a similar relationship between keys on the R manual and their octave counterparts on the L and B manuals by pointing to several keys and saying that they "took the same name from each other." Table 1 illustrates
56 Bandambira's system of classification of mbira keys and pro-

Table 1
Classification of Mbira DzaVadzimu Keys Based on Bandambira's Explanation of His System

Keys	Names	Explanations
L1[a]	*Benzi* (mad person)	Frightens you or makes you start; makes you feel awake; makes the heart feel wild or excited like a mad person; makes you dance wildly; has a sharp voice that leads the mbira.
B1	*Gadzanga* (from *kugadza,* "to put in a stable position")	Controls the excited feeling of the *benzi,* the high pitch; controls the high pitches, cools the feeling down to normal; settles the piece and holds it together; without this, there can be no mbira music.
B2 R1 R4	*Shumba* (the lion)	The animal in which the powerful spirits live.
B3 L3 R5	*Zanga zanga* (ideophone representing the swaying of a person going into a trance)	One of the most important pitches; the mother of the mbira; makes you shake but not in the sense of dancing (that is, physical manifestation of spirit possession).
B4 L2 R6	*Mvundura* (from *kubvundura,* "to stir up")	Makes your heart full; changes your heart; makes you dance; changes your feelings.
B5 L4 R7	*Nhiura* (big drum)	Lifts up your lungs; makes you feel like shaking your body.
B6 L5 R8	*Tida* (no literal meaning)	Shouts from far away, sings aloud; makes people feel like singing to it; makes you raise your voice in song.
B7 R3	*Duri* (mortar)	Like stamping millet (referring to the rhythmic sound of mortar and pestle being used to pound millet).

[a]Keys L1 and B1 are the only keys tuned an octave apart to which Bandambira assigned different names, distinguishing their effect upon the lis-

vides his explanation of the names he used for each group of keys.

The terms by which Bandambira referred to the keys of the *mbira dzavadzimu* can be regarded in large part as praise names, names that praise each key for its musical quality and for its effect upon listeners.

In addition, some of the terms give a clue to the musical function of the keys. For example, *benzi* (L1), which "excites" the listener and "leads" the mbira, is the key on which certain classic mbira pieces are generally begun, although, as will be discussed further in this chapter, the beginnings and endings of a piece are not rigidly defined and can vary from one player to another and from one rendition to another. *Gadzanga* (B1), which is an octave below the *benzi*, takes its name from the verb *kugadza*, meaning "to put in a stable position," and often it has this literal function as well. It is the lowest pitch on the mbira and serves as a focal point or tonal center for many mbira pieces. In other pieces, *zanga zanga* (B3), which is described by Bandambira as "the mother of the mbira" and "one of the most important keys," has this function. In contrast, *duri* (B7) refers to a mortar. During certain variations on mbira pieces, the *duri* produces rhythmically regular patterns which can perhaps be likened to the sound of a mortar and pestle "stamping millet." Finally, *shumba* (B2) can be regarded as having a symbolic meaning.[c] According to Bandambira it refers to the powerful "lion spirits" (*mhondoro*) who reside in their animal hosts un-

---

tener and their musical function. He indicated that R2 and, by implication, R9, took the name of either *benzi* or *gadzanga*, depending on which one of these lower pitches they were played with. Bandambira called L6 *whindingwi* in relation to its counterpart, R2.

[c] Roumeguère-Eberhardt (1963) has reported much more elaborate symbolism associated with the Venda and Lemba *mbila dzamadeza* (which she erroneously calls *deza*); they are morphologically identical with the *mbira dzavadzimu*. She claims that the *mbila* symbolizes the entire social structure of the village as well as the cosmological teachings of the initiation ceremony, the *domba*. While her interpretations have been quoted elsewhere in the literature (Bebey, *African Music*, pp. 82–84; Berliner, "Soul of Mbira: An Ethnography," pp. 33–37; and Wachsmann, "Interrelations," pp. 402–403), Blacking ("Review of 'Pensée' " p. 30, for example) has considered this aspect of her work to be quite dubious. One might further question the validity of her assertions since the *mbila* was originally taken from the Shona people, among whom, apparently, no such deep symbolism exists in relation to the mbira.

til they find a suitable human medium. Such possession results when mbira music is performed at religious ceremonies.

Although the general tuning plans for mbira of the same type are for the most part identical (the only exception to this rule that I have discovered among *mbira dzavadzimu* is that on several antique instruments the positions of keys B1 and B2 are reversed; see Plate 21), various tuning procedures are used by musicians and the actual tunings can vary considerably from one instrument to another. In the construction of a new mbira, many blacksmiths such as John Kunaka forge the lowest key on the instrument (B1) first, and proceed to make new keys alternately for the L and B manuals, working their way from the center of the instrument out to the left side. They then forge the lowest key on the R manual (R1) and work their way stepwise up the ascending scale from the center of the mbira out to the right side. Using another approach, some blacksmiths work their way outward from the center in both directions, adding keys alternately to the right and to the left manuals, after forging the lowest key on the mbira. During either process, mbira makers tune the new instruments methodically, from all possible angles. First, as each new key is added to the soundboard they tune it to the pitch of the corresponding key on a "model" instrument, usually one owned by the maker, that is well in tune. Next they tune corresponding keys on different manuals in octaves, checking these against equivalent keys on the model instrument. With the addition of each new key, the blacksmiths compare the tuning of the entire sequence of intervals on a particular manual, from the center of the manual outward, to that of the model instrument. When enough keys have been added to the soundboard, the makers test its tuning periodically by playing a portion of a piece with the unfinished mbira. Finally, it is not uncommon for mbira makers ultimately to test the tuning of the completed instrument by playing a composition with the model mbira and the new mbira simultaneously (Plate 26): the craftsman plays the right-hand part on the model instrument and the left-hand part on the newly made instrument. He then switches the instruments from one hand to the other and continues to play both mbira, stopping to make minor changes in the tuning of the new instrument until the two instruments sound as if they are one.[d]

[d] Blacksmiths are known for their skill at making mbira and are often mbira virtuosi themselves. Some mbira players like Simon Mashoko de- 59

Once purchased, the new mbira is kept well in tune. Musicians differ in their ability to tune mbira; it was a point of pride for John Kunaka that his uncle, a skilled mbira player, relied on his nephew's assistance in tuning his instrument. Sometimes players tune their mbira by comparing its pitches, one at a time, to those of another, properly tuned, instrument. The latter procedure is often used by members of mbira ensembles checking to make sure that their instruments are in tune with each other before performing in public. At other times, they tune their mbira during a performance, occasionally stopping to retune a key when they hear a discord in the music. The importance of correct tuning to Shona musicians was demonstrated to me one evening when Luken Pasipamire did not have time to examine his instrument before a formal musical event. Upon discovering that a number of keys on his mbira were out of tune with those of the other players in his ensemble, he compensated throughout the performance by changing his part so as to skip over the "bad" keys.

The tunings that players of *mbira dzavadzimu* adopt either as individuals or collectively as members of the same group can vary considerably, and players differ greatly in their commitment to a particular tuning.[e] For instance, John Kunaka first played an mbira with the tuning used by his mbira teacher. Later he switched to his own tuning and kept it for about ten years, and he has recently changed to another tuning which he plans to keep for a "long time." Hakurotwi Mude has changed tunings even more frequently than Kunaka. Over the past several years Mude has used five different mbira tunings with his group *Mhuri yekwaRwizi*. He usually keeps the same tuning until he hears another musician or ensemble using another that appeals to him more than his own. He then adopts the new tuning.

There can be a risk of damaging the instrument by switching

velop an expertise at building mbira without ever becoming professional blacksmiths. Mashoko feels that it is an important skill for an mbira player to have so that he can repair his instrument when necessary.

[e] The tuning practices among mbira players apparently differ from one type of mbira to the next. Andrew Tracey ("Matepe Mbira Music," p. 47) reports that in the northern part of Zimbabwe there is a standard tuning for the mbira that tends to be constant over long periods of time. This has not been my experience with tunings in central Zimbabwe where the *mbira dzavadzimu* is played.

too frequently from one tuning to another on the same instrument: in changing an mbira's tuning, it is necessary to bend and reshape the tails of the keys slightly (the tail is at the top end of the key at the opposite end from the spatulate playing tip; it clings to the end of the mbira soundboard and supports the tension of the keys over the bridge). After repeated manipulation, the mbira keys can become misshapen, and the playing ends of the keys, instead of forming an even line across each manual, stick out at different angles, leaving a jagged line and uneven gaps between keys. Moreover, the strength of the keys is weakened by continual bending and readjustment, sometimes to the point of breaking under forceful playing. Therefore, although players of *mbira dzavadzimu* sometimes change their mbira tunings, they do not change the tuning of their instruments from one piece to another, as is the practice with other melodic instruments in some parts of Africa.[f] They play their entire repertory for the mbira in the tuning they have adopted. As will be discussed later, the mbira player's repertory takes on a new character when the musician adopts a different tuning for his instrument.

Mbira players use the Shona-ized English word *chuning* to refer to a number of interrelated aspects distinguishing the overall sound of certain mbira from that of others. These include tone, sound projection, pitch level, tuning, variation within octaves, relationships of corresponding intervals among the three manuals, and presence or absence of tuned overtones.[g] The mbira player distinguishes the *chuning* of his own instrument from others by its fullness of sound, its ringing quality, and its relative highness or lowness (that is, the absolute highest pitch and the absolute lowest pitch in the mbira's three-octave range). One musician explained to me in a typical fashion that the *chuning* he used for his instrument was the second "highest" of four known in his area and that he selected it because it had a "big"

[f] For example, as Anthony King reports ("Construction and Tuning of the *Kora*," p. 126), musicians in The Gambia use three different tuning systems in the performance of the repertory of the *Kora* (a twenty-one stringed harp-lute).

[g] This material comprises my research to date on *mbira dzavadzimu* tunings. While I would have liked to have been able to posit a theory of Shona mbira tuning in this chapter, the complexity of the matter makes it premature at this time. My purpose is only to discuss those aspects of tuning considered important by musicians.

61

(loud) voice rather than a "small" (soft) one. Its sound was so full that people enjoyed listening to him perform solo. The pitch level of different *mbira dzavadzimu* commonly varies as much as a fourth, with the lowest key of the instruments ranging from approximately G_2 to C_3.[h]

Factors other than abstract consideration of the sound sometimes enter into the musician's choice of a higher or lower *chuning*. One performer lowered the pitch level of a newly made mbira because the playing action of the keys was very stiff and he considered them too difficult to play. He moved the keys over the bridge of his mbira, lengthening the playing end. This made them more flexible, and consequently lowered the pitch level of his mbira as well. On another occasion, Dumisani Maraire suggested that the lowest tone on his *karimba*-type mbira should match the lowest tone that the singer can reach comfortably. Similarly, Mude, who takes pride in being able to sing with any mbira *chuning*, favors those which he says are "good" for his voice, that is, those in which the pitches of the B manual fall within his natural range. At the same time, however, Mude likes to sing with different *chunings* for a change because he says the change "molds his voice" and "makes it grow," that it gives him the opportunity to extend his range.

In addition to the variable of pitch level among *mbira dzavadzimu* with different *chunings*, there are significant differences in the actual size of their corresponding intervals. Hakurotwi Mude revealed the importance of this aspect of *chuning* on one occasion when he purchased several instruments from an mbira maker whose *chuning* had moved him deeply. After performing the new mbira, Mude decided that its pitch level was a little too high for his taste (B1 of the new mbira was just over one "whole tone" above that of B1 on his previous mbira). Instead of lowering the *chuning* himself, however, Mude suggested that the instruments should be returned to the maker for this purpose, so as not to risk losing its special character (that is, the actual sequence of intervals that characterized the new mbira).

Within the range of *chunings* available for the *mbira dzavadzimu* there are some comprised of intervals that are quite simi-

---

[h] To hear the difference in relative highness or lowness of mbira *chunings*, compare Muchatera Mujuru's mbira with that of John Kunaka (*The Soul of Mbira*, side II, bands 2 and 3 respectively).

lar to those of a Western major scale, deviating from them only in microtones and others comprised of intervals that differ as much as a semitone (100 cents) or more from those of a Western major scale (Table 2).[1] In comparing the mbira of five well-known musicians with whom I worked in Zimbabwe, considerable variation was found in the size of corresponding intervals from one *mbira dzavadzimu* to another (Table 3). Two methods were used for obtaining the pitch measurements of the five mbira represented in Table 3. First, I asked several musicians who owned these mbira (for example, Hakurotwi Mude and Ephat Mujuru) to select from a set of fifty-four forks tuned 4 c.p.s. apart (from 212 c.p.s. to 424 c.p.s.) the individual forks which each thought matched the tuning of the keys on his respective instrument. The fact that they sometimes said that the pitch of an mbira key fell between two tuning forks demonstrated that the musicians could discern fine variations in tun-

Table 2a
Western Major Scale (Just Intonation)
Compared with Two Mbira Tunings

Western Major Scale Intervals in Cents	Kunaka's Tuning Intervals in Cents (R_2–R_9)	Deviation of Mbira Tuning with Respect to Major Scale
C		
112	98	−14
B		
182	173	− 9
A		
204	201	− 3
G		
204	170	−34
F		
112	129	+17
E		
182	181	− 1
D		
204	196	− 8
C		
0	0	0

[1] In Tables 2a and 2b the Western major scale is compared to the tunings of the mbira's R manuals because those keys are arranged, and often played, in a scale-wise fashion.

Table 2b

Western Major Scale Intervals in Cents	Bandambira's Tuning Intervals in Cents (R_2-R_9)	Deviation of Mbira Tuning with Respect to Major Scale
C		
112	251	+139[a]
B		
182	137	− 45
A		
204	158	− 46
G		
204	163	− 41
F		
112	204	+ 92[a]
E		
182	204	+ 22
D		
204	185	− 19
C		
0	0	0

[a] Especially great deviation.

ing. While the tuning forks provided a useful means of collecting tuning measurements in the field directly, the method had obvious drawbacks. For example, in some parts of the mbira's range the method required musicians to make judgments of the tuning of particular keys based on octave transposition.

In order to check the kinds of results obtained from tunings measured by the first method, I used a second method for an additional sample of mbira tunings. Measurements of these mbira (see Kunaka's and Gondo's mbira tunings in Table 3) were made from tape recordings and a dual trace oscilloscope. One of the two traces was a sinusoid or pure tone generated by an oscillator; its other trace was generated by the pitch of each mbira key. The time base of the oscilloscope was synchronized with the sinusoid. As each pitch of the instrument was sounded, the frequency of the sinusoid was adjusted until the two traces were stable, one to the other, indicating that the frequency of the sinusoid was the same as the fundamental frequency of the pitch of the mbira key. The frequency of the oscillator was then measured with an electrical frequency counter. Finally, the frequencies of the pitches of the mbira keys measured by both

Table 3
Comparison of the Tunings of Five Mbira DzaVadzimu

Intervals Between Adjacent Keys	Mujiru Tuning	Mude Tuning	Bandambira Tuning	Kunaka Tuning	Gondo Tuning	Greatest Deviation Among Intervals
R manual						
R8-R9	240	260[a]	251	98	192	162[b]
R7-R8	*128*	173	137	*173*	161	45
R6-R7	151	172	158	201	*151*	50
R5-R6	*219*	214	*163*	170	182	56
R4-R5	143	*118*	204	129	136	86[b]
R3-R4	156	180	204	181	218	62
R2-R3	190	231	185	196	*179*	52
R1-R2	839	791	884	826	873	93[b]
L manual						
L5-L6	264	*128*	193	161	182	136[b]
L4-L5	97	139	*169*	164	164	72
L3-L4	415	381	306	390	328	109[b]
L2-L3	263	*211*	*118*	209	191	145[b]
L1-L2	624	702	681	712	709	88[b]
B manual						
B6-B7	414	376	*418*	412	349	69
B5-B6	105	*158*	153	154	151	53
B4-B5	314	37	179	178	186	277[b]
B3-B4	156	286	*96*	210	164	190[b]
B2-B3	117	115	199	*92*	157	107[b]
B1-B2	126	174	355	455	323	329[b]
Means of Measurement	T.F.[c]	T.F.	T.F.	OSC.[d]	OSC.	

NOTE: Absolute pitches of these tunings are given in Appendix II.
[a] The largest and smallest intervals between the corresponding keys on the five mbira are italicized.
[b] Especially great deviation   [c] T.F. - Tuning forks   [d] OCS. - Oscillator

methods described above were converted to cents, using Robert W. Young's table.[4] It is important to note that the data on mbira tunings collected by the second method complemented that collected by the first method and revealed the kinds of differences from one mbira tuning to another discussed in this chapter.

The amount of deviation among the intervals of adjacent keys on corresponding manuals of the different mbira (Table 3) varies from just under a quartertone (45 cents) in the R manual of the instruments to just over a minor third (329 cents) in the B manual. Looking at the individual manuals, the deviation varies from 45 to 162 cents on the R manual, from 72 to 145 cents on the L manual, and from 53 to 329 cents on the B manual. On the basis of these figures, it appears that the highest degree of correspondence among the respective intervals of the different mbira occurs in the highest register of the instrument (for example, R7–R8, R6–R7), and that the least correspondence is found in some of the intervals of the lowest register (for example, B1–B2, B3–B4, B4–B5).

The range of difference among Shona mbira tunings in Table 3 is also evident in a larger sample of tunings collected by the author compared with five tunings for the *mbira dzavadzimu* published previously.[5] Such diversity among mbira tunings and the range of variation possible between adjacent scale degrees within a particular mbira tuning (for example, in Table 4 the successive intervals in Mude's tuning of the B manual vary from 37 cents to 286 cents), call into question the prevailing theory of Shona mbira tunings, which is that "mbira makers and players use a distinctive, well defined scale, with only slight variation in different parts of the country. . . . It can be described as a seven-note scale, *with all the intervals equal.*"[6]

Another factor that distinguishes the sound of mbira with different *chunings* is the internal relationship among the intervals of each instrument. Mbira differ in the way in which their octaves are tuned and in the amount of variation among other corresponding intervals within the instrument's registers. This is shown in a comparison of the mbira of Gondo and Mude. While most of the corresponding intervals on Gondo's instrument are tuned within a quartertone of each other, the intervals on Mude's mbira show greater deviation (Table 4). At certain points (see figures indicated with arrows) they are tuned over a semitone apart. In addition, the octaves of the two instruments have a different character (Table 5). In Gondo's

Table 4
Corresponding Intervals in Different Mbira Registers in Cents

Descending scale degrees	Mbira keys	Low register	Mbira keys	Middle register	Mbira keys	High register	Greatest deviation
Gondo's Tuning							
7–8	B6–L1	198	L5–6	201 [a]	R8–9	192	9
6–7	B5–6	151	L4–5	164	R7–8	161	13
5–6	B4–5	186	L2–L4	137	R6–7	151	49
4–5	B3–4	164	L3–L2	191	R5–6	182	27
3–4	B2–3	157	R1–L3	180	R4–5	136	44
2–3		—[b]	B7–R1	187	R3–4	218	31
1–2		—[b]	L1–B7	151	R2–3	179	28
Mude's Tuning							
7–8	B6–L1	206	L5–6	128	R8–9	260	132 [c]
6–7	B5–6	158	L4–5	139	R7–8	173	34
5–6	B4–5	37	L2–L4	170	R6–7	172	135 [c]
4–5	B3–4	286	L3–L2	211	R5–6	214	75
3–4	B2–3	115	R1–L3	141	R4–5	118	26
2–3		—[b]	B7–R1	180	R3–4	180	0
1–2		—[b]	L1–B7	170	R2–3	231	61

[a] The largest and smallest corresponding intervals in the different registers of the mbira are italicized.
[b] These spaces are vacant because the second degree of the scale is omitted in the tuning plan of the bass register of the *mbira dzavadzimu*.
[c] Especially large intervals.

Table 5
Tuning of Octaves on Two Mbira DzaVadzimu

Groups of Keys Tuned One "Octave" Apart	Gondo's Mbira Deviation from a perfect octave (1200 Cents)	Mude's Mbira Deviation from a perfect octave (1200 Cents)
R9	+19	+148
R2	+11	− 61
L1	−21	−224
B1		
R4	+70	0
R1	− 6	− 48
B2		
R3	+39	0
B7		
R5	+26	− 23
L3	+17	− 22
B3		
R6	+17	− 20
L2	+44	−103
B4		
R7	+31	− 18
L4	− 5	+ 36
B5		
R8	+28	+ 16
L5	+ 8	+ 17
B6		

mbira the octaves are usually augmented, while on Mude's mbira they are frequently diminished.

The presence or absence of tuned overtones is an additional factor in distinguishing the *chunings* of different mbira. John Kunaka, for example, reported that the instruments he builds are different from those constructed by other local blacksmiths because he "gives two voices" to the lowest pitch (B1) on his instruments. To achieve this he forges keys which produce an overtone of approximately a fifth or a third, two octaves above the fundamental pitch. He regards these tuned overtones as "helping" the music during the performance of an mbira piece. His preference is for an overtone of a fifth, but he feels the third also helps the music. He distinguishes such tuned overtones from others which "do not help the music" and are therefore ignored by the performers.

As a result of the variables described above *mbira dzavad-zimu* can sound substantially different from one another. This is illustrated by the transcriptions of an excerpt from the classic piece "Nyamaropa" as performed on each of the instruments examined above (Examples 1 and 2). For the purpose of comparison in these examples the corresponding phrases have been moved to the same basic range, so that the respective keys L1 of the different mbira are equivalent to G_4 on the staff. (The actual pitches of these keys are given in parentheses to the left of each example.) Arrows indicate pitches between thirty-five and fifty cents above or below the pitch level indicated in the staff notation. In Example 1, transcription A (Kunaka's mbira) contains dotted circles and numbers that isolate features of the piece. These features are compared with the corresponding features of the "Nyamaropa" transcriptions B–E in Example 2.

Column 1 in Example 2 illustrates the varying nature of the octaves of "Nyamaropa," which on different mbira may be either augmented or diminished nearly a semitone. Column 3 shows the differences among corresponding simultaneities that arise during the piece when it is performed with different *chunings*. As indicated by the transcriptions, the equivalent simultaneities can vary from approximately a perfect fifth (Kunaka's mbira) to a tritone (Mujuru's mbira). Columns 2 and 4 show the degree to which the corresponding melodic patterns of the piece can be transformed from one mbira to the next. Particular intervals of the corresponding phrases vary from slightly under a minor third to a quartertone (50 cents) in relation to one an- 69

1. *An Excerpt of Nyamaropa Performed in Five Mbira Chunings*

other (compare Mude's and Kunaka's mbira, column 4). These examples illustrate the range of variation that can result when musicians select one *chuning* over another in which to perform their repertories for the mbira. While the basic relationships among the melodic/rhythmic phrases of the pieces remain approximately the same, the compositions take on a different character.

Mbira players are sensitive to the differences among particular mbira *chunings*: the effect of hearing a new mbira *chuning* can be jarring to the performers. On one occasion a musician offered to teach me an mbira piece that he had played many times before. Since my mbira was more readily available than his own, he asked to borrow it in order to demonstrate the piece for me. My instrument, however, was tuned differently from his. As a result, he became disoriented as soon as he began to play. After several attempts, the mbira player apologized to me and said he would have to go back to his own instrument in order to "remember" the piece again. Only after playing it several times on his own mbira was the musician able to teach me the composition on mine. My own reaction to mbira tunings in Zimbabwe was often similar to that of the musicians with whom I travelled. It was sometimes disorienting at first to listen to a different *mbira dzavadzimu* tuning. It took a short period of readjustment to accept a new collection of pitches as a point of reference for the appreciation of the instrument's repertory.

In other instances, however, musicians respond appreciatively to a different mbira *chuning*. On one such occasion, Hakurotwi Mude broke down in tears upon hearing the performance of an mbira piece played on a new mbira. He explained to me later that it had been the *chuning* of the musician's instrument that had moved him so deeply. Mude was in fact so moved by the performance that he commissioned the other musician, also a

2. *Corresponding Features of Nyamaropa in Five Mbira Chunings*   71

blacksmith, to make several mbira for him so that he could adopt the player's *chuning* for his own ensemble. This incident epitomizes the sensitivity of Shona mbira players to the subtle differences that distinguish various mbira and reflects the great significance different *chunings* can have for musicians.

The musician's conception of *chuning*, then, includes a complex of the interrelated aspects of an mbira's sound described in this section. Mbira regarded by musicians as having different *chunings* comprise a unique combination of these aspects. Among players of *mbira dzavadzimu*, the choice is largely a matter of personal taste.

The Repertory of Mbira Players

Mbira players have repertories of composed pieces (*rwiyo*, singular; *nziyo*, plural) which have been passed down orally and aurally from generation to generation. Although the Shona consider singing to be an integral part of mbira music, the compositions for the *mbira dzavadzimu* appear historically to have been instrumental pieces rather than having been derived from earlier songs. Musicians report that such pieces as "Nyamaropa," for example, date back to the origin of the *mbira dzavadzimu*, and they are performed only on the mbira.

Although individual musicians have a command of a varying number of mbira compositions (from ten to twenty or more), the number of mbira pieces in existence in some areas is quite sizable. Some virtuosi report that they know as many as a hundred pieces. In comparing the repertories of different musicians, one sometimes finds that the same pieces have different names. These differences can be minor, without significant changes in the meaning of the pieces. For example, "Taireva" ("We shall speak out") is known by some musicians as "Taisireva"; "Mukatiende" ("Wake up and let's go") is sometimes called "Bukatiende." A more significant difference occurs in the case of the composition that Pasipamire and Magaya know as "Nyamaropa" but which Kunaka learned as "Chipembere."[j] In spite of such differences, there is a high degree of correspondence among the repertories of musicians who play the same type of mbira.

[j] According to Kunaka, the piece played by Magaya and Pasipamire, which is commonly regarded as "Nyamaropa" by performers today (see Example 3) is actually a simplified version of the original "Nyamaropa" which was more complex rhythmically and was characterized by a more active bass line.

Each piece in the repertory of mbira players can be identified by its title, although the precise meaning of the composition's name has in some cases been lost. In other cases, musicians may attach different meanings to a title. Sometimes they explain the names of mbira pieces in terms of their historical or contemporary function in Shona culture. For example, "Nyamaropa," which literally means "meat and blood," has been described to me as "referring to the period after a hunt when meat is all around," as "a war song to arouse feelings before the battle," as "the scene of a battlefield after fighting when blood and flesh is everywhere," and as having "to do with the blood of a beast when it is sacrificed for the [ancestral spirits]."[7]

Within the general repertory of mbira players musicians distinguish individual pieces by their independent parts, history and function, formal features, and relative difficulty. Mbira compositions contain at least two basic parts that can be performed together by different musicians. The first part is called the *kushaura* ("to lead the piece, to take the solo part") and the second part is called the *kutsinhira* ("to exchange parts of a song; to interweave a second interlocking mbira part"). The first of the two parts contains much of the melodic essence of the piece, while the second often provides a contrasting rhythmic part. Together the two patterns form the basic structure of the composition.[k] If only one musician is present at a musical event, he features the *kushaura* part in his performance, because the *kutsinhira* part by itself does not always signal the identity of the piece to listeners.

On the basis of history and function, Ephat Mujuru divided sixty-eight pieces of his repertory into five categories: traditional pieces for the *mbira dzavadzimu*, traditional pieces for drums and chorus that have been adapted to the mbira, adaptations for the *mbira dzavadzimu* of *karimba* pieces associated with the *shangara* dance, newly composed pieces for the mbira, and story-songs accompanied by the mbira. Compositions in the first two categories are generally considered to be suitable for performance at religious ceremonies. Pieces from the latter three categories, on the other hand, are used primarily for entertainment at secular events. (It should be pointed out that although pieces that are regarded as being primarily for entertainment

[k] A musical example of two separate parts as they appear in a piece is provided on p. 93 and is discussed in the third section of this chapter, "The Anatomy of an Mbira Piece."

73

are not ordinarily played at religious ceremonies, pieces designated for religious ritual may be performed outside of ritual context.)

In discussing traditional mbira pieces designated for religious ritual, it is not uncommon to hear musicians praise particular compositions they consider to be the oldest and most important for the mbira. For example, the performers with *Mhuri yekwaRwizi* stressed the importance of such pieces as "Nyamaropa," "Nhemamusasa," "Kuzanga," "Muka tiende," "Mandarendare," and "Shumba." These were said to have been among the most favored tunes of Chaminuka and to have given him the power to dream about the future, to bring about miracles, and to make himself invincible. It is also said that these are effective pieces for bringing about the possession of spirit mediums today.

In addition to having dissimilar social functions and historical backgrounds, the pieces within the repertory of mbira players can differ considerably in formal features. Musicians refer to these features of mbira pieces in various ways, reporting, for example, that some compositions are played with "different mbira keys" (that is, they utilize a different selection of the mbira's pitches) while others use the "same keys, played differently." This means that the same basic pitches may be used in a number of pieces, employed differently in each to produce that piece's characteristic melodic and rhythmic patterns. Musicians make another distinction between pieces with a "high voice" overall and others with a "low voice," that is, the tonal centers of the pieces differ. Additionally, some pieces are "bigger" than others and are more suitable for extensive elaboration and variation. Sometimes musicians describe several pieces that share a number of basic elements in common as belonging to the same "family." These are often pieces that have historically been derived one from another. In such terms, then, musicians associate or distinguish mbira pieces on the basis of numerous formal aspects: harmonic structure (to be discussed below), characteristic rhythmic and melodic patterns, the pitches which comprise them, tonal centers, the number and length of the basic phrases, amount of variation associated with each piece, and the relationship between the piece's *kushaura* and *kutsinhira* parts. These features of mbira music are discussed below with the series of transcribed examples of mbira compositions illustrative of the repertory of mbira players.

Most mbira pieces consist of a forty-eight beat pattern divided into four major phrases of twelve beats each, repeated in a continuous cycle throughout the performance of the piece. A transcription of the *kushaura* part of the classic *mbira dzavadzimu* piece "Nyamaropa" illustrates this basic structure (Example 3).[1] The phrases that comprise "Nyamaropa" are arranged vertically (Sections I–IV) to facilitate comparison of their thematic and harmonic structures.. Typically, a basic motive is altered slightly in each phrase of the composition. The most radical transformation takes place at the beginning of the fourth phrase, at which point the first part of the motive moves up one scale degree.

In addition to the thematic transformation from one phrase to the next, the sections of the piece can be distinguished on the basis of their harmonic/melodic content. Mbira music can be regarded as contrapuntal in the sense that the parts of its compositions are characterized by the presence of a restricted set of two or sometimes three pitches played either simultaneously or consecutively, as melodic fragments. This is illustrated by the diagram beneath the transcription in Example 3, where the pitches distinguishing each harmonic or melodic unit and their scale degrees in relation to the emphasized tonal center of the piece are indicated in brackets. As shown by the diagram, the distinct harmonic feeling within the sections of Shona mbira music is commonly created by intervals of approximately an octave, a fifth, or a third, or by their inversions.[8] As mentioned in the section on tunings, there can be considerable variation among corresponding scale degrees on different mbira. The harmonic color of a section of an mbira piece depends upon the instruments on which it is performed. Reference in general terms to harmonic segments characterized by the presence of certain intervals in mbira music really concerns a class of particular intervals rather than fixed ratios (in other words, a perfect fifth on one instrument can be so different as to be a tritone on another). What is important to note is that the corresponding intervals within a class have the same relative functions within the piece, even when played on instruments with different tunings. Henceforth I will use the term harmonic progression to refer to the changing groups of pitches which characterize the

[1] A performance of the standard version of "Nyamaropa" (with its combined *kushaura* and *kutsinhira* parts) can be heard on *The Soul of Mbira*, side I, band 3.

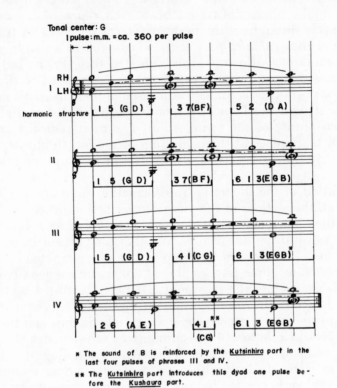

Tonal center: G

I pulse: m.m. = ca. 360 per pulse

* The sound of B is reinforced by the Kutsinhira part in the last four pulses of phrases III and IV.

** The Kutsinhira part introduces this dyad one pulse before the Kushaura part.

3. Nyamaropa (Kushaura)

In the transcriptions of mbira music, the smallest unit of time is represented by the vertical lines spaced evenly on the staff from left to right. (Stems with flags have been omitted because their use would tend to give the impression of rigid, fixed note-groupings, and this is not true to the character of Shona mbira music.) To illustrate the various melodic patterns of mbira music that are often created at different pitch levels of the piece, three varieties of note-heads are used:

O for pitches of the upper melodic lines, ● for pitches that comprise the middle voices, and ♀ for pitches forming the lower melodic patterns. The boundaries between particular notes in adjacent registers are flexible. Pitches from one register can combine with neighboring pitches from another to form new melodies.

Notes above the staff are played on the mbira with the right hand. The only exception to this is B_4, which is produced by key R1 and appears in the transcriptions in parenthesis with the symbol (o). All the other notes on or below the staff are played with the left hand. The note-heads designate only approximate pitches.

various segments of an mbira piece (for instance, in Example 3, Section I, the movement from pitches 1+5 to 3+7 to 5+2), and I will use the term harmonic rhythm to refer to the rate at which harmonic changes occur (for instance, in Example 3, Section I, the harmonic rhythm consists of four, three, and five pulses).

The piece examined above, "Nyamaropa," is known by musicians as one of the most ancient mbira compositions. According to many musicians, it was the first piece composed for the instrument. It is also considered to be especially important because it is the prototype of many other mbira pieces, including such classics as "Kariga Mombe," "Mahororo," "Mandarendare," "Chipindura," "Nhimutimu," and "Chaminuka ndimambo."

The relationship between "Nyamaropa" and two representative members of the "Nyamaropa" family, "Mahororo" and "Kariga Mombe," is shown in Example 4. In the transcriptions the phrases of each piece are arranged linearly and the symbol ᴧ indicates the main beat of each piece established by the accompanying gourd rattle pattern; for example, the complete *hosho* pattern, discussed on p. 113, would be approximated as follows: ♫♩ The three pieces considered together illustrate that class of mbira compositions which musicians describe as using the "same mbira keys, but played differently." As is apparent from the harmonic schemes provided below each transcription, the corresponding sections of each piece utilize the same basic pitch collection and follow the same general progression. (The harmonic structures outlined in Example 4 take into account pitches added by the *kutsinhira* parts; note the overlapping of the harmonic structure and phrase structure of the mbira pieces.)

At the same time, each piece has its own distinguishing characteristics. For example, while the overall harmonic movement is the same, each has a slightly different harmonic rhythm. This is evident in comparing the harmonic changes in the first phrase of "Nyamaropa" and "Mahororo." In "Nyamaropa" the changes produce a rhythmic pattern of four, three, and five pulses, while in "Mahororo" the pattern is three, three, and six pulses. The rhythmic relationship among the melodic lines also differs from one piece to the next. "Nyamaropa" comprises two contrasting rhythmic parts. Within each basic six-pulse unit, the upper voice—played by the right hand—occurs every two pulses, and 77 the lower voice—played by the left hand—has a three-pulse pattern, sounding on the first and third pulse. In the performance of "Mahororo" the hands interlock on every other underlying pulse, creating the effect of a basic six-pulse structure. "Kariga Mombe" consists of a sequence of dyads in which the upper and lower voices are heard simultaneously on every other underlying pulse. A three against two pattern exists between the mbira part and the *hosho*, with the mbira in three and the *hosho* in two. The individual patterns coincide every second *hosho* beat. (The grouping of the *hosho* in two does not indicate a downbeat-upbeat pattern; each *hosho* beat indicated in the transcription is played as a downbeat.) Characteristics such as these allow listeners to recognize the identity of individual pieces within a particular family of compositions, even when they are based on the same collection of pitches or follow the same overall harmonic progression.

Among mbira pieces unrelated by family, other formal differences exist as well. Some pieces considered as a whole have higher or lower "voices" or tonal centers. The two most common tonal centers among pieces for the *mbira dzavadzimu* are the lowest pitch on the instrument (G_3 in the transcriptions) and the pitch a fourth above this (C_4 in the transcriptions). Bandambira emphasized the importance of these pitches (Table 1), describing the former as the pitch "which settles the mbira and holds the piece together" and the latter as "one of the most important pitches; the mother of mbira."

Two classic mbira pieces with different tonal centers are "Nyamaropa" (Example 3), which has a low tonal center, and "Nhemamusasa" (Example 5), which has a high tonal center.[m] It is interesting to note that "Nyamaropa" and "Nhemamusasa" share basic elements of harmonic and thematic structure in spite of the difference in their tonal centers: they follow the same overall harmonic progression, and the form of their thematic development is very similar. Each section of both pieces consists of a basic motive which varies in a slightly different musical direction. The most dramatic change occurs in Section IV, when in "Nyamaropa" the first part of the motive is transposed up a scale degree, and in "Nhemamusasa" the entire phrase is transposed up a scale degree.

[m] The *kushaura* part to "Nhemamusasa" by itself may be heard on side I, band 1(a) of *Shona Mbira Music*.

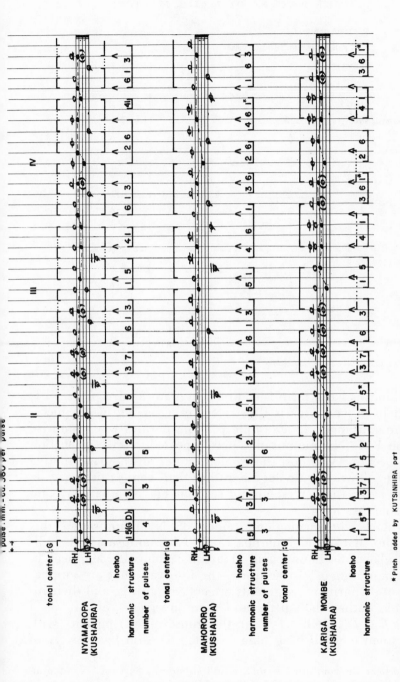

4. *Pieces Derived from Nyamaropa*

* Pitch added by KUTSINHIRA part

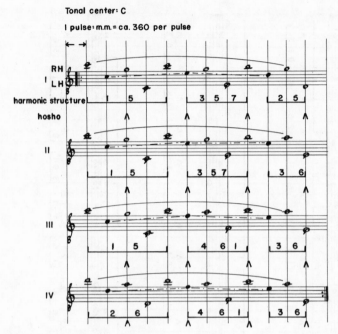

Tonal center: C

I pulse: m.m. = ca. 360 per pulse

5. *Nhemamusasa (Kushaura)*

While this basic form is common to many mbira pieces, it is varied in others. This is illustrated by a version of the piece, "Nyamamusango" in Example 6.[n] The phrases that comprise Section I of "Nyamamusango" are repeated exactly in Section II. In Section IV almost the whole first part of the basic motive is moved down a scale degree, rather than being raised a scale degree as in the corresponding sections of "Nyamaropa" and "Nhemamusasa."

Similarly, the harmonic movement of "Nyamamusango" differs from that of "Nyamaropa" and "Nhemamusasa." As indicated above, Sections I and II are harmonically identical in "Nyamamusango." In addition, the intervals that are emphasized in its harmonic segments are octaves, thirds, and their inversions, rather than fifths and their inversions, and it has a strong *C-G-D* (pitches 1-5-2 in the transcription) polarity with a common embellishing tone *F* (pitch 4), and less variety of

[n] To hear the combined *kushaura* and *kutsinhira* parts of "Nyamamusango," listen to side II, band 4 of *Shona Mbira Music*.

embellishing tones such as *A* and *E* (in contrast to the preva-
lence of pitches 3 and 6 shown in Examples 3 and 5).

Melodic contour is another feature by which mbira pieces can
be distinguished. In many mbira pieces it is common for the
outer melodic parts—the high-tone melody and the bass melody
—to move in contrary motion to one another. Frequently there
is a basic funnel movement in which the outer melodic lines
begin as much as an octave and a fifth to two octaves apart and
gradually move toward each other, coming to rest an octave
apart. "Nyamamusango" offers an example of contrast to this
basic form. Its outer voices move essentially in parallel or
oblique motion. In the lower voice of Sections I and II there is
a repeated pattern that also characterizes the piece.

There are still other distinguishing features in the relationship between the outer voices of mbira pieces. For example, while
most *kushaura* parts utilize all three registers of the mbira, several pieces such as "Kariga Mombe" (Example 4) eliminate the
bass register so that their outer voices are contained within two

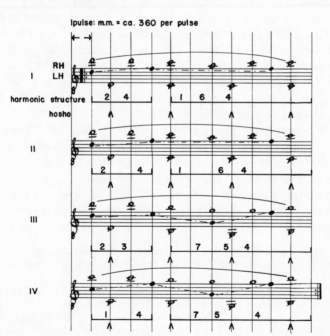

6. Nyamamusango (Kushaura)

octaves rather than three.[o] In still another format, the outer voices change in relation to one another throughout the piece. For example, in the piece "Chaminuka we" a melodic line in the bass and middle register alternates in relation to a constant high-tone melody. This creates the effect of a call and response pattern between the upper and lower voices of the piece.[p] Additional distinguishing factors in mbira pieces include the length and number of phrases that make up its basic structure and the pitches they utilize.

All of the mbira pieces examined thus far have followed the basic form of four phrases of twelve beats each. Example 7 illustrates pieces that offer a variation on this basic structure. The first, "Kuzanga," is a traditional piece for the *mbira dzavadzimu* with the same tonal center as "Nhemamusasa" (Example 5). "Kuzanga" has phrases of nine beats each, however, rather than twelve. Its harmonic pattern also differs in some respects. While Sections II and III of "Kuzanga" follow a harmonic progression similar to corresponding sections of "Nhemamusasa," its Sections IV and I center around the fifth scale degree above the tonal center, varying the structure of "Nhemamusasa."

The second transcription in Example 7 is "Baya wabaya," a traditional piece for drums and chorus adapted for the *mbira dzavadzimu*. While its tonal center and harmonic progression are the same as in "Nyamaropa," its phrases are eight beats long (3+2+3). This represents a considerable contrast to traditional mbira pieces, whose characteristic phrases are in multiples of three pulses in length, rather than two.

The third transcription in Example 7, that of "Chemutengure," illustrates an *mbira dzavadzimu* adaptation of a piece traditional to the small type of *karimba*.[q] It consists of two phrases rather than four, and its basic progression is equivalent to that of the first two phrases of "Nyamaropa." "Chemutengure" and "Baya wabaya" also exemplify mbira pieces which musicians say "use different mbira keys," that is, particular

[o] An example of a piece which eliminates the bass register in its *kushaura* part is the version of "Taireva" found on *Shona Mbira Music*, side I, band 3.

[p] Parts of the version of "Chaminuka we" on *Shona Mbira Music*, side II, band 5, provide an example of this effect.

[q] The small type of karimba from whose repertory "Chemutengure" is adapted often does not have the fourth degree of the scale represented on its keyboard. A performance of "Chemutengure" by Maraire on one such karimba is on *Mbira Music of Rhodesia*, side I, band 1; see discography.

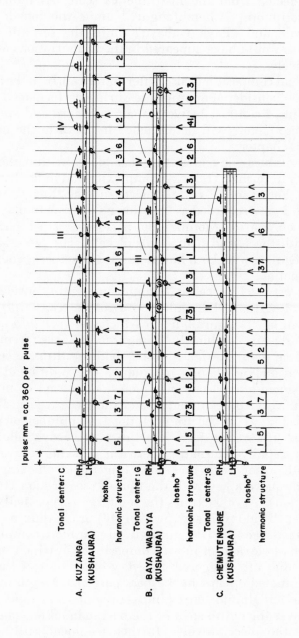

*Examples B and C show complete hosho patterns

7. *Mbira Pieces with Various Phrase Lengths*

pitches selected from the instrument's scale. As indicated in the transcriptions, "Chemutengure" omits the fourth degree of the scale and "Baya wabaya" omits the seventh degree. These notes would have appeared in the transcriptions as A and F respectively.

Individual compositions also differ significantly in the amount of variation considered appropriate during performance, and in the amount of contrast between their *kushaura* and *kutsinhira* parts. These factors will be discussed in detail in the next section of this chapter.

Finally, mbira players distinguish pieces within their own repertories in terms of relative complexity and difficulty in performance. For example, certain pieces such as "Kariga Mombe" (Example 3) are regarded as "beginner's pieces." In playing the *kushaura* of "Kariga Mombe" the performer is primarily concerned with the L and R manuals of keys. The piece is rhythmically regular, with both hands playing together, generally in parallel motion.

In contrast, such pieces as "Dangurangu" are considered the province of virtuosi. Example 8 provides a transcription of a solo version of "Dangurangu" in which the *kushaura* and *kutsinhira* parts are combined. "Dangurangu" is a far more advanced piece than "Kariga Mombe" both in ultimate complexity of form and in playing technique. The right-hand part of the piece includes sections in which a succession of pitches is played on every consecutive pulse of the piece (see circled portion of Section II in the transcription). A number of playing techniques are called for. Sometimes successive pitches are played by rapidly alternating between plucking upward from underneath a key with the index finger and plucking downward from above a key with the thumb (see Section IIb in the transcription). At other times the same key is repeatedly struck with either the index finger (Section IIc) or the thumb (Section Ia). Such passages in "Dangurangu" are far more complex than those of most versions of mbira compositions in which the high-tone melodies are staggered on every other beat of the piece. The wide melodic leaps in the bass part of "Dangurangu," in which the left thumb must jump—sometimes as much as five inches—over the entire span of the bass manual on consecutive pulses of the piece, involve further technical skill (Section IIId). These techniques require a great deal of strength, endur-
84 ance, and agility on the part of the player.

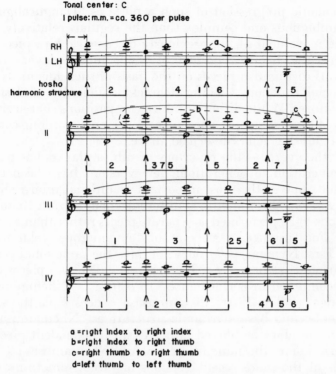

Tonal center: C
I pulse: m.m. = ca. 360 per pulse

a = right index to right index
b = right index to right thumb
c = right thumb to right thumb
d = left thumb to left thumb

8. Dangurangu (Solo Version Combining Kushaura and Kutsinhira)

In addition to the technical mastery required to play virtuoso pieces like "Dangurangu," the formal aspects of such pieces are considerably more complex than other compositions in the repertory of musicians. For example, in contrast to many mbira pieces in which the basic melodic/rhythmic pattern of the first section is repeated throughout the piece, "Dangurangu" is comprised of melodic/rhythmic patterns which change in relation to one another in every section of the piece. One prominent feature of this piece is the powerful bass line, the irregular rhythm of which only occasionally coincides with the beat of the *hosho*. The differing melodic/rhythmic configurations in the right- and left-hand parts of this piece epitomize the complexity of Shona mbira music. They result in that independence of the upper, middle, and lower melodic parts of the piece which produces the effect of several instruments being played at once.[r] Finally,

[r] For a demonstration refer to the version of "Dangurangu" on *The Soul of Mbira*, side II, band 4.

85

the harmonic progression of such a piece as "Dangurangu" is more ambiguous and complex than the regular, relatively predictable movement of the previously discussed mbira pieces.

Within the diverse repertory of Shona mbira players, then, musicians distinguish pieces on the basis of such factors as history, social function, varying degrees of difficulty, and structural features. While different mbira compositions share certain aspects of their structure, each piece represents a unique combination of all the factors described above.

Over the years, as the repertory of mbira players has passed from generation to generation, new versions have been composed for some of the most important traditional mbira pieces. These versions are sometimes different enough from the older renditions to be performed as separate pieces rather than as variations. For instance, a version of "Nyamaropa yekutanga" ("The First Nyamaropa") does not have the same tonal center and harmonic structure as "Nyamaropa." The two pieces cannot be combined in performance.[8] In contrast, "Nhemamusasa yekutanga" ("The First Nhemamusasa") does have the same tonal center and basic harmonic structure as "Nhemamusasa," and can therefore be played either as an independent piece or as a variation on the standard version of "Nhemamusasa."

Titles of the more recent versions of pieces sometimes contain the names of their composers or the names of the villages where they were composed: "Shumba yaNgwasha" is the version of "Shumba" composed by Ngwasha; "Nyamaropa yeDambatsoko" is the version of "Nyamaropa" composed at Dambatsoko. Newer renditions of ancient pieces often have their own set of variations in both the *kushaura* and *kutsinhira* parts.

Development of new pieces for the mbira and creation of new versions of traditional pieces are attributed by musicians to three sources: dreams, deliberate composition, and accidental discoveries made in the process of playing the mbira. Musicians report that a person can learn new pieces through dreams in which he is assisted by ancestral spirits. John Kunaka remarks that the "new" pieces a person learns in dreams are actually the ancient pieces of the spirits who are teaching him. This interesting theoretical point is consistent with Muchatera Mujuru's

[8] Versions of "Nyamaropa" and "Nyamaropa yekutanga" are on *The Soul of Mbira*, side I, band 3, and *Shona Mbira Music*, side II, band 1, respectively.

story about Zimba Risina Musuwo (given in the preceding chapter). In that story mbira pieces first belonged to the spirits, who later taught them to the people. The music existed in the spirit world, then, even before the mbira appeared among the Shona.

Some pieces are deliberate compositions; Ephat Mujuru composed one such song, "Muchatera wauya," in honor of his grandfather. The origin of other new compositions is unanticipated discovery in performance. While playing a sequence of pitches, for instance, a musician sometimes reaches for a particular key but misses it, hitting another instead, and finds that he likes its sound as well. Such accidents during the performance of mbira music can lead to the creation of new versions of older pieces or to new pieces altogether.

Although there are new compositions in the general repertory of players of *mbira dzavadzimu*, their number is small in comparison to the large body of traditional pieces. This does not mean, however, that the repertory of an individual musician is fixed. Musicians regularly expand their repertory by learning new variations on traditional pieces and by learning additional mbira classics from the vast repertories of expert players.

Several factors have contributed to the conservative nature of the mbira repertory. One is the inherent fascination the traditional pieces hold for Shona musicians. Factors such as variation, improvisation, and other subtleties of the music keep traditional pieces fresh from performance to performance. The practice of changing mbira tunings may limit the need for new compositions: when performers tire of the sound of the traditional mbira pieces in one tuning they can adopt another and thereby give their mbira pieces slightly different, fresh characters.

Finally, a significant factor restricting the adoption of new mbira pieces for the *mbira dzavadzimu* is the closeness of its tradition to religious worship. Musicians tend to regard newly composed pieces less seriously than traditional pieces, considering them unsuitable for performance at religious events. According to mbira players who perform professionally at spirit possession ceremonies, the mediums' spirits most appreciate and respond to the traditional pieces they remember from the time when they lived in the world as human beings. This belief must have the powerful effect of insuring survival of the old mbira classics.

87

The Anatomy of an Mbira Piece: "Nhemamusasa"

While Shona mbira compositions can be viewed in terms of their harmonic aspects, their most characteristic feature is the complexity of the relationship among the interwoven melodic lines. As mentioned previously, musicians themselves observe that a single mbira can produce the effect of two or more instruments being played simultaneously. One explanation for the apparent complexity of the music lies in a phenomenon known as "inherent rhythms."[9] Inherent rhythms are those melodic/rhythmic patterns not directly being played by the performer but arising from the total complex of the mbira music. They are the product of the psycho-acoustic fact that the ear does not perceive a series of tones as isolated pitches, but as a gestalt. For example, in mbira music in which the hands typically play large melodic leaps, the ear does not necessarily follow the precise linear melodic patterns being played; it picks out pitches of a similar level and groups them in separate independent phrases. Compositions of the Baroque period in which there is a contrapuntal dialogue between the upper and lower voices, such as the Bach unaccompanied violin and cello suites, create this effect in Western music. Transcription A of Example 9 illustrates inherent rhythms by showing three major resultant lines that arise from the *kushaura* part to "Nhemamusasa."

In the performance of "Nhemamusasa" the right hand plays the high-tone melody on every other pulse of the piece. This part interlocks with the left-hand part, which consists of the alternation between pitches in the middle and the bass register on every two pulses of the piece. As this *kushaura* part repeats in a cycle, the three resultant lines sound independently of each other. A number of factors enhance the independence of the parts. First, each melodic line begins and ends at different points in the forty-eight beat cycle of the piece and has a different relationship to the main *hosho* beat. Second, the rattles attached to the mbira's soundboard and to the calabash respond at different levels of intensity to the various melodies, at times emphasizing the melodic rhythm of the bass part. Third, the practice of tuning octaves slightly differently within the overall tuning arrangement of the instrument may enhance the differences among the melodies heard at the three pitch levels of the piece.

In addition to the major stratification of the melodic parts that results when mbira music is performed, there are also changes

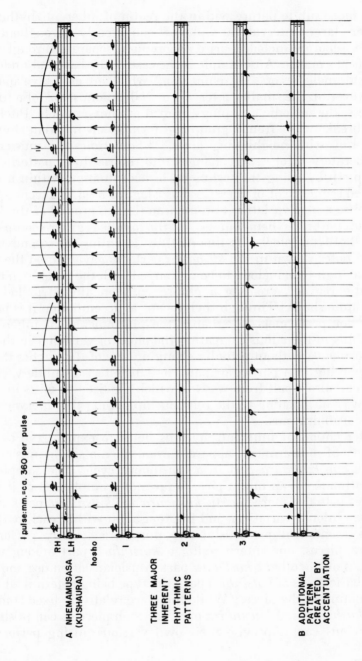

9. *Nhemamusasa: Inherent Rhythms*

of a more subtle nature within the realm of inherent rhythms. When large intervals are played consistently throughout a piece, separate melodies arise and remain separate throughout the performance. An example is the case of the bass and middle register melodies of "Nhemamusasa," which are an octave apart. However, in the smaller intervals in "Nhemamusasa," of a fifth or less, the melodic groupings formed are not as stable. Pitches can break away "from a group and form a new inherent rhythmic line with neighboring notes."[10] Sometimes the musician deliberately brings such changes to the resultant patterns of the piece by using the technique of accentuation within a repeated sequence of pitches. Cosmas Magaya used this technique to cause a new variation to come into the foreground of the *kushaura* part of "Nhemamusasa" in the middle register (compare line B of Example 9 with line A2). By accenting the second and third notes shown in the *kushaura* part, Magaya caused the G_5 in the high-tone melody to be regrouped with the melody in the middle register, creating a phrase with an altered melodic/rhythmic shape.[t] Through such means as accentuation it is possible for performers to enhance the phenomenon of inherent rhythms in their music, creating the effect of variation in their performance without actually changing any of the pitches they are playing in a particular pattern. This effect of subtle variation can also result from ways in which the listener shifts his or her way of listening to the relationship among the interwoven lines of mbira music.[11]

The notion of inherent rhythms helps to explain the complexity of mbira music, apparent even when a single musician plays one *kushaura* part in a continuous cycle. The complete performance of an mbira piece is far more complex, since it includes both the characteristic *kushaura* and *kutsinhira* parts and the traditional variations and improvisation within each part.

As mentioned previously, two musicians usually perform mbira pieces, one interweaving a *kutsinhira* part among the pitches of the other's *kushaura* part. Musicians often use one of two basic types of *kutsinhira* part, the type being determined by the nature of the piece. (While there are relatively fixed standard *kushaura* and *kutsinhira* parts for each piece, accomplished musicians can improvise their own versions during perform-

---

[t] The beginning of "Nhemamusasa," on *Shona Mbira Music*, side I, band 1(a), uses this pattern.

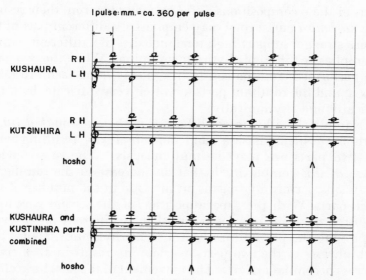

10. *Nyamamusango: Excerpt of Kushaura and Kutsinhira Parts Combined*

ance.) For example, such pieces as "Kuzanga," "Shumba," "Dande," and "Nyamamusango" use a *kutsinhira* part either identical or very similar to the *kushaura* part.[u] The *kutsinhira* part falls one beat behind the *kushaura* part; the parts interlock so that the second player in effect echoes the first musician's pitches. An excerpt from "Nyamamusango" in Example 10 illustrates this basic arrangement. As indicated by the transcription, it is common in pieces of this nature for the bass melody of the *kushaura* part to coincide with the main *hosho* beat. Performers of *kutsinhira* parts of this type often emphasize their bass pitches, thereby increasing the rhythmic tension between the two parts.

A second type of *kutsinhira* part is more appropriate for such pieces as "Nyamaropa" and "Nhemamusasa."[v] The *kutsinhira*

[u] "Dande," "Shumba," and "Nyamamusango" are on *Shona Mbira Music*, side I, band 2 and side II, bands 3 and 4, respectively.

[v] "Nhemamusasa" is on *Shona Mbira Music*, side I, band 1; "Nyamaropa" is on *The Soul of Mbira*, side I, band 3. There are some pieces, moreover, which are suitable for both kinds of the arrangements described above: for example, the version of "Taireva" on *The Soul of Mbira*, side I, band 2, has similar *kutsinhira* and *kushaura* parts, while the version on *Shona Mbira Music*, side II, band 2, has differing parts.

91

parts of these compositions differ in character from their respective *kushaura* parts; they may emphasize a different part of the mbira's range, support high-tone melodies of a different nature, or emphasize different rhythmic groupings. When the two parts are performed simultaneously, fragments from each are interwoven and the resultant parts are often very intricate, both melodically and rhythmically.

Example 11 illustrates differing *kushaura* and *kutsinhira* parts for "Nhemamusasa" and the complexity resulting when the two parts are played simultaneously.[w] The most obvious cause of this complexity is that an increase in the number of musicians performing means an increase in the number of melodic parts. With the superimposition of the second part upon the first, new pitches cluster together at different pitch levels, improving the possibilities for inherent rhythmic activity. Second, phrases of the two parts overlapping result in an increase of cross-accentual activity. The movement of the bass lines clearly reflects this. At the beginning of the transcription the bass line of the *kutsinhira* part comes in just one pulse ahead of the *kushaura* bass line. However, since the bass of the *kushaura* is played every four pulses and the bass of the *kutsinhira* is played every three pulses, their phrases coincide on every twelfth beat, creating a basic polyrhythm of three against four. In a manner typical of certain pieces with differing *kushaura* and *kutsinhira* parts, the bass line of the latter coincides with the main *hosho* beat.

The last line in Example 11 shows the overall resultant pattern created when the *kushaura* and *kutsinhira* parts are combined; they interlock, creating new rhythmic/melodic configurations at each stratum of the instrument's range. In the high-tone melodic part a characteristic rippling effect is created by the rapid succession of pitches on consecutive pulses of the piece. In the middle and bass parts, there are new rhythmically regular patterns characterized by repeated pitches. The repeated pitches are especially prominent in the middle voice, but also

---

[w] Transcribed Examples 11–15 coincide with the first musical example on *Shona Mbira Music*, side I, which includes similar or identical versions of "Nhemamusasa." As indicated by Examples 11 and 15, the major area of contrast between differing *kushaura* and *kutsinhira* parts is found in the middle and lower voices of the music. The upper voice of the *kutsinhira* generally follows or anticipates the melodic patterns of the upper voice of the *kushaura* part.

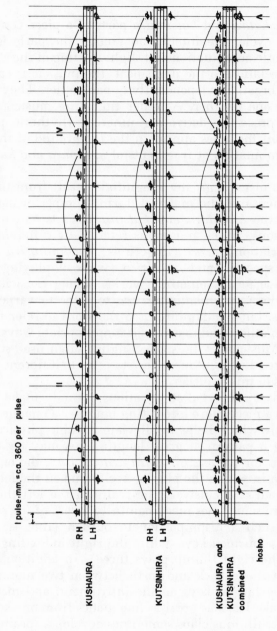

11. *Nhemamusasa: Kushaura and Kutsinhira*

occur in the bass part at the beginning of each twelve-pulse phrase.

As the *kushaura* and *kutsinhira* parts of a piece continue in an ongoing cycle, the interaction among the parts is lively. Through subtle accentuation and slight shifting of the rhythmic patterns in relation to the main beat, the musicians can cause the parts to breathe independently of each other. They seem to rebound off one another. At other times the musicians mesh their parts precisely, activating inherent rhythmic patterns. New resultant melodies appear in the foreground of the music from the combination of fragments of *kushaura* and *kutsinhira* parts.

Variations of even greater magnitude result from the introduction of new melodic material during the performance of a piece. Both the *kushaura* and *kutsinhira* parts can introduce these variations, which musicians refer to by different terms: *musaku* (variation), *zvara* (fingerings), *madunhurirwa* (exaggeration in speech), and *miridziro* (ways of playing).[12] The usage of these terms sometimes varies among musicians: Kunaka used the word *madunhurirwa* to refer to variations on mbira pieces, but Bandambira used the word to refer to pieces derived from others and to errors or inappropriate ways of playing pieces. Musicians who speak English often use "styles" or the Shona-ized English "mastyles" to refer to different versions or variations of mbira pieces.

Mbira players report that variations not only make the performance of a piece more interesting but offer a change of playing technique which helps to alleviate possible physical strain in repeating a pattern at great length. This may be a special consideration for players of *mbira dzavadzimu*, the only large Shona mbira in which the playing technique on the left side of the instrument is exclusively the realm of the left thumb. Its musicians are sometimes made painfully aware of the problems created by such a disproportionate burden (that is, the left thumb plays fourteen keys, while the right index finger plays seven and the right thumb plays three). In addition, the left thumb must move back and forth between two manuals consisting of the largest keys on the instrument, and may be required to make leaps as great as five inches from one key to the next. As a result, musicians sometimes develop a sprain in their left wrist (possibly tendonitis) that requires treatment by a n'anga (see p. 237).

94 *n'anga* (see p. 237).

The versions of a piece that musicians play during a performance fall into three basic categories. First, there is often a pair of standard *kushaura* and *kutsinhira* parts that performers consider to be most basic to the piece. Second are traditional variations that have been passed down aurally from one generation to the next and form a permanent part of the musicians' repertories. Third are variations that are the creations of the individual performers. These are often discovered during the process of improvisation which comprises part of the performance of mbira music, and then become a permanent or semi-permanent part of the musician's repertory.

The amount of variation and improvisation that takes place during the performance of a piece is the result of a number of factors, including not only the knowledge and skill of the mbira player but also the character of the piece itself. There are several pieces, such as "Kuzanga" and "Nyamamusango," which, according to Shona musicians, are not suited to a great deal of elaboration.[x] The variations associated with them tend to be few and subtle in nature. In contrast, such pieces as "Nyamaropa" and "Nhemamusasa" are very well suited for elaboration. Musicians are usually familiar with many different versions of such pieces and may alternate them during a performance. The context of a performance can also be a consideration. Musicians stress, for example, that for the learner the experimentation involved in developing new variations and imitating the styles of other performers should never take place at the *bira*; at such an event mistakes in mbira playing could have a detrimental effect on the possession of the medium. Therefore students should play only basic *kushaura* parts at a *bira*.

Variations on a piece can involve change at any of the pitch levels of the music. Lines A, B, and C in Example 12 illustrate three variations on the standard high-tone *kushaura* part of "Nhemamusasa." Any of these patterns may be played in relation to the left-hand lower-voiced part of the piece, shown at the bottom of the example. Each of the variations shown produces a different melodic contour in the upper part of the piece. In variation A the pitches indicated in parentheses can be

[x] Several such pieces—"Dande," "Shumba," "Nyamamusango," and "Chaminuka we"—are on *Shona Mbira Music*, side I, band 2 and side II, bands 3–5. Musicians sometimes play without much elaboration pieces capable of supporting many variations, as, for example, the version of "Taireva I" on *Shona Mbira Music*, side I, band 3.

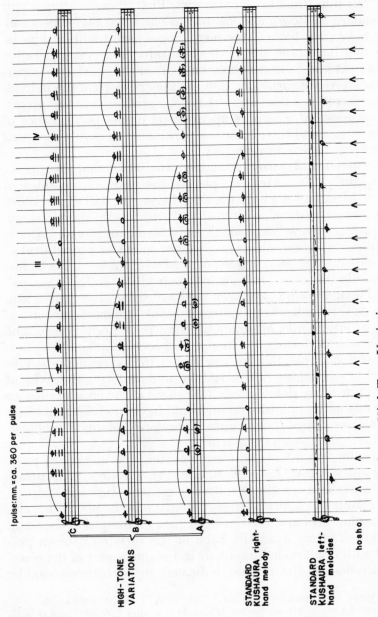

12. *Nhemamusasa: Kushaura High-Tone Variations*

played together with those above them as dyads. This common form of coloration used in the upper voice of mbira music usually involves dyads or simultaneities of octaves, thirds, or fifths, or their inversions. Variation C illustrates a standard melodic pattern which can be adapted to many mbira pieces: it consists of two stepwise descending phrases, each containing repeated pitches and encompassing a full octave in range. Usually the player begins a performance with a basic, characteristic version of the piece (Example 12, Standard parts) and then introduces the more extended melodic patterns (Example 12, A–C) as he develops the complexity of the piece.

The high-tone melodies of the *kushaura* and *kutsinhira* parts of mbira pieces interlock in performance, as was illustrated in Example 11. Often in this interaction between the two musicians the first introduces a variation utilizing a characteristic high-tone pattern in the *kushaura* part and the second imitates this pattern one beat behind in the *kutsinhira* part. (The *kutsinhira* player may also perform high-tone patterns anticipating the part of the *kushaura* player by one beat.) When, after several repetitions of one pattern, the first player switches to another, the second player follows suit. The *kushaura* player sometimes deliberately challenges the *kutsinhira* player in this respect and the interaction between them can be very spirited. During a performance musicians often alternate between playing high-tone patterns in a strictly imitative fashion and departing in different musical directions, playing contrasting melodic parts against each other, but returning from time to time to the performance of high-tone patterns characteristic of the piece so that its identity will not be obscured by their improvisations.

Variations can also be focused on the lower melodic parts of the music. Musical terminology used by the mbira players with whom I studied distinguishes such variations on the basis of their concentration in the middle register of the instrument (that is, the L manual), the bass register (that is, the B manual), or both registers. Variations on the L manual of the mbira, diminishing or eliminating the use of the bass pitches, are *kushaura* or *kutsinhira kwepamusoro*, the leading or the interweaving of the upper ones (that is, upper keys). Variations on the B manual, minimizing or eliminating the middle register, are *kushaura* or *kutsinhira kwepasi*, the leading or interweaving of the lower ones. Variations that include the use of both L and B manuals are *kushaura* or *kutsinhira kwepamusoro nepasi*, 97 the leading or interweaving of the upper and lower ones. The *kushaura* and *kutsinhira* parts of "Nhemamusasa" (Example 11) illustrate the latter type. During performance of a piece the characteristic high-tone patterns play in relation to the changing variations in the lower voices and vice versa. Not all mbira pieces are considered suitable for all types of variation; some have only certain types of variation associated with them. In addition, some kinds of variation, *kushaura kwepasi*, for example, are uncommon, although mbira players sometimes use them for contrast to a particular *kutsinhira* part performed by a second musician.

Within the categories discussed above, some of the variations of the standard *kushaura* or *kutsinhira* parts are subtle. However, because of the limited number of pitches on which mbira pieces are based and because of the phenomenon of inherent rhythms, changes such as the substitution of one or two pitches in a melodic sequence can cause whole new phrases to appear in mbira music. The left-hand parts of several versions of "Nhemamusasa" (*kushaura kwepamusoro nepasi*) illustrate this (Example 13a, 1 and 2). The standard *kushaura* part, which we have examined previously, is shown in the first line of the example. Just below it is a variation (version 1) in which the new pitches, A_4, G_1, and G_4, are indicated with arrows. Lines A and B below this part show two resultant patterns that emerge from the introduction of the new pitches. Since these pitches are sufficiently close to both the middle and the bass melodies, they can form inherent rhythmic phrases with either, as the transcription illustrates.

Within a melodic sequence individual pitches can be replaced by their harmonic counterparts an interval of a third, fourth, fifth, or octave away. Such substitutions give rise to new melodic/rhythmic patterns without disturbing the harmonic rhythm of the piece. A comparison of version 2 of Example 13a with the standard part reveals such pitch substitution to be a common principle underlying the formation of variations in Shona mbira music. The changes that have taken place in relation to the standard *kushaura* part are indicated in version 2 with arrows.

This basic principle also operates in the formation of variations of the types *kushaura kwepamusoro* and *kushaura kwepasi*; see Example 13b, versions 1 and 2, respectively. In version 1, the octave equivalent from the middle register of the instrument replaces each pitch in the bass line of the standard part to

I pulse: mm. = ca. 360 per pulse

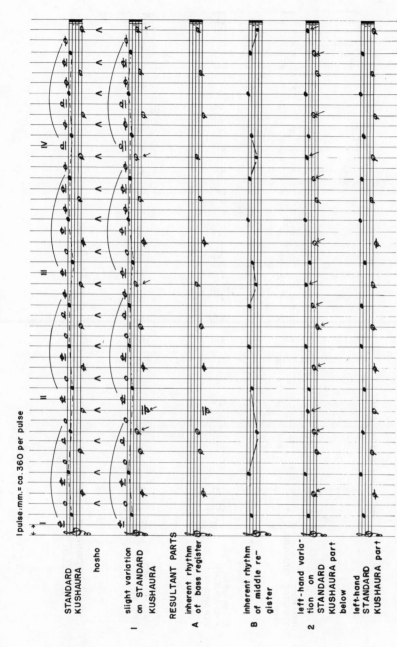

STANDARD KUSHAURA

hosho

1 slight variation on STANDARD KUSHAURA

RESULTANT PARTS

A inherent rhythm of bass register

B inherent rhythm of middle re- gister

2 left-hand varia- tion on STANDARD KUSHAURA part below

left-hand STANDARD KUSHAURA part

13A. Nhemamusasa Variations: Kushaura KwePamusoro NePasi

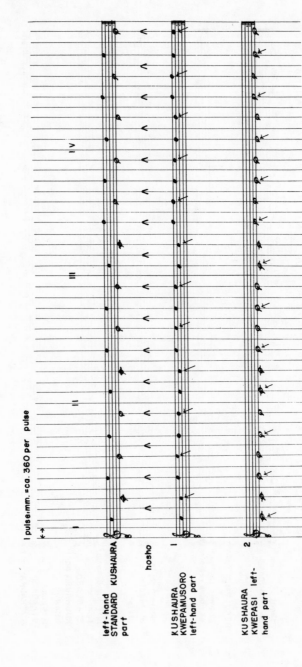

13B. Nhemamusasa Variations: Kushaura KwePamusoro, Kushaura KwePasi

left-hand STANDARD KUSHAURA part

hosho

KUSHAURA KWEPAMUSORO left-hand part

KUSHAURA KWEPASI left-hand part

I pulse:mm. =ca. 360 per pulse

form the *kushaura kwepamusoro* (see notes designated by arrows in transcription). Similarly, in version 2 the octave counterpart in the bass register of the instrument replaces every pitch in the middle register of the standard part to form the *kushaura kwepasi*.

In another approach to forming variations, musicians sometimes alter a pattern by deleting certain pitches within the overall part, causing new melodic/rhythmic phrases at various strata of the music. A variation on the standard *kushaura* part of "Nhemamusasa" in which the mbira player deletes every third pitch in the bass melody while performing the complete melodic patterns in the upper parts of the piece exemplifies this approach.

During the performance of an mbira piece the musician tends to concentrate his variations on one side of the instrument at a time. He will hold a particular pattern in the lower voices of the mbira music constant while gradually varying the high-tone melody. After settling upon a high-tone pattern, he holds this constant and introduces variation in the middle or lower register of the instrument. In a typical performance of the versions of "Nhemamusasa," the performer begins by playing the standard part in a continuous cycle and introduces the new pitches of version 1 (Example 13a) in the lower parts of the music while keeping the high-tone melody the same. After some time elapses, the player switches to one of the characteristic stepwise descending high-tone patterns (Example 12), while keeping the lower voices constant. After several repetitions of this new combination of variations, he alters the lower parts (as in version 2, Example 13a), while keeping the descending stepwise high-tone melody constant, and so on. In a similar manner, he can switch from these *kushaura kwepamusoro nepasi* parts to *kushaura kwepamusoro* or *kushaura kwepasi*. Such changes minimize or eliminate the use of particular registers of the instrument, causing old patterns to fade away and new ones to come into focus.

The performer of the *kutsinhira* parts has the same, or a greater, range of possibilities for variations available to him during a performance. Example 14 illustrates some of these possibilities. The first *kutsinhira* part, examined in Example 11, utilizes both the middle and bass register of the instrument and exemplifies a *kutsinhira kwepamusoro nepasi*. The second example illustrates a *kutsinhira kwepamusoro* part, minimizing the   101

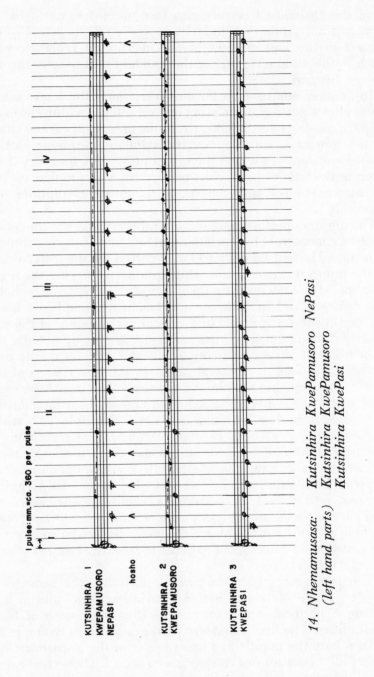

14. *Nhemamusasa:*   *Kutsinhira KwePamusoro NePasi*
     (left hand parts)   *Kutsinhira KwePamusoro*
                     Kutsinhira KwePasi

use of the bass register of the mbira. The third example mini-mizes the use of the middle register and is a *kutsinhira kwepasi* part. While these parts share a similar rhythmic structure they differ considerably in melodic contour. There are also *kutsinhira* parts to "Nhemamusasa" which depart from the basic rhythmic structure shared by these variations. One such part is a *kutsinhira kwepamusoro* part comprising a series of pitches that sound on every pulse of the piece.

In comparing the three *kutsinhira* parts in Example 14, one finds the same underlying principle for the formation of *kutsinhira* parts as for the formation of *kushaura* parts: variations occur by rearranging at different pitch levels and in different sequences the pitches characterizing each harmonic segment of the piece. Corresponding pitches among the three *kutsinhira* versions are identical or bear an intervallic relationship to one another of a third (tenth), or a fifth (twelfth), or their inver-sions. At the same time, the harmonic principles operating in mbira music are flexible, providing the basic underlying struc-ture of the music within which melodic/rhythmic parts inter-weave and vary. The musicians, rather than confining them-selves to the pitches that comprise the harmonic segments of a piece, may add other pitches—non-harmonic tones—as embel-lishments at various pitch levels within the melodic fabric of the music.

In the performance of an mbira piece there is no designated order in which variations need appear. In addition, just as dif-ferent high-tone patterns combine with various lower-voiced *kushaura* and *kutsinhira* parts, these parts, in turn, can com-bine in many different pairs. All combinations of the *kushaura* and *kutsinhira* parts for "Nhemamusasa" examined thus far can, theoretically, interlock in various pairs. It is often the case, however, that musicians have preferences in this regard. A per-former sometimes feels that one high-tone pattern is best suited to a particular *kutsinhira* part, and when switching from one *kutsinhira* part to another he changes his high-tone melody accordingly. Musicians who perform together within the same mbira ensemble learn each other's musical tastes in this respect and they accommodate each other by playing pairs of *kushaura* and *kutsinhira* parts that they agree are best suited to one an-other. In such groups, when the *kushaura* player switches to a second *kushaura* part the *kutsinhira* player then changes over to the most appropriate *kutsinhira* counterpart. Often they favor 103

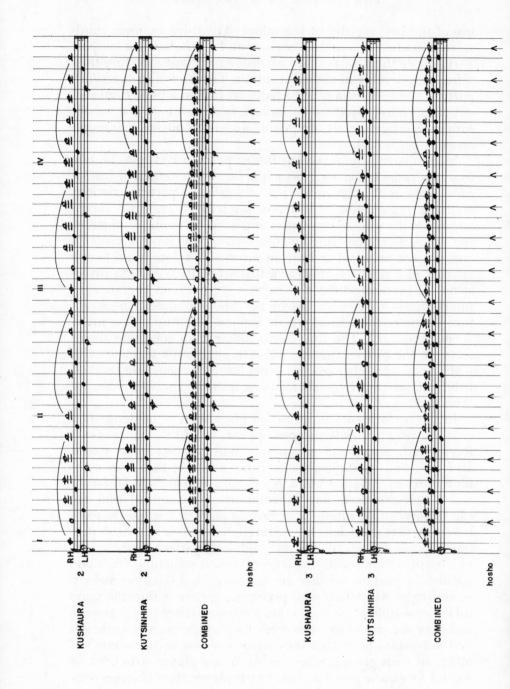

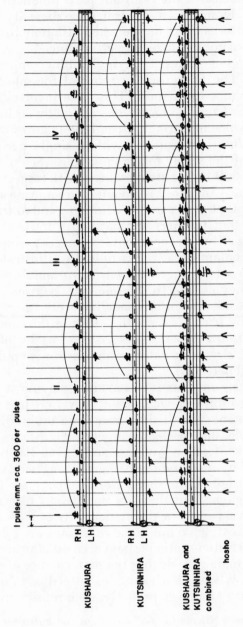

15. *Nhemamusasa: Three Pairs of Complementary Kushaura and
Kutsinhira Parts*

the selected pairs because of the resultant parts produced when they are combined. Example 15 illustrates the diversity of the overall resultant patterns that emerge when different *kushaura* and *kutsinhira* parts combine during a performance.[y]

Two other *mastyles* or "ways of playing" mbira compositions are acknowledged. The first, usually reserved for solo mbira playing, is the province of virtuosi. This style involves either the alternation of *kushaura* and *kutsinhira* parts by an individual[z] or the performance of parts that combine features of both *kushaura* and *kutsinhira* variations, with a single performer creating the effect of the whole mbira ensemble. (See p. 84 for a description of the skill such a style requires with respect to the piece, "Dangurangu.") In fact, it is a point of great pride among some mbira players that they can mix *kushaura* and *kutsinhira* parts so effectively that listeners approaching a musical event believe that they hear "two or three" mbira players performing. An excerpt of "Nhemamusasa" (Example 16) illustrates the relationship of such solo parts to the *kushaura* and *kutsinhira* parts from which they derive. In the solo part (version b) the performer plays a steady *kutsinhira* bass line every three pulses and at the same time tries to create the effect of the combined *kushaura* and *kutsinhira* upper voices (version a) by playing comparable melodic/rhythmic patterns on consecutive pulses of the piece (see circled patterns).

Controversial among musicians is a modern playing style associated with young mbira players, one of newly created variations offering an abrupt stylistic departure from the traditional versions (for example, unexpected changes in rhythm, melodic contour, or harmony). Cosmas Magaya and Luken Pasipamire referred to such variations as *majimba* ("jokes" or "trick styles" for the mbira; not originally a Shona word). "They are fun to play," reported Magaya, "but they are not always nice mbira music." Young players make a distinction between good and bad variations in this style. While some musicians are selective in playing "good" variations, others stand accused of using "bad styles" in an illegitimate way during the performance of pieces that they do not know well. For example, instead of following the melody or rhythm of a piece properly, such musicians bluff

[y] Hear these and other "Nhemamusasa" *kushaura* and *kutsinhira* parts on *Shona Mbira Music*, side I, band 1 (a-c).

[z] Kunaka alternates the *kushaura* and *kutsinhira* parts of "Nhimutimu" on *The Soul of Mbira*, side II, band 2.

Plates

1. KANGE. *An mbira player seated in performance.*

2. TETE, MOZAMBIQUE. *Thomas Baines' nineteenth-century sketch of an mbira and an ornately decorated calabash resonator, (National Archives of Rhodesia, Salisbury)*

PLATES 3–13
THE VARIETY OF
AFRICAN MBIRA

3. NIGERIA. *Wood, 10⅗″ × 3⅗″
(Smithsonian Institution, Washington, D.C.)*

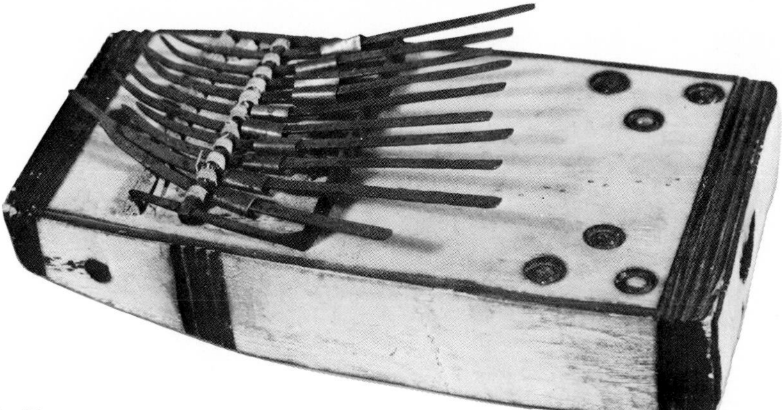

4. Yombe, Zaire. *Wood, metal, fiber, 6⅗″ × 3⁷⁄₁₀″ (Musée Royal de L'Afrique Centrale, Tervuren)*

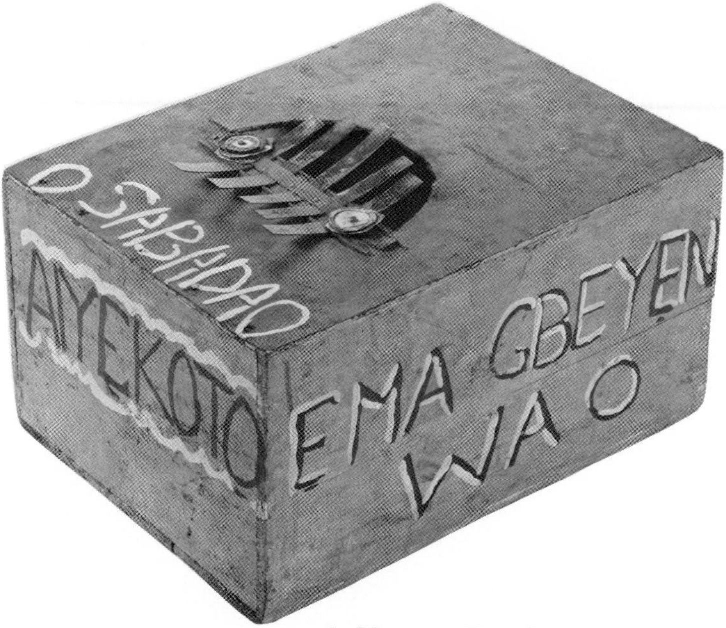

5. Nigeria. *Wooden packing crate, metal, 13⅕″ × 8⅘″ × 7⅕″ (Smithsonian Institution, Washington, D.C.)*

6. *(Left)* Luvale, Zambia. *Wood, metal, wire, 10⅗″ × 5⅘″ (The Livingstone Museum, Livingstone)*

7. *(Below)* Nigeria. *Wood, fiber, 13″ × 10½″ (Museum Für Völkerkunde, Berlin)*

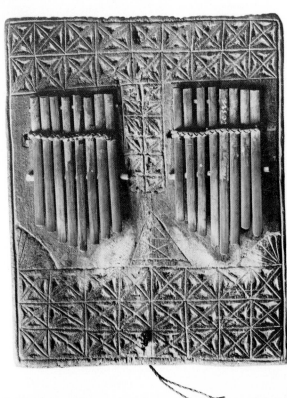

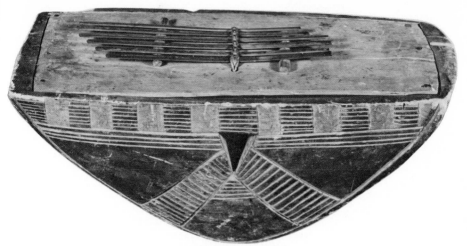

8. FANG, GABON. *Wood, metal, fiber,*
5¾″ × 12″ × 5⅕″ (Musée Royal de
L'Afrique Centrale, Tervuren)

9-10. LUBA, ZAIRE. *Wood,*
metal, elephant tusk, skin,
33¾″ (Musée Royal de
L'Afrique Centrale, Ter-
vuren)

11. IBO, NIGERIA. *Wood, polychrome, 16⅖″ × 4″ (Horniman Museum, London)*

12. MBANJA, ZAIRE. *Wood, fiber, 25″ (Musée Royal de L'Afrique Centrale, Tervuren)*

13. ZANDE, ZAIRE. *Wood, fiber, 23¾″ (Musée Royale de L'Afrique Centrale, Tervuren)*

14. *The playing technique of the* mbira dzavadzimu

PLATES 15–19.
FIVE TYPES OF
SHONA MBIRA

15. (Above) The matepe *and its relative, the* hera *(left)*

16. (Right) A karimba-*type called the* ndimba

17. (Below) Mbira DzaVadzimu

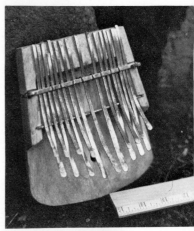

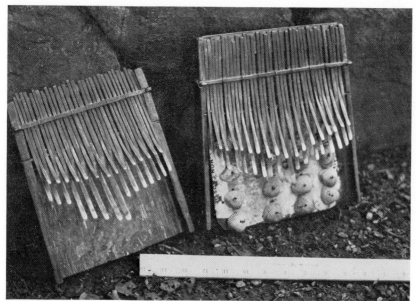

18. Njari

19. Mbira DzaVaNdau

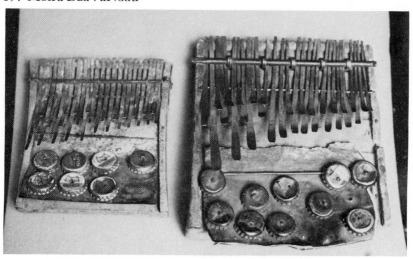

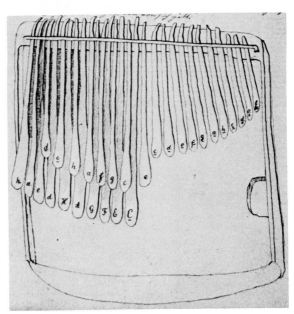

20. *Carl Mauch's drawing of a nineteenth-century* mbira dzavadzimu *(Hauptstaats-archiv Stuttgart)*

21. *Muchatera Mujuru's twenty-five key* mbira dzavadzimu

22. *Dried gourds purchased by Webster Pasipamire and Erick Muchena*

23. *A stitched gourd resonator*

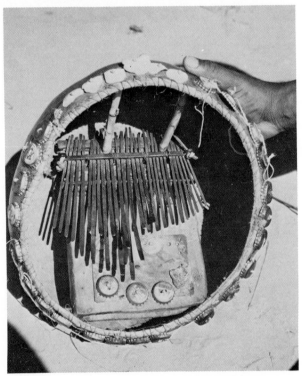

24. *A* matepe *propped in a resonator with hoop support*

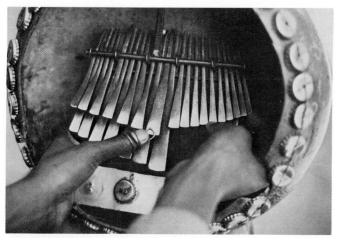

25. *The use of a protective "ring" for playing the* mbira dzavadzimu

26. *John Kunaka, playing a newly-made mbira together with his own model instrument*

27. An mbira ensemble: Erick Muchena, Cosmas Magaya, and a friend

28. Hosho

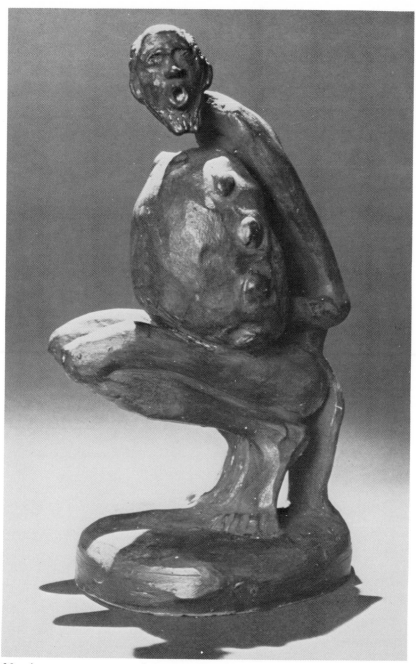

29. A contemporary sculpture of an mbira player by Taylor Nkomo

30. The nephew of John Kunaka

31. *(Above) Justin Magaya*

32. *(Right) Erick Muchena*

33. *The mbira players of Muchatera Mujuru*

34. *A nineteenth-century painting of an mbira player by Thomas Baines; made in Mozam-bique where such traditional Shona mbira as the* matepe *are said to have originated (Royal Geographic Society, London)*

35. *Indirect teaching: Cosmas Magaya (left) and Luken Pasipamire*

36. *Simon Mashoko: Singing, dancing, and playing the mbira*

37. *A landscape of the Mondoro Tribal Trust Land*

PLATES 38–42.
A *BIRA* AT MUDE'S VILLAGE.
(I am grateful to Hakurotwi Mude for his kind permission to take these photographs of the bira *and to reproduce them in this work.)*

38. The exterior of the round-house where the bira *was held*

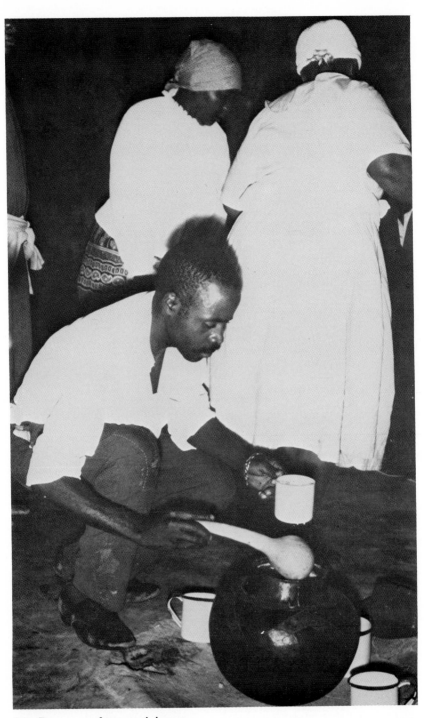

39. *Beer served to participants*

40. *(Above) Mbira players accompanied by* hosho *and hand-clapping*

41. *(Left) Participants dance to the music*

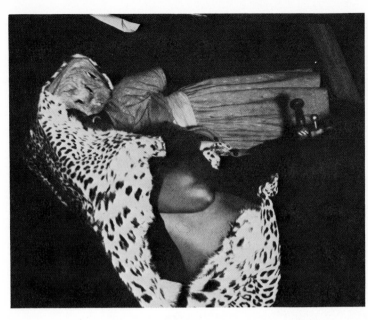

42b. Suddenly, as if possessed by the music, the participant leaps to his feet and dances in a frenzy

42a. One participant dressed in leopard skins, the characteristic dress of some mediums, listens to the music as others dance

43. *A professional spirit medium at Dambatsoko Village: Muchatera Mujuru (right) and his official attendant, Wafawanaka Mupfururi*

44. *Cosmas Magaya*

45. *Luken Pasipamire*

46. *Ephat Mujuru*

47. *John Kunaka*

48. *Simon Mashoko*

49. *John Hakurotwi Mude*

50. *Mubayiwa Bandambira*

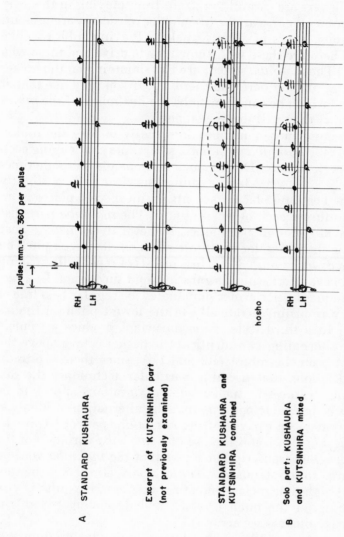

16. *Nhemamusasa: Excerpt of Solo Version Mixing Kushaura and Kutsinhira*

their way by erratically and repeatedly playing certain pitches that they think will fit the structure of the piece. The older and more experienced musicians generally look down upon the use of the *majmba* style, even when skillfully performed, and younger players are careful to refrain from playing in this way at a *bira* or on other occasions when older musicians are present. In the strong words of John Kunaka, "Playing mbira is like driving. There are those who know how to drive and those who don't. . . . [The *majimba* styles] are like slamming on the brakes and jerking, turning here and there. . . . If you play like that at Nyandoro [which he considers to be the birthplace of the *mbira dzavadzimu*] they will throw you out!"

When young musicians meet informally to play the mbira, they often play *majimba* variations, sometimes challenging each other in performance. During such sessions players sometimes deliberately play very fast, rushing ahead or falling slightly behind the beat and placing accents in unexpected places in an attempt to throw each other off guard. The *majimba* parts use a number of different techniques. Some of these include very fast double-thumbing for rhythmic effect on the lowest pitch on the *mbira dzavadzimu* (B1). This consists of repeatedly striking the same key, alternating thumbs in rapid succession. In a second technique the performer punctuates the regular bass line of a piece by returning erratically to the lowest pitch on the instrument. In a third style, some musicians produce a tremolo effect by alternating two identical pitches an octave above the lowest pitch on the mbira (R2 and L6); since there are traditional variations that use this particular technique, the distinguishing features in such *majimba* variations appear to be the kinds of irregular patterns that the alternation of identical pitches creates. An excerpt of the *kutsinhira* part of "Taireva" (Example 17) illustrates the use of a *majimba* variation of the latter type. The transcription shows that the *majimba* version, if compared to the standard *kutsinhira* part, eliminates the conventional high-tone melody, creating a series of irregular rhythmic patterns at the pitch level G_4 and displacing two of the normal bass pitches (see arrows).

Young musicians who enjoy playing *majimba* variations use them sparingly during a performance. When performers do introduce them into the music, they usually only play these parts for one or two cycles of the piece. As Magaya explained, "They are good for a change, but too much will spoil the music."

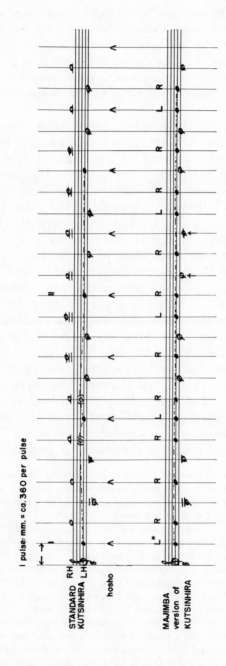

17. Taireva Excerpt of Kutsinhira, Majimba Style

Mbira players, then, are careful to balance new and old material in their performances. Cosmas Magaya, for example, distinguishes variations in his repertory that are traditional and therefore suitable for as many cycles of the piece as he considers appropriate, from recently composed variations that he plays for only a few cycles before returning to the more conventional parts.

In the performance of an mbira piece, then, the *kushaura* player usually begins with a version he considers to be a standard one, to signal the identity of the piece to listeners. The musician can begin the part at any point in the piece's cycle. What is most important in the music is the interrelationship among the different lines as the cycle of the piece is set into motion. The first player usually begins slowly with a basic version of the piece, then gradually increases its tempo and complexity.[aa] This gives the *kutsinhira* player a chance to get his bearings in relation to the *kushaura* part and to find an appropriate point at which to enter the music with a second, interlocking part. After the *kutsinhira* player joins the *kushaura* player, the *hosho* player then adds the basic rhythmic accompaniment, and together the three musicians accelerate to the appropriate tempo for the piece.[bb]

As the first player changes his part the second player follows suit. They may play variations of the same basic type (for example, a *kushaura* and *kutsinhira kwepamusoro nepasi*), or they may interweave variations of different types (for example, a *kushaura kwepamusoro* and a *kutsinhira kwepasi*). With each change new patterns result in the music. A predominant bass

[aa] As illustrated by "Taireva" (version I on *Shona Mbira Music*, side I, band 3), mbira players sometimes warm up by playing a phrase or more of the piece before the formal beginning of the performance.

[bb] The underlying pulse of mbira pieces (represented in the transcriptions as the distance between two vertical lines) is commonly M.M.=360. However, the tempo of the pieces can vary with their performing contexts from approximately M.M. = 250 to 450. To compare various tempos, listen to the version of "Nhemamusasa" performed by Mude's ensemble at a spirit possession ceremony and the version of "Nyamaropa" performed by Muchatera Mujuru for his own relaxation and meditation; *The Soul of Mbira*, side I, band 1 and side II, band 3, respectively. Usually in the performance of a piece at a formal event, the tempo begins slowly and then increases to a peak at which it remains for the duration of the piece. As illustrated by "Nyamamusango" (*Shona Mbira Music*, side II, band 4), sometimes the tempo increases over a period of several minutes before the musicians settle on the desired tempo.

line suddenly disappears and may or may not reappear several cycles later. A new melodic line appears in the middle register of the instrument, subtly changing melodic contour. For a period of time, the interlocking high-tone melodies mirror and echo each other. Then one musician switches to a counter-melody and the two parts rebound in opposite directions. As the piece is repeated cycle after cycle its formal aspects take on a certain ambiguity. Melodic lines begin and end at different points. An overall rhythmic pattern of two against three shifts into six pulses. The harmonic rhythm created by a particular set of variations becomes temporarily blurred as new melodic variations cause the pitches of each section to overlap. The music becomes "kaleidophonic." [13]

A piece can last anywhere from a few minutes to a half hour or more, depending upon the mood of the performers. At the end of the piece the tempo decreases, the *hosho* player drops out, and the mbira parts trail off. The point in the cycle at which the musicians end the piece is as arbitrary as the point at which they begin it; it differs from one musician to another and from one performance to the next. Some musicians conclude a performance with a musical "tag" at whatever point in the piece's cycle they feel like stopping. For example, Kunaka sometimes signals the end of the piece to other musicians in his ensemble by producing a tremolo effect, rhythmically alternating the performance of two keys (R2 and L6) with the identical pitch, G_4.

In Shona terms, then, an mbira piece such as "Nhemamusasa" is not a single fixed structure with a well-defined beginning and ending. It is rather a set of cyclical, harmonic, and melodic/rhythmic structures, comprising the kernel of a self-contained universe of musical ideas that performers elaborate through variation. Since there is no prescribed order in which to play variations, and because of such factors as the interaction between the musicians and the element of improvisation, each performance of a piece is a unique musical event. For an audience attuned to the subtleties of mbira music, the performance of a composition consists of an ever-changing stream of musical ideas.

5.

In Performance: The Shona Mbira Ensemble and the Relationship Between the Mbira Player and the Mbira

The *mbira dzavadzimu* can be a solo instrument, but at formal religious or secular musical events it is usually part of an mbira ensemble. The typical mbira ensemble consists of two or three mbira players, a gourd-rattle or *hosho* player, and one or more singers, who are often the mbira players themselves (Plate 27). During such special events as rainmaking ceremonies, however, as many as fifteen to twenty or more mbira players may perform together. The accompanying rhythm of the *hosho* and the vocal styles associated with the mbira are considered to be an integral part of the music. Performers sometimes whistle along with the music, and if a singer's hands are free he or she can accompany the music with handclapping patterns. Although it is common for some types of mbira ensembles (for example, *njari* and *matepe*) to include drums, this is not often the case with ensembles of *mbira dzavadzimu*.[a]

The typical accompanying instrument, *hosho* (Plate 28), consists of a pair of hollowed gourds with either seeds or kernels

---

[a] Providing an exception to this rule is *Shona Mbira Music*, side I, band 3, a recording of an event in which Mude decided to add a drum to his group "just for a change."

of dried corn placed inside them. The player must be able to throw the seeds from side to side in the gourd, slapping them in a cluster against each side. Without the proper control, the seeds slosh around inside the gourd, producing a dull sound and a weak, ambiguous beat. Special gourds that lend themselves naturally to the purpose grow in some parts of the country. These gourds have a large bulb at one end and a curved handle. In other parts of the country musicians use round gourds fixed with stick handles. In cities or other regions where it is difficult to obtain gourds, cans fixed with stick handles may be used as *hosho*.

Although an mbira group often has its own *hosho* player, a few villagers sometimes bring their *hosho* to a musical event and play them in synchronization with the professional player. During the course of such events the villagers' *hosho* pass from player to player as each one tires. While many people play *hosho* to some degree, a highly skilled player is always in demand. Few people have both the feeling for precise timing that the *hosho* part requires and the endurance to play evenly for piece after piece throughout the night. The natural tendency for an amateur *hosho* player is to drag the tempo as his or her arms begin to tire. It is not uncommon during the evening's performance to hear the leader or singer with an mbira group shout out "Kurumidza *hosho*!" ("Be quick, hosho [player]!").

The *hosho* player of the mbira ensemble establishes the dominant beat of the music. The most typical *hosho* pattern accompanying the *mbira dzavadzimu* is a three-pulse figure with emphasis on the main beat. This pattern can be represented approximately as follows: ♪♫ ♪♫ with the main beat of the figure indicated by the pyramid (▲). The sixteenth- and eighth-note parts of the pattern actually come slightly earlier than indicated by the notation.[b] As indicated in the transcriptions, the *hosho* pattern's dominant beat falls on every third underlying pulse of the mbira music. Mbira players sometimes express this basic pulse by nodding their heads slightly as they perform.

While a single gourd rattle can produce the typical *hosho* pattern, it is most common for the player to use a pair. A forward stroke of the lower-pitched gourd usually produces the

[b] This rhythmic pattern accompanies most of the pieces for the *mbira dzavadzimu* on *The Soul of Mbira*, and all of the pieces on *Shona Mbira Music*.

main beat and a back stroke of the higher-pitched gourd introduces the sixteenth-note segment of the rhythm.

By subtly changing the rhythmic relationship between the two gourds within the three-pulse pattern, performers develop their own style of playing. I have heard some players slur the sound of the *hosho* in such a way that the overall effect is that of one continual percussive phrase, changing pitch and timbre and culminating on the main beat like the crack of a whip. It is usually the case that except for these subtle changes in the phrasing of the three-pulse pattern the same basic *hosho* part accompanies every piece throughout the evening's performance of an ensemble of *mbira dzavadzimu.*

Handclapping patterns called *makwa* may supply additional rhythmic accompaniment to the mbira music. Because participants clap with their hands cupped, their rhythmic patterns have a loud, hollow, drumlike quality that varies in timbre and pitch from one performer to another. Four typical handclapping patterns appear in Example 18; all of these coincide with the first main beat of the *hosho* in each of the twelve-pulse phrases of the mbira pieces. The handclapping patterns used by Shona musicians vary greatly in complexity of rhythmic configuration and in phrase length. Pattern A (Example 18), the simplest *makwa* part, coincides with the main beat of the *hosho* rhythm, occurring on every third pulse of the mbira music. At their most complex, however, the *makwa* patterns are a virtuoso form of drumming. Such parts range from a rapid-fire three-pulse figure that synchronizes with the complete *hosho* pattern, to long, powerful, improvised rhythmic lines characterized by complex off-beat phrasing.[c]

Makwa patterns combine in many ways and usually participants perform at least two contrasting patterns simultaneously. As these patterns interlock they create a number of resultant phrases with different rhythmic relationships to the mbira piece: when pattern B joins pattern A it articulates a triple subdivision of the first pattern and produces a resultant part which repeats four times during every phrase of the mbira piece; when pattern C combines with pattern A, together they create a polyrhythm of two against three which repeats twice during every phrase of the piece. During a performance, then, the *makwa* parts con-

---

[c] *Makwa* patterns accompany the performance of mbira pieces on *The Soul of Mbira*, side I, band 1, and on *Shona Mbira Music*, side I, band 3 and side II, band 1.

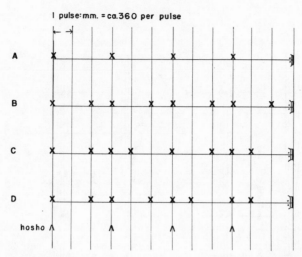

18. *Handclapping Patterns*

tinually change with respect to one another, producing a steady flow of varied rhythmic patterns in the background of the mbira music. These patterns in relation to the mbira parts demonstrate a cardinal principle of African music which has been called the "clash of rhythms."[1]

During an mbira performance, there are three basic styles of singing that form an integral part of the music: *mahon'era* (or *mahonyera*), *huro*, and *kudeketera*.[d] At a formal religious event like a *bira* or at informal events like beer parties, both the musicians and the participating villagers freely perform any of these styles in which they feel competent, alternating them at will to the mbira music.

Mahon'era is a soft, syllabic style of singing, usually in the singer's lowest comfortable range. It interweaves with the lower parts of the mbira music. Example 19 illustrates a *mahon'era* part sung to "Nyamaropa" by Hakurotwi Mude. As the transcription indicates, the *mahon'era* parts often comprise four ascending melodic phrases beginning in the bass register of the mbira and corresponding, for the most part, with the four seg-

[d] These vocal styles are on most of the recordings on *The Soul of Mbira* and *Shona Mbira Music*. Mude's performance of vocal parts similar to those transcribed in Examples 19–22 are on "Nyamaropa" (*The Soul of Mbira*, side I band 3) and "Nhemamusasa" (*Shona Mbira Music*, side I, band 1c).

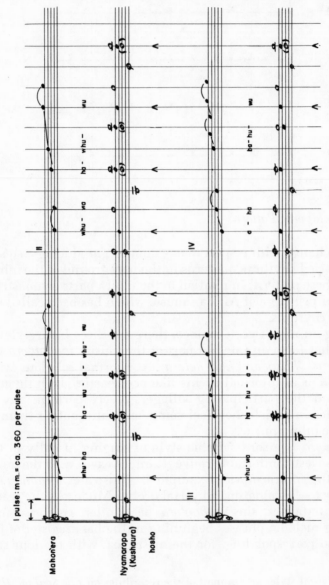

19. *The Mahon'era Vocal Style for Nyamaropa*

ments of the mbira piece. In range, the *mahon'era* phrases can encompass as much as an octave or more.

The degree to which the *mahon'era* parts follow the basic structure of an mbira piece is apparent from a comparison of the pitches in the transcribed vocal phrases and those in the corresponding sections of "Nyamaropa." Each pitch in the vocal parts consists of one of the pitches that constitute the corresponding harmonic section. In addition, when part of the first phrase of "Nyamaropa" transposes up a scale degree in Section IV of the piece, the corresponding phrase in the *mahon'era* also transposes up a scale degree. In this fashion the *mahon'era* parts follow the basic harmonic and melodic form of an mbira piece.

In the course of singing *mahon'era*, performers sometimes use their voices to outline the different resultant parts they hear arising from the complex of lines of the mbira music, using such syllables as "hiya—hiya—hiya" or "whu—ha-whu-ha—whu-uu." Maraire describes this style of singing as the result of the mbira player "having inside with the mbira." "Having inside with the mbira" implies being able to hear all of the inner melodic/rhythmic parts of the mbira's voice. The *mahon'era* parts resulting from this process are somewhat like personal, vocalized "transcriptions" of the mbira music, in which the singer shows to the listener the phrases the performer hears in the mbira music. By utilizing a sophisticated technique the singer relies not only upon inherent melodic/rhythmic patterns, but also draws pitches together from different strata of the music, combining them to form a motivic basis for his or her vocal parts. As a result of this sensitive interplay between the instrument and the voice, it sometimes seems as if the mbira continues to sing a pattern emphasized by a vocalist after the vocalist has stopped singing it.

In contrast to the low, soft, and introverted *mahon'era* style, the *huro* style comprises melodic lines that are high and penetrating. It utilizes non-verbal syllables and various vocal techniques, the most characteristic of which is a highly developed form of yodelling (*kunguridzira*).[e] At its simplest, a *huro* yodelling phrase consists of such syllables as "wo-i-ye, i-ye, i-ye, i-ye" rendered in a descending saw-tooth pattern in which "i" is the falsetto tone:

[e] Performers who have not developed the skill of yodelling frequently sing the basic melodic *huro* parts in a falsetto style.

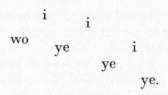

As in the *mahon'era* style, different singers have developed very different personal styles of yodelling, and from their phrasing, choice and mixture of syllables, and tone of their voices, they are easily recognizable.[f] For instance, Simon Mashoko, a well-known singer and *njari* player, sometimes begins his *huro* phrases with the syllables of the word *baba* (father) using the following general melodic contour:

Hakurotwi Mude often begins his *huro* passages with the non-syntactic syllables *hongore*:

He sometimes alters this passage by adding the syllables "ye . . . re . . . re" to the end of the phrase, or by beginning the phrase on the second syllable: "ngo-re . . . ," etc.

Mude describes the art of singing *huro* as "the molding of the voice to the mbira [music]." In this respect, the performance of *huro* sometimes involves an imitative response to the high-tone patterns of the mbira music, much as the *mahon'era* does to the lower melodic parts.[g] Often, however, this approach is used merely as a point of departure for the performance of more

---

[f] Performances by Hakurotwi Mude and Simon Mashoko on *The Soul on Mbira*, side I, band 3, and side II, band 1, respectively, exemplify the differences in individual *huro* styles among mbira players.

[g] The vocal performances on *Shona Mbira Music*, side II, bands 4 and 5, demonstrate how closely the *mahon'era* and *huro* parts sometimes follow the patterns of mbira music.

independent and extended *huro* melodies interwoven among the polyphonic lines of the mbira music. In the transcription of one *huro* passage from Mude's performance of "Nhemamusasa," the symbol ⌐● represents a skip, from the falsetto tone to the pitch below, that is frequently close to an interval of a third or a fourth (Example 20).

As indicated by the transcription, *huro* phrases usually begin in the upper register of the mbira music. They have a descending melodic contour, encompassing a range of as much as an octave or more, and they frequently overlap the phrases of the mbira music. Like the *mahon'era* parts, the *huro* phrases follow the basic structure of the mbira music; their lines comprise pitches which often anticipate or follow those of the mbira and are largely consistent with the corresponding harmonic sections of the piece. Non-harmonic tones function as decorative pitches (see arrows).

In the performance of mbira music, *mahon'era* and *huro* styles not only intensify the mood but serve as vehicles for vocal improvisation and variation. The performance of the vocal styles, therefore, is similar to that of the mbira music itself. Like the mbira players, Shona singers have a storehouse of basic patterns and musical formulae from which they draw patterns and combine them in different ways during a performance. These patterns consist of riffs and phrases that the singer has learned over the years which fit the structure of particular mbira pieces. The performer's vocal phrases, like those of the mbira music itself, are not fixed; they change over the years as the singer or mbira player discovers new parts through experimentation and through listening to other performers. Performers like Hakurotwi Mude are specialists in this, and other musicians have adopted their creations of new *huro* and *mahon'era* parts. On one occasion when I played a tape of a group I had recorded in the field for the members of *Mhuri yekwaRwizi*, they laughed with enjoyment at the singer's performance and declared, "He's trying to copy Mude. He must have heard him on the radio."

From one performance to the next, a wide range of factors can contribute to subtle transformations of the basic vocal parts. These factors include, among others, melodic contour, timbre, accent, dynamics, vibrato, rhythmic phrasing, and choice of non-syntactic syllables. Performers can also adapt the patterns in their repertories from one vocal style to another. For example, I have heard Mude sing in his lowest range as *mahon'era*   119

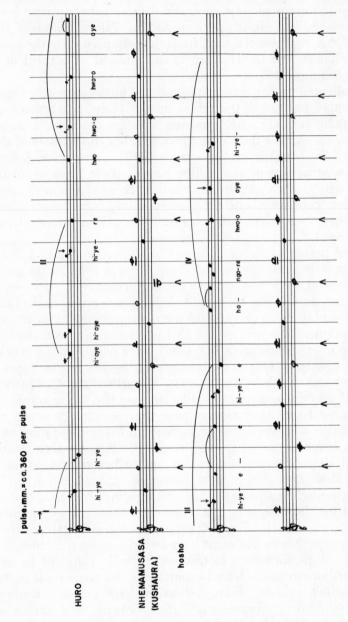

20. *The Huro Vocal Style for Nhemamusasa*

parts phrases he had years earlier sung as *huro*. In the performance of *huro* and *mahon'era*, then, the singer draws on a continually evolving repertory of vocal patterns, recombining and
alternating parts in different ways depending on the singer's
mood and, at times, on the melodic parts he or she hears arising
from the mbira music.

The third vocal style sung with mbira music is a verbal,
poetic style called *kudeketera*. The *kudeketera* song texts accompanying the *mbira dzavadzimu* include poetic lines associated with particular mbira pieces, other lines appropriate to any
mbira piece, and lines improvised in response to events taking
place at the time of the performance. The song texts deal with
a wide range of themes, reflecting many different aspects of
Shona culture. *Kudeketera* texts will be discussed in some detail
in Chapter 7.

Example 21 illustrates a characteristic style of singing *kudeketera*. Its melodic lines have a stepwise descending contour
encompassing the range of a fifth to an octave. The transcriptions illustrate the manner in which the *kudeketera* lines typically weave in and out of the polyphonic fabric of the mbira
music, touching fragments of the mbira music in unison at certain points and departing from them at others. It is not uncommon for poetic lines to overlap with the phrases of the instrumental parts. Like the non-verbal vocal styles previously
discussed, the *kudeketera* melodic patterns follow the general
harmonic movement of the piece. They begin and end on harmonic tones; the non-harmonic tones appear as decorative
pitches (see arrows), sometimes anticipating the pitches of the
mbira.

Another important aspect of the *kudeketera* vocal style is the
effect of the tonal pattern of the spoken language upon the song
texts. The diagram on the right in Example 21 compares the
spoken and sung tonal patterns of the poetic lines.[2] As in transcription 1, the sung lines of *kudeketera* sometimes follow the
tonal pattern of the spoken line precisely. However, as in transcriptions 2 and 3, the tonal patterns of *kudeketera* phrases can
change in varying degrees when they are sung rather than
spoken, and when they are sung with different mbira pieces
(see circles). In general, the tendency is for the melodic phrase
of *kudeketera* to be largely consistent with that of the spoken
line, following or at least being tempered by the tonal laws of
the Shona language.

121

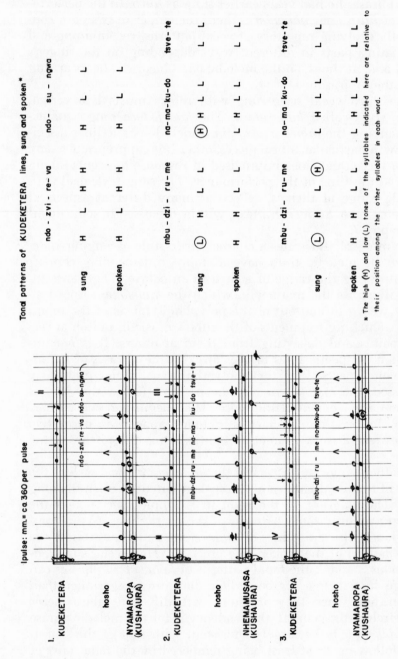

21. *Kudeketera Vocal Style for Nyamaropa and Nhemamusasa*

Singers report that in the performance of *kudeketera* accompanying the *mbira dzavadzimu* the mbira plays a role in several respects. First, it is from the stream of images, associations, and feelings evoked by the music that the performers draw the themes of the texts. Second, the structure of the particular mbira piece affects the *kudeketera* vocal style. When two or more musicians play simultaneously, their parts produce a continual stream of interwoven melodies, providing the singer with musical ideas that he or she can adapt for vocal parts. (The examples provided here, however, show *kudeketera* lines to have a similar contour regardless of the melodic patterns played in the mbira music. Although pitches for the vocal parts are often selected from the mbira music and singers are concerned with following the rhythm of the mbira music, I have not yet determined the degree to which singers are influenced by the actual melodic patterns of an mbira piece in singing their poetic lines.) Third, the performance of the music stimulates the singers, giving them, as Mude says, "more power for singing," and adding to the overall excitement of the event.

As mentioned previously, during an mbira piece the singer alternates among *mahon'era*, *huro*, and *kudeketera* styles. Example 22 provides a transcription of an excerpt of a performance of "Nhemamusasa" by Hakurotwi Mude in which an interlude of mbira music follows a line of *kudeketera*. This leads to a section of *huro* which ends with a *mahon'era* phrase. In this manner the interaction between the vocal parts and the mbira parts changes throughout the performance of an mbira piece.

In the process of singing *kudeketera*, the performer, deeply moved by the sound of the mbira, responds vocally, drawing upon the images and feelings that the music brings about. The vocal styles intensify the mood of the piece and are used by the singer as a means of interacting with the mbira. Performers weave their vocal parts into the polyphonic fabric of the mbira music, following its basic structure and sometimes imitating its inner melodic/rhythmic parts. The sensitivity to the music this requires is one of the factors distinguishing good from poor singing. Mbira players and listeners criticize some singers for "going one way while the mbira goes another" or for "forcing the voice to the mbira," while performances by great singers such as Mude illustrate the degree to which the vocal parts are an integral part of Shona mbira music, contributing to the uniqueness of each performance.

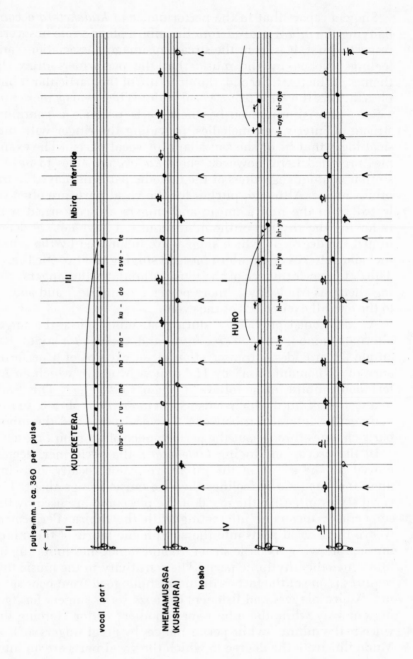

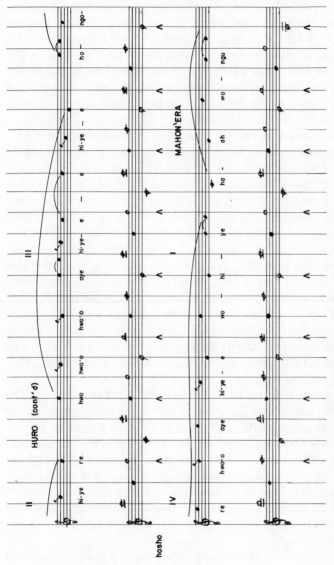

22. *Vocal Styles Alternated in Performance of Nhemamusasa*

Mbira ensembles often have professional names that identify the players as part of the family of a common ancestor, relative, or chief. For instance, the name of the group *Mhuri yekwa-Rwizi* means "Family of (Chief) Rwizi." Chief Rwizi presides over a portion of the Mondoro tribal trust land in which the group's leader and some of its members live. The name of another group, *Mhuri yekwaChaminuka*, means "Family of Chaminuka," indicating that its members trace their ancestry back to a medium for Chaminuka.

Just as the names of the groups suggest family ties, the rapport and encouragement between and among group members during performances are consistent with the mutual support one associates with familial relationships. For example, in one group with which I frequently travelled, three mbira players in their twenties affectionately assigned each other nicknames consisting of single syllabic words without meaning. In the course of performance they called out each other's nicknames. Upon hearing his name, the musician played with extra vigor. They also periodically exchanged glances and smiles and shouted such encouragements to one another as "Pisa!" ("Set on fire!"). One of the mbira players when deeply moved by the music shook his head dramatically from side to side. Such gestures serve to reinforce the feelings of solidarity among the members of the mbira ensemble, reflecting their appreciation of each other's contributions to the performance.

Mbira ensembles often have a leader who takes charge of the organizational aspects of the group: he makes arrangements for professional engagements, calls the ensemble together for rehearsals, and makes decisions about the repertory of the group. In such ensembles the leader can keep the identity of the group intact when some readjustment of the group's personnel is necessary. For example, *Mhuri yekwaRwizi*, an ongoing organization for over a decade, has revolved around its leader and featured singer, Hakurotwi Mude, while the other personnel of the ensemble have changed.

The disruptions within mbira groups are partly a result of growing transience within the African community. A musician with one group may visit or move permanently to another part of the country because of demands made upon him by his family. Changes of personnel can also result from conflicts within the group. In one ensemble a musician was asked to leave after ignoring warnings about his reluctance to rehearse with the group and his unwillingness to learn new pieces. Dissatisfaction among members of a group arises for many other reasons as well, including problems with the way in which performers interact musically, difference in personal taste over the adopted *chuning* of the group, disagreements over the way in which the business transactions of the ensemble are handled, and so on.

While mbira groups at times find themselves engaged in the conflicts one expects to find in any family, musicians generally show a great deal of admiration and respect for each other's abilities. Two unrelated incidents serve to illustrate this camaraderie. On one occasion two mbira players with *Mhuri yekwa-Rwizi*, Cosmas Magaya and Luken Pasipamire, listened to a playback of a recording I had made of their group the previous evening. They were especially moved by the performance of the group's singer, Hakurotwi Mude. "There's no one who can sing like that," Pasipamire remarked. "Mude's a real composer. God gave him that." Moved by the beauty of Mude's singing, in an unselfconscious pantomime he embraced the speaker of the tape recorder and kissed the sound-filled space. He then joined the general laughter that greeted his charade.

On another occasion, Mude was driving his mbira players through the bush after a reunion with them. He threw a glance at the musicians practicing in the back seat of the car. Turning his attention back to the route through the tall grass, Mude sighed aloud and smiled deeply. "Ahhhh," he said to me, "I am happy when I hear music like that; that's good music they're playing. When I hear music like that, I am just going to the God."

The Relationship Between the Mbira Player and the Mbira

In the performance of mbira music there is an intimate bond between the mbira player and his instrument. This intimacy is to some degree inherent in the physical relationship of the mbira player to his mbira. When the musician performs, his instrument's sound is amplified and projected directly back to him by the gourd resonator. Thus enveloped by the sound of his instrument, he is closest to the music and in the best position to appreciate its nuances and subtleties. Hakurotwi Mude once commented that the gourd resonator acted like the strainer in making tea. Certain subtleties of the mbira's sound, like the tea   127 leaves, are contained within the gourd, shared only with the player, while the basic music is allowed to pass through to the listeners.

Personification of the instrument by some musicians, who refer to the music that arises from the mbira as its voice, indicates the intimate nature of the relationship between the mbira player and his mbira during a performance. The sculptured soundboards of some mbira, the keys of which are fastened to the hollowed chests of wooden human figures, represent, perhaps, a similar personification of the mbira. When an mbira player strikes the keys of such an instrument, the mbira reflects its sound back to the musician as if it were singing to him (Plates 12 and 13). Some performers imply as well that the instrument has a strong will of its own. For example, Simon Mashoko relayed a story to me about the mbira, indicating that the instrument has the power to remind its performer of his obligations toward the music. When Mashoko was a young musician, he was once told by more experienced mbira players that if he stored his mbira in his calabash underneath his bed and ignored it for several days or more, the instrument would call to him, waking him in the middle of the night. First the calabash would sound as if a low pitch on the mbira were being played: "Kow! . . . Kow! . . . Kow! . . ." Then, if still ignored, the mbira would sound one key at a time: "Ngi . . . Ngi . . . Ngi . . ." ringing from beneath the bed. "When this happens," said Mashoko, "the mbira is telling you, 'You must play me now!' That is how we know [the mbira] is holy." When I asked Mashoko if he had ever experienced this phenomenon himself, he replied, "Many times."

Other musicians such as Dumisani Maraire personify the role of the mbira in the performance of mbira music.[3] In this context the mbira is said to be capable of making musical suggestions to the player during the performance of an mbira piece.[4] If as the musician plays a particular finger pattern he inadvertently strikes a different key than the one for which he has aimed, it is not necessarily viewed as a mistake. Rather, if the mbira player likes the new pitch he can interpret it as the mbira's suggestion for the next variation and can incorporate it into his performance. Maraire's reference to the creative use of unanticipated variations in the performance of a piece is similar to that mentioned earlier by Kunaka as one of the sources of new mbira compositions.

The personification of the mbira by some musicians reflects their sensitivity to and appreciation of the musical feedback they receive from the mbira during performance. As Maraire reports, "To me an mbira is a lively instrument. It amazes me whenever I hear all these different things coming out without any changes in my way of playing. This is not because I am playing different patterns without knowing what I am doing, but because, as I give the mbira more, I get more from it."[5] The musical feedback Maraire describes is the result both of the acoustic properties of the mbira and of the complex nature of mbira music itself.

To begin with, each mbira key does not merely produce a single pitch; it produces an aggregate of sounds. When a key is struck, its fundamental pitch is sometimes accompanied by prominent overtones. As the key vibrates, its basic pitch becomes alternately flat and sharp. Maraire reports that in the Garwe dialect three tones are distinguished within each key, "The basic pitch [dziro], the high vibration [maungira] and the low vibration [maungira e pasi]."[6] The vibration of one key occasionally also sets into vibration another key on the mbira tuned in unison to it, resulting in a mixture of different timbres of the same pitch. Furthermore, as mentioned in the introduction to this chapter, since there is no way of dampening the keys on the instrument after they are struck the pitches of the mbira tend to overlap one another when they are played in succession. The gourd resonator, which sustains the "lifetime" of each pitch played on the mbira, enhances this sound mixture. The cyclical nature of mbira music, in which the beginning and the ending of phrases can be ambiguous, and the phenomenon of inherent rhythms, which causes the listener to perceive the melodic parts of a piece differently from the way they are actually played by the performer, add to the music's complexity. As the interwoven melodic/rhythmic patterns of mbira music interact throughout the performance of a piece, new phrases seem continually to emerge from the music.

Finally, the mbira's vibrators or buzzers contribute to the overall complexity of the sound. Bringing out various rhythmic patterns and occasionally vibrating in sympathy with the pitches played, the buzzers sound slightly out of phase with the music. At times it is as if they echo or paraphrase the figures played, while at other times they seem to bring out their own phrases or to create the effect of a drone.

129

As a result of all this the performer is confronted with a basic fact: the music reflected back to him by his resonator as he plays seems to be more complex than that which his fingers alone produce. It is, then, real musical feedback that the musician receives from his instrument. It may well be that this feedback is responsible for some musicians' personification of the mbira and its role in the music-making process.

In a sense, then, one can regard mbira music as the product of a "duet" between the player and the mbira in which the relationship between the musician and his instrument is a primary one, rather than as the product of a solo performance.[7] In Maraire's words, when a mbira player performs, "He is not trying to please people. . . . What he is doing is that he has a friend [that is, the mbira]. This friend is of the same musical quality with him. He teaches his friend what to do and his friend teaches him what to do."[8]

In effect, the mbira player has a dual role in this process. On the one hand, he is the performer, initiating the music. On the other hand, he continually receives new musical patterns from the mbira as if he were a member of the audience. This involves a delicately balanced exchange between the mbira player and his instrument.

The ultimate extension of the musician sharing with the mbira is his vocal accompaniment to the music, and most mbira players do sing with their instruments. Usually when the mbira player sings he simplifies his mbira playing to some degree. Musicians speak of the considerable skill that simultaneous performance of the mbira and vocal styles requires and caution that one must not allow singing to affect one's mbira playing adversely. Musicians criticize mbira players who miss mbira keys or who unconsciously vary the tempo of the piece when they sing with the music. Those who feel unsure of their ability in this regard may hum or sing softly to themselves. As one mbira player explained to me, even though he did not sing out loud to the music he was always "singing silently in [his] heart." Maraire describes the interaction of the mbira player's voice with the mbira as follows: the mbira player "gives his vocal melodies or vocal sounds to the mbira, and at the same time lets the mbira vary the melodies in a way the voice cannot do. He listens to it, following it vocally, commenting with different sounds, cheering it."[9]

130   In this sharing between the "two friends of the same musical

quality," the mbira player initiates the basic pattern of a piece and listens to the complex of parts projected back to him by the mbira. He hears the sequence of pitches, the interplay of the overtones, the buzzing of the vibrators, the overlapping phrases, and the resultant parts arising from the music. In reaction to the mbira's voice, the musician gradually elaborates upon the piece, listening for the mbira's suggestions, introducing new variations, and responding with a wide range of vocal expression, singing poetic lines, yodelling, humming, whistling, and so on. Maraire sums up the relationship between the mbira player and his instrument:

> So in simple terms, I can say that the mbira is always in front, giving new materials to its player, and the player follows behind, emphasizing these [materials] while at the same time asking for more. What more can one say of such an instrument but that it is a friend indeed?[10]

This rapport between the mbira player and the mbira forms the essence of a performance of mbira music.

In many respects, mbira music is music for meditation. It is not uncommon for an mbira player to go off by himself, to be alone with his mbira and his thoughts. As the mbira player performs, he dwells on any of a wide range of subjects, which are reflected in the poetic lines sung with the mbira. Hakurotwi Mude emphasized the way in which mbira music stimulates his imagination: "When I play the mbira in Highfields [Salisbury]," he reports, "I can see places as far as my home in Mondoro or farther, and in my mind I am just [transported] there."

The mbira player, enveloped by the sound of the music, entranced by its repetitive, cyclical nature, and captivated by its subtle variations, may find his state of consciousness transformed. Several performers reported that playing mbira music made them feel "dreamy" or "sleepy." Others said that the music made them "peaceful," "calm," and "unafraid," as mbira music was said to do in folktales discussed earlier. Another player remarked that the effect of playing mbira was sometimes like that of smoking marijuana, and once, after I had been playing the mbira with a great deal of force, I was jokingly warned by other mbira players that if I continued to play in that fashion all the time I would one day be found wandering in the forest, not knowing my own name. Furthermore, non-musicians among the Shona sometimes imitate mbira players by staring

131

blankly into the space before them, totally absorbed in their own thoughts, as they mime the performance of the mbira. This absorption has also been represented in modern sculptures of mbira players in Zimbabwe; Mude, upon seeing one such sculpture (plate 29) for the first time, said emphatically, "That is Mude!" Many Shona people informed me that mbira music was "very deep" in its effect upon listeners as well as upon performers, and that it required full attention. A traditional line of poetry sung with mbira music which states, "I cannot plow, my music is playing," reflects this attitude.

The power of mbira music to affect the performer was dramatically demonstrated to me one morning just after sunrise, at the conclusion of a ceremony for the ancestral spirits. I was seated on the ground beside Hakurotwi Mude, among the people of his village and the guests from neighboring villages who had participated all through the night in the singing, dancing, and drinking. Exhausted from exertion and lack of sleep, people chatted quietly among themselves and watched children gleefully chasing unsuspecting dogs and chickens that had wandered into their midst.

As if oblivious to all that was going on around him, Mude sat quietly and stared without expression off into the distance. An mbira was balanced on his knee and his fingers methodically worked their way over the keys. Mude's small son Edson walked over and stood with his hand on his father's shoulder, but Mude showed no sign of recognition. Mude twisted his head to the side and stared somberly over his shoulder. Soft music flowed steadily from his mbira.

As Mude played the mbira his eyes became clouded. Tears welled up and fell silently down his cheeks. It was some time before anyone noticed what was happening. Finally, Mude's father-in-law walked over and knelt before him. Careful not to interfere with the playing of the mbira, the old man pulled a handkerchief out of his pocket and blotted up the tears on Mude's cheeks. Tears flowed so steadily that the old man saw it was to no avail. He stood up and silently motioned to all the other villagers seated around to follow him into the large kitchen where the *bira* had previously been held. So as not to embarrass Mude, we left him with his music and his tears.[h]

[h] I am grateful to Hakurotwi Mude for his permission to relate the incident about this sensitive aspect of mbira music.

It is not uncommon in Shona culture to hear of mbira players who have been moved to tears while playing the mbira. This expression rises out of the intimacy of the relationship of the mbira player with his instrument, and out of the broader associations of the mbira's sound in Shona culture. Mbira players have offered a number of explanations. Several lines of poetry that are sung to the mbira eloquently reflect one explanation:

The mbira, when it sounds, makes me feel pity [compassion].
Misfortune, when it comes to a man who doesn't want it, sticks like bee's wax.
Thinking hard, without speaking, there followed the falling of tears.[11]

Luken Pasipamire once explained, "Sometimes when you are playing mbira nicely, you will cry, for the mbira makes you think too much." Thus, as in the incident involving Mude, mbira music can move a person to think deeply about his or her troubles or those of others. The troubles can be personal, social, or political; the latter is a constant source of pain and frustration for Africans who see themselves as exploited in the hands of an antagonistic European political system in Zimbabwe.

The association of the mbira with traditional Shona religion and the worship of ancestral spirits also explains the power of the mbira to move its player to tears. According to Ephat Mujuru:

much of African history has been handed down . . . in song. [As you play mbira and sing] you can see the panoramic scenes of those bygone days and the vague dreamy figures of the past come into . . . focus in the modern time. . . . You can almost see your ancestors limping toward the living world again. . . . So deep is such retrospection that many find their eyes filled with tears.[12]

And Maraire reports:

Many mbira players have told me that they started playing after a tragic happening had disturbed their lives. . . . My own teacher, Sekuru Jeke Tapera, told me that he started playing the mbira after the death of his mother. The image of his mother was always coming before him. . . . Like most other mbira players, he adopted the mbira for comfort in his sadness.[13]

The association of the mbira with the world of the ancestors is a strong one for Shona listeners. One man who looked melancholy during an mbira performance explained to me afterwards that the music had made him think of his departed grandfather, over whose loss he still grieved.

A third explanation for the tears of mbira players emphasizes the emotional effect of the mbira music as resulting from the power of its abstract sound, rather than from its cultural associations. Ephat Mujuru pointed out that at occasional high points in an mbira performance the sheer ecstasy of the experience sometimes so overwhelms the mbira player that he can be moved to tears in a state of "overgladness." As a student of the mbira, my teachers sometimes forewarned me that a variation I was learning was so moving that it would one day make me cry.

The incident in which the other villagers left Mude with his mbira and his tears epitomizes the freedom of expression that grows out of the intimate relationship between an mbira player and his instrument. On this occasion, the mbira music apparently had a cathartic effect. About twenty minutes after the musician's father-in-law beckoned the villagers to follow him into the round-house where the *bira* had been held, Mude appeared at the entrance, visibly cheered. He joined the company of his family and friends without hesitation and the incident was never mentioned.

Catharsis is only one element in Shona mbira music. The mbira has many extra-musical associations in Shona culture, and musicians regard their instruments with a complex of emotions and attitudes. The playing of the mbira can at times have an effect contradictory to catharsis. A player who happens to be in a cheerful mood may become sad as a result of thoughts and feelings brought about by the mbira music.

In fact, sadness is an appropriate and sometimes a desired response to mbira music. Hakurotwi Mude once voiced scorn to me over a type of mbira played in another part of the country: "Can it make you feel sad? Can it make you think deeply? No, it is for playing in the beer halls." On another occasion, referring to his own mbira, he stated emphatically, "The *mbira dzavadzimu* is not played for pleasure." Many Shona mbira players would receive this statement with general agreement. Its meaning will become apparent later in the discussion of the mbira in the context of traditional Shona religion.

The facial expressions of performing musicians often give clues to the meaning their music has for them. Mbira players, both privately, when playing for themselves, and publicly at religious ceremonies, often look serious, meditative, introspective, and occasionally sad or somber; this effect of the music and basic attitude toward the instrument is apparent in the performances of young as well as older mbira players (Plates 30–33). It is also the case, however, that performances sometimes have an exhilarating effect upon the mbira players; they smile and laugh aloud with thorough enjoyment when playing (Plate 36). On one such occasion Luken Pasipamire reported that the music made him feel as if he was flying. Because of the intimate bond between the mbira player and his instrument, the musician is free to express his emotions while performing, whether through tears or through laughter. In Shona culture mbira music supports the full range of human emotion from depression to ecstasy.[1]

Within the range of moods brought about by mbira music, one typical of many mbira performances was captured beautifully by the painter Thomas Baines in the mid-nineteenth century. (Plate 34). For the dignity and grace of the mbira player's posture, and for the serious introspective and meditative quality of his expression, Baines' work might have been painted in Zimbabwe today.

The aspects of mbira music discussed in this last section offer insight into that mystique surrounding the mbira demonstrated in stories from Shona history and oral tradition. The most powerful effect of mbira music occurs in the context of traditional Shona religion, at a *bira*, in which the mbira music induces a spirit to possess its entranced medium.

[1] The degree to which listeners respond emotionally to the mbira is, of course, an individual matter. Mubayiwa Bandambira reports that he has seen other mbira players cry while thinking of departed relatives, but he himself is not affected in this way by the music. He is also skeptical of the assertions of some people that mbira music can actually heal illness. In the words of Bandambira, "If someone is healed by listening to mbira music, then he was not very sick to begin with."

6.
Learning the Mbira

"Sometimes when you are learning a song," said John Kunaka (Maridzambira),

> you do not have time to finish it. You may be left knowing only the first section, leaving three parts unfinished. But the ancestral spirits may hear you and offer their help. They can come while you are playing the mbira in a dream and tell you to play this key, or that key. Or, the spirit himself can play mbira in the dream, showing you what his fingers are doing, so that you can see clearly. He can show you new styles and variations, telling you where to add or to take away different keys. When you wake up the next morning, you can go quickly to your mbira and play the way that the spirit has shown you. . . .
>
> In many dreams I have had, the spirit has come as an old man with white hair and a white beard. Although I could not see his face I could see his hands clearly, playing the mbira. In the last dream in which I saw him, he was playing a beautiful old mbira with very large keys—the basses were three-quarter inches wide. Someday I will build an mbira just like the one in the dream.

Learning the Mbira

The Shona believe that the ability to play the mbira results from a combination of inherited and achieved skills. It is a specialized role; not everyone can become an mbira player. Mbira players usually attribute their mastery of the mbira to two sources: the spirits, through dreams, and their colleagues, through direct and indirect teaching.

Considering that mbira music is the music of the ancestors 136 and that it is of central importance in traditional religious ritual, the Shona belief that the spirits play an important role in the process of learning the mbira is not surprising. The first interest a person shows in the mbira and the person's early manifest skill in mbira playing are often interpreted as the reappearance of the long-dormant talent of an ancestor who was himself a skilled player. In contemporary Zimbabwe, as new and old ideologies mix younger musicians express a slightly modified view of this role of the spirits. A person could conceivably learn to play the mbira without the help of an ancestor, but he would most likely have to struggle harder to learn, and he would have less chance of becoming a really great mbira player.

Biographical sketches of mbira players indicate that the spirits play two roles in assisting in the learning process of musicians (see Chapter 9). The first, as expressed by both Luken Pasipamire and Ephat Mujuru, is that of encouragement. Each of them saw in a dream a spirit figure, an old man, who expressed his wish for the dreamer to work hard and to succeed as an mbira player. Mujuru and Pasipamire both interpreted the old men as being the spirits of departed relatives who had at one time performed as expert mbira players for Chaminuka in the court of Chitungwiza. In Pasipamire's case the dream initiated his commitment to the mbira, while in Mujuru's case it came at a discouraging time in his life and renewed his determination to continue his course as an mbira player.

To show respect for the spirits, there is sometimes a certain amount of ritual involved with the learning of mbira. When John Kunaka had learned to play the mbira, there was a special ceremony at his village. His family brewed beer and hired mbira players in order to tell the ancestors of his acquired skill, and Kunaka himself did not play on that occasion. In another instance, a musician, before considering whether to accept me as an mbira student, made a special trip to his home to "ask the permission" of the spirits. Friends of his explained that this ritual was really a way of informing the spirits of his intention so that they would pave the way and guide him in teaching; another friend pointed out that this practice allowed the musician to announce his intention formally and to receive ritual support, so that if any misfortune occurred in his village thereafter, his transaction with me would not be considered the cause. Ephat Mujuru informed me shortly after I had begun studying the mbira with him that an old man (that is, an an- 137 cient spirit) had visited him in a dream, commending him for his efforts and ordering him to work hard with me. As in the instances above, the spirits can encourage both the student and the teacher in the learning process.

The second function of the spirits was described by Kunaka at the beginning of this chapter: they themselves can serve as teachers. Muchatera Mujuru, Ephat's grandfather, also tells stories, typical of those of mbira players, of his encounters with ancestral spirits. He reports that when he was very young, two old men used to come to him in dreams and teach him the mbira. He recognized them as Zhanje and Makunde, both great mbira players in the Mujuru family; they had played for Chaminuka in his court at Chitungwiza. Mujuru remembers the dreams as being "as clear as daylight." The old men told him what to play on the mbira, and he would awake the next morning and perform the new parts he had learned during the night.

It is prestigious for an mbira player to have been taught in dreams by a spirit, particularly by a spirit well-known for his expertise on the mbira or for his general powers. This fact makes musicians skeptical of some of their colleagues' claims; for example, one prominent mbira player said that he had been taught by the great tribal spirit, Chaminuka himself, but other musicians doubted this. There are also differences of opinion regarding certain theoretical aspects of learning from dreams. Some mbira players stated that they learned their first pieces in this fashion, but such assertions were questioned by other performers who maintained that a person must first be taught to play several tunes by living musicians as a prerequisite for learning others in dreams. Kunaka said that in his experience with such matters, the same teacher sometimes reappears in different dreams. Only one piece is taught during a visit, but the same spirit may return a month or so later to demonstrate a new variation on the same piece or a different piece altogether.

In addition to the role the ancestral spirits play in the development of mbira students, indirect teaching on the part of advanced mbira players is frequently part of the beginner's learning experience (Plate 35). Through this method the student learns by observing and imitating the performance of other skilled players without actually being given lessons. This kind of learning goes on in Shona villages in many areas of endeavor. When young girls play together, for instance, they sometimes wrap dolls on their backs and carry toy buckets on their heads in imitation of their mothers, practicing the skills they will need as adults. Indirect learning takes place in dance as well. An infant, bound on its mother's back, bounces along with her as she dances at musical events. When the child is old enough to stand, he or she is encouraged to learn the most basic movements, bobbing up and down to the music. Gradually, by imitating parents and other relatives, the child develops the coordination necessary for more complex steps. The music does not slow down for the child's benefit, nor does anyone necessarily explain the steps or provide practice of them out of the context of performance. This same teaching process is part of the experience of mbira players, who, as Luken Pasipamire expressed it, must learn by "pinching" knowledge from more experienced musicians. The teacher does not slow down his playing or separate the piece into its component parts to make learning easier; he simply allows the younger player to watch his fingers move on the keys and to memorize the piece.

Reflecting on this practice, Pasipamire's uncle Selestino laughed and recalled how his young nephew used to hang over his shoulder, wide-eyed, every time he played the mbira. Then he would ask to borrow the instrument and would try to work out the parts by himself. Musicians report that if the performer from whom they wish to learn is not interested in sharing his knowledge, they must be quick in "pinching" the mbira part before the performer notices them and, by shifting the position of the instrument on his lap, hides his fingers in his gourd resonator.

This visual component of learning mbira music is often as important as the aural. Because the resultant parts that arise from the music differ from those which either hand plays separately, and because duplicate pitches exist on the instrument's soundboard, it is difficult to learn an unfamilar piece or a complex variation solely by listening, although players can develop considerable skill in this.

With the advent of radio programs devoted to traditional African music, young musicians are able to listen to and copy some of the best mbira players in Zimbabwe; Ephat Mujuru, a devoted student of Mubayiwa Bandambira, used to listen to the radio program regularly, hoping to learn a little more of Bandambira's style each time one of his recordings was played. Finally, the atmosphere of the traditional Shona village, in which members of one age group are in a position to benefit from the

139

experiences of the others, is conducive to transmission of mbira music through indirect teaching methods. Just as a teenage student watches over the shoulder of an older uncle playing mbira, when the teenager himself borrows an instrument on which to practice he soon finds his own younger brothers and cousins surrounding him, closely observing his mbira performance.

In addition to indirect methods of learning mbira music, in which a student draws upon and synthesizes bits of knowledge from many different sources, there are also more direct learning situations. Experienced musicians sometimes work directly with students, encouraging them and taking on the responsibility for their education. Various arrangements between the student and the teacher are possible in order to facilitate this approach to learning. For example, some advanced mbira players teach their students intensely for short lesson periods, either at prearranged times or whenever they happen to be in the mood. Others invite a student to remain at their place of work and teach while they carry on their other chores. On one occasion at which I was present, John Kunaka, a well-known musician and blacksmith, pounded away at mbira keys beside his coal fire and homemade bellows and carried on an animated conversation with other villagers seated beside him. In the background, twenty feet away, a young student sat by himself practicing the mbira. Although Kunaka appeared to be paying little attention to the student, he would periodically excuse himself from the conversation, lay aside his tools, and go to the student to correct a mistake he had heard.

There are also several ways of learning mbira pieces. In one common approach, the teacher breaks each piece down into its component phrases and teaches them to the student one at a time. Because the basic structure of mbira pieces is cyclical, with an ambiguous beginning and end, teachers sometimes arbitrarily choose a point in the piece at which always to start and to finish their demonstrated version, so as not to confuse the beginner. By this method, students memorize each phrase, learning one after another until they have mastered all four segments of the piece and can play them in succession unfalteringly.

Teaching methods vary a great deal in this respect. Some of Jege Tapera's students at Kwanongoma College remember him as an extremely uncompromising teacher who challenged them by continually changing his playing of pieces during consecutive lessons. First he showed a student a composition, performing it over and over until the student had grasped it. At the next lesson, however, when the student played the piece for him again, Tapera invariably acted upset at the student's rendition, insisting that it was not the pattern he had demonstrated before. The student would then humbly relearn the piece during this lesson, practice it diligently, only to return at the next lesson and receive the same treatment. In this manner Tapera forced his students to learn new material, teaching them, as well, the important lesson that an mbira piece is not a single fixed part but a set of musical patterns which support a range of variations and interpretations.[1]

In another approach, the mbira player teaches his student each thumb part separately. Usually players of the *mbira dzavadzimu* who employ this method teach their students the left-thumb part of the piece first. Next the students are taught the right-thumb part, and then they learn to coordinate the two. After gaining control of the first two parts, they learn the right-index-finger part, which contains the high-tone melody. Many musicians who learn indirectly use this approach as well: that is, looking over the shoulder of the performer, they concentrate on the movement of the player's left thumb, trying first to copy that. Since all the bass keys are on the left side of the instrument, the left-thumb part provides a complete linear outline of the piece. Additionally, the bass keys are larger than those on the upper manuals of the mbira, so that the left-thumb movements of the player are the easiest to observe. Once a musician has learned the bass line from another player, he can figure out the right-hand melody part to the piece himself.

It is sometimes the case that learners begin by studying a smaller type of mbira than the one that they eventually master. Several musicians with whom I worked received their first experience with mbira music on a small *karimba* (with its own repertory, playing technique, etc.) before distinguishing themselves as outstanding performers of the *njari* or the *mbira dzavadzimu*. One ethnologist reports that some players of the *munyonga*, a *matepe*-like mbira, originally learned to play on an mbira of six to twelve keys.[2] A small mbira provides the musician with an opportunity to explore his interest and ability in mbira music on simple instruments before graduating to the larger Shona mbira with their capacity for complex variations.

In spite of the differences in teaching method, there are a number of overriding similarities in the attitudes of musicians 141 regarding the skills beginners should master and the proper course for their development as mbira players, ranging from the technique of plucking mbira keys to the appropriate circumstances under which students should experiment with the subtle nuances of the pieces and with variations.

All teachers emphasize the importance of students learning a proper approach to the instruments and to the music. This includes a concern for precision and force in striking the mbira keys so as to bring out their true full sound, as well as a concern for rhythmic accuracy. These skills first are developed by learning one or a few mbira pieces rather than a large repertory. Teachers are aware of the likelihood of students developing bad habits in an attempt to progress too quickly, and they warn of the consequences of trying to learn too much new material in a short span of time. More than one overzealous student has had the experience of learning several mbira pieces at one sitting, only to find himself mixing up the different pieces or forgetting them altogether the following day. It is important for beginners to develop control of their instruments slowly and deliberately, building a solid foundation on a small number of pieces which can gradually be expanded into a full repertory of compositions and variations.

Mbira teachers also stress the importance of a student having, or being willing to develop, a good memory, since the repertory for the mbira is passed down aurally. Simon Mashoko emphasizes this point in his autobiographical narrative. As a beginner, Mashoko carried his mbira everywhere with him, even into the fields where he worked, so that he could continue diligently to practice new material that he had learned.

In a typical beginning lesson, once a student has learned the finger pattern for a particular piece he must play the part slowly and evenly through many repetitions. Once Luken Pasipamire instructed me to play the basic pattern of a piece in this manner, and then left the room. He returned twenty minutes later, satisfied to find me still playing the same part in the same way. Such drill not only reinforces the student's knowledge of the piece but also strengthens the student's fingers. This is a practical consideration, because at a religious ceremony the musician must have the endurance to play through the entire evening, with each piece continuing for as much as half an hour or more.

Once a beginner has mastered the basic pattern of several compositions, it is not uncommon for his teacher to suggest that

142

they perform in public together. In such a performance, the student repeatedly plays the basic *kushaura* patterns to the pieces he has learned while his teacher creates variations on them within the framework of the *kutsinhira* parts. This practice enables the student to develop the skill of keeping the steady rhythm of the basic pattern without being thrown off by the other parts being played around him. Additionally, once he has the confidence to listen to his teacher's playing without losing his own bearings, he can begin to get a feeling for the range of variation permissible in the elaboration of an mbira piece, even before he is taught to play variations. The skill of being able to play with other musicians is important because the mbira player must hold his own in an ensemble of two or more mbira players and a complex of musical parts: *hosho* accompaniment, clapping and singing, etc. An mbira player who is insecure about his playing may find that the subtle changes of the powerful *hosho* accompaniment alone can throw him off the rhythm. Luken Pasipamire stressed the attitude that if an mbira player has a sizable repertory but is unable to play with others or does not play with proper strength and control, he is not considered a "player." Conversely, a musician with a very limited repertory who can play with others with good sound and control is considered a "player." He would be welcome to perform at a religious ceremony, even if he had to compensate for his limited repertory by repeating many songs during the evening.

In beginning lessons students may watch their fingers as they play. As they progress, however, their teachers encourage them to free themselves of the habit. As one mbira player put it, "To play mbira, your fingers must have eyes." This is important for two reasons. First, in order to play with sensitivity, listening closely to the mbira and responding to the other musicians, an mbira player cannot be preoccupied with the mechanics of playing. Second, there is a practical consideration. When performing late at night, next to a smoky fire or inside the dimly lit place of the *bira*, a player is not always able to see his fingers in the gourd resonator. Moreover, the shape of the opening of the gourd resonator itself sometimes blocks the performer's view of his instrument.

Muscle relaxation is important in playing the mbira. Developing the strength and control to play without becoming tense is sometimes a challenge for beginners. When a student tries to force himself to play too hard or too fast for an extended period 143 of time, his muscles become tense and easily exhausted. Because of the long hours performers play in the *bira*, control over muscle relaxation is essential. It is a valued compliment when a teacher comments that a student's fingers are becoming loose or flexible.

In order to strengthen the muscles required for mbira playing, students practice frequently for short intervals of time, alternately playing and resting, rather than practicing intensely for long periods. Pacing one's self in performance is necessary for more advanced players as well. Rather than doing flexibility exercises or playing scales before a performance, an mbira player warms up as he plays. Usually, therefore, pieces begin slowly and gradually accelerate to their peak speed. For the same reason musicians sometimes begin the evening performance at a *bira* with some of the least technically demanding pieces, such as "Kariga Mombe," advancing to more difficult pieces as they feel ready for them.

A beginning student of the *mbira dzavadzimu* usually first learns the *kushaura* or lead part of an mbira piece. After learning the *kushaura* parts to several compositions he then learns the *kutsinhira* parts. As a matter of personal taste, some musicians specialize in either the first or the second part to mbira pieces. Others methodically learn both the *kushaura* and *kutsinhira* parts of mbira compositions. Gradually mbira students expand their repertories not only with new pieces but with the traditional variations on the classic pieces they have mastered.

Once a student has developed confidence in his playing, he begins to experiment with the subtleties and nuances of the compositions. By slight changes in the rhythmic relationship between the two interlocking hand parts he can effect a change in the total feeling of the piece and its overall phrasing. By shifting accents to different keys or alternating accents from one hand to the other, new parts spring out from the polyphonic fabric of the piece. As the student progresses, he develops enough control to add new high-tone embellishments to the basic mbira parts, thus increasing the complexity of the mbira music. He can listen to the music in different ways, almost as if he were a member of the audience and his hands were playing independently of his body. At this stage the mbira player achieves the level of playing described in Chapter 5, in which the musician exchanges ideas with the mbira. This relationship of exchange between the mbira player and his instrument presents one of the greatest challenges for the learner.

When I first began to study the mbira, I listened "too carefully" to the resultant parts arising from my instrument and was often thrown off by the discrepancy between what my fingers were playing and what I heard. I often lost my place in the music after repeating a basic pattern a number of times. My teacher, Dumisani Maraire, would say to me at such times, "You are taking too much from the mbira, you must give more" (that is, "Do not listen so carefully to the voice of the mbira, but concentrate on what your fingers are doing"). As I developed more control of the mbira I was confronted with the opposite problem. Sometimes I changed too quickly from one variation to another or played a variation that represented too abrupt a departure from the one before it. At such times Maraire said, "You are giving too much to the mbira, you must take more from the mbira" (that is, "Listen more to the mbira's voice; allow yourself to be affected and moved by its mood and what it is saying"). Once a student understands this principle of sharing ideas with the mbira, he begins to develop the sought-after rapport between himself and his instrument.

Ultimately, out of this relationship with his instrument the advanced student discovers new variations on the pieces he has learned and goes on to develop a personal playing style of his own. While the development of new variations is a creative aspect of mbira playing, musicians instruct their students to confine their experimentation with mbira music to performances at secular events outside the place of the *bira*. This is because a student trying out new variations or trying to improvise might make a mistake while performing that could have a detrimental effect on the possession of the medium. Learners restrict themselves to the most basic *kushaura* parts when performing at religious ceremonies.

Musicians who also teach emphasize the serious nature of the commitment involved in learning to play the mbira. Kunaka stresses the difficulty of the task and says he often turned students away, especially those who would not work up to his expectations. He considers teaching the mbira "too big a job" for the potential rewards unless a student is really serious. He has returned money to students who showed neither the talent nor the discipline to learn well after they began to study with him. 145

On the other hand, Ephat Mujuru emphasizes the need for more musicians to involve themselves in teaching. As a man very much concerned with the reaffirmation of traditional African ways of life in the face of the acculturative process taking place in Zimbabwe today, Mujuru is emphatic about the importance of passing on the art. "If we do not teach younger people to play the mbira," he asks rhetorically, "then who will play mbira for our spirits when we have left this life?"

Except among very good friends or closely related family members, the relationship between teacher and student is a professional one, requiring some form of payment. The student sometimes pays in the form of goods or exchange of services. Luken Pasipamire paid his first teacher's fee in goats. Hakurotwi Mude has built up a sizable herd of cattle as a result of professional services as an mbira player, including teaching. Cosmas Magaya, who is the son of an herbalist, reports that he received his first lessons from one of his father's clients, who taught him mbira in lieu of cash payment for his father's treatments. The arrangements vary, of course, from one player to the next. It is not uncommon for a teacher to charge on the basis of the number of compositions taught, rather than on the number of meetings arranged with the student. Sometimes the fee is adjusted according to the ability of the student to pay. Instructors often agree to receive partial payment before the lessons have begun and final payment upon satisfactory completion.

Much direct teaching and general professional collaboration takes place among mbira players who are related to one another. Mbira players who travel in the same family circle frequently practice, perform, and share knowledge of the mbira repertory with each other. For example, Luken Pasipamire's first teacher was Banibus, an older nephew. Luken, in turn, taught his own brothers Felix and Jealous, who later served as mbira teachers for two other relatives, and so on. Such teaching situations are flexible and the teacher/student roles can be reversed. It is not uncommon for one musician to teach a beginner several tunes and for his student, after learning further from other musicians, to return to teach his first instructor new pieces.

Many times one finds musicians from one family performing together professionally. For example, band leader and singer Hakurotwi Mude has been related to all the various mbira play-

146

ers who over the years have formed the nucleus of his famed ensemble, *Mhuri yekwaRwizi*.

The question arises as to whether the relationships pointed out above reflect what might be in effect a broadly extended family guild of mbira players. The fees that outsiders pay, as distinct from the active and free sharing that takes place within family lines, suggests this possibility. It could be the case, however, that professional relationships grow naturally out of the greater geographical proximity of relatives, rather than from a deliberate attempt to perpetuate a family guild. It is apparent, however, given the available data, that the mbira player, like other professionals, tends to band with others who share his specialized interest. These associates are to a large degree made up of musician relatives of the player. Within this community a grandfather, father, uncle, cousin, or brother may teach a beginner. Clearly, familial connections reinforce the transmission of mbira music within the Shona community.

Within a family, mbira players sometimes share or delegate the responsibilty for teaching and performing. For example, when Cosmas Magaya was younger, his father often made the professional arrangements for his son's performance at religious ceremonies. Another young player in the tribal trust lands once reported to me that when his grandfather, who had taught him to play, became too old to play himself, he acted as his grandson's promoter. This young musician inherited his grandfather's mbira and seven gourd resonators.[a] In other instances, highly skilled mbira players have offered sons or close relatives as teachers to prospective students after they themselves had made the initial arrangements. In these cases, the junior members accepted the obligation and the senior mbira players profited. This is justified in terms of repayment or exchange of services, for the senior player initially taught the junior player his skill. This practice also reflects the attitude that a beginner does not necessarily need to learn from an expert. He can study for a period of time with a competent young musician before he will warrant the attention and instruction of a master player.

It should be pointed out that the methods by which mbira players learn their art are by no means mutually exclusive. As

[a] This is an unusually large number of resonators for an individual player to own, but, as a friend remarked, the young mbira player, like an herbalist, wished to live surrounded by the things of his practice.

147

reflected in the biographical sketches later in this work, an mbira player's education often includes a variety of learning situations. In Luken Pasipamire's case, dreaming about the mbira, which he subsequently interpreted as "encouragement from the spirit world," led to his apprenticeship with an advanced musician. Cosmas Magaya, on the other hand, had to learn the mbira indirectly, thereby proving his genuine interest and ability, before an expert would take him seriously and accept him as a student. Among advanced musicians, learning directly and indirectly from their colleagues and from dreams plays a role in their continuing development as mbira players.

Finally, Shona musicians recognize that for serious mbira players there is no end to learning and to developing their art; it is a lifelong process and a lifelong devotion. The growth and development of performers' styles became apparent to me when on my second trip to Zimbabwe I had the opportunity to play variations on mbira pieces that I had learned from tapes made during my first visit. Upon hearing my performance, one of my teachers, Cosmas Magaya, listened quizzically at first, as if the variations sounded faintly familiar to him. Suddenly he laughed with delight, remarking, "Ahhhh, I remember those styles; that is the way I used to play two years ago!"

After I had completed my third research trip to Zimbabwe, mbira player Mondrek Muchena advised me:

> Now you have seen for yourself how deep the music is. Each time you have come to us, you have found us having learned more music; each time you have come, you have learned more things yourself. And it will always be this way for you as well as for us.

Musicianship Among Mbira Players

I once asked John Kunaka how many different levels of skill and musicianship mbira players recognized. In his answer he distinguished among musicians in five different categories:

> When a man is beginning to learn the mbira we say he is "mudzidzi" (student). He is still learning, so we don't allow him to play at the bira.
> After he has begun to develop, we say "Akugona zvishoma" (He is able [to play mbira] a little). He can go to the bira with what he knows, only playing the kushaura parts of pieces together with his teacher.
> Next, we say "Akugona" (He is able). He can go to the bira

148

with someone else [a more advanced player] and can play either the *kushaura* or the *kutsinhira* parts to the pieces that he has learned.

Then we say, *"Akuridza chaizvo"* (He plays beautifully). He can go to the *bira* with someone else or he can go alone. If you tell him to play the *kushaura* or to play the *kutsinhira*, he can do it while other things are going on around him [that is, he is not distracted or thrown off by other musical activities at the *bira*]. Only, he has yet to master all the pieces for the mbira and he is just beginning to add his own variations.

Finally, when a man is at the top, we call him *"sha sha"* or *"nyanzvi."* We say *"Inyanzvi"* (He is a champion). He can go to the *bira* alone and compete with others. He can learn a new piece just from hearing it played for the first time and can make up his own *kutsinhira* part on the spot. He knows all the compositions for the mbira and can create his own variations.

When I asked him to rate several mbira players on the scale that he had described, and suggested three names, two younger musicians who were present looked up with interest. Without hesitation the mbira player rated the first two musicians: one was "able" and the other a rank higher, "able to play beautifully." At the third name he hesitated. It was the name of a well-known mbira player. Finally, after much deliberation, he announced, *"Mudzidzi."* The two young mbira players broke out in hilarity. "Ahhh, no!" one exclaimed after catching his breath, "not *mudzidzi*, no." The mbira player did not face the younger musicians but looked off into the distance. "Yes," he repeated, *"mudzidzi!"*

Kunaka's differentiation of five levels of musicianship among mbira players and his exchange with the other performers above reflect the degree to which musicians judge each other's skill and standing in their profession. It also suggests the element of personal rivalry that occasionally colors these judgments.

Competition is very much a part of Shona mbira music today. It is not always simply a personal matter but exists among mbira groups as well. The leader of a famous mbira group often appeared with his ensemble at musical events to give a sample of his playing and to prove his position. "They will see that I am the champion," he once said to me on his way to a *bira*. On another occasion at which I was present, an mbira group declined to perform when the same man challenged them. They maintained that they were not allowed to use the music of the ancestors for competition. However, on a later occasion the 149 leader of that group boasted to me that his own relative was an mbira player "to be feared" for his playing. Rivalry also occurs between mbira players of different regions. The mbira players in a Mondoro village reported to me that in another village of the country people were good singers but did not play the mbira well. Competition is found in other aspects of the mbira music performance. One singer informed me that when he sang, others were "shy" about joining in.

Musicians tend to regard each other's performances with highly critical ears. Although I have often heard the general feeling expressed among mbira players that one "is not allowed to" or at least "should not" blame or oppose the playing of another mbira player, privately they often make judgments. A number of different criteria form the basis of these judgments and reflect those aspects of the performance of mbira music important to the musicians themselves. The criteria mentioned here are based on criticisms that I heard numerous mbira players repeat about each other's performances. The judgments musicians made seemed to me to fall into two categories: those implying a common standard of general musicianship, and those based on personal or regional taste.

The first category includes consideration of the skills required for basic control and ultimate mastery of the mbira. Some relate to the practice of teaching mbira music. For example, accomplished musicians should be able to play all the mbira's pitches with precision, bringing out the full sound of each key. Lesser musicians are not able to keep strict time and hit the keys unevenly, with the result that only some keys ring well. Other factors which indicate the musician's skill are his power to project the sound of the mbira and his endurance. John Kunaka claimed, for instance, that he "could give the mbira voice to a hundred people." I heard several mbira players criticized for playing with "the soft hands of a woman." Another musician, in sizing me up as an mbira player, once approached me and asked "For how long can you play the mbira?" On another occasion a musician boasted that he could "chase away from a *bira*" a virtuoso in the region, who, he said, no longer had the strength he had had when he was younger. As mentioned above, powers of physical endurance are important in performance at a *bira*. It is said as well that an expert "having good hands" has the flexibility necessary to play any mbira of his own type.

A less able musician would have to struggle to perform on an mbira other than the one to which he was accustomed.

In addition to the mbira player's basic control of his instrument, the requirements of general musicianship encompass the following criteria: care of the mbira, knowledge of the repertory associated with the instrument, ability to create variations, and skill at performing with others. To begin with, a good musician keeps his mbira well tuned and in good repair. I once heard strong criticism of a highly respected performer after a demonstration in which he played with one key out of tune and with another improperly bound to the soundboard so that it started vibrating loosely, making extraneous " qwak-qwak" sounds.

Musicians sometimes criticize individual mbira players for their limited knowledge of mbira pieces and lack of interest in pieces performed outside their own village. Musicians are also sensitive to the degree of mastery evident in the selection of pieces within an individual's mbira repertory. For example, students often start with basic compositions, such as "Kariga Mombe," that do not demand great technical skill, while champions can play with ease the most difficult mbira pieces, such as "Dangurangu." Experts also have extensive repertories and can learn new pieces quickly. This is epitomized by a story told to me by Ephat Mujuru about the great virtuoso Mubayiwa Bandambira. According to the story, Bandambira surprised his early teachers with his capacity to learn almost immediately after his father presented him with his first mbira. "He's playing it better than I now," his teachers exclaimed when Bandambira returned to them the day after each lesson. "Come and teach me back!" they insisted.

There is often playful boasting among mbira players regarding their knowledge of the mbira repertory. Their reputations sometimes reflect their skill with specific pieces. One musician reported to me that his favorite pieces were "Muka tiende," "Dande," and "Taireva." When he played them, he said, he was a "terrible man." Another musician who performed with him said that when he himself played "Nyamaropa yekutanga" no other musician in the area could overtake him. When the name of a third musician came up, the two players said that he was a "terrible man for singing," but that he could not overtake them on mbira. However, there was one piece on which they agreed that he was a master. When this singer played "Manda-rendare" on his mbira, he was "to be feared" by all other players. Since within the general mbira repertory individual players can specialize in either *kushaura* or *kutsinhira* parts, villagers will sometimes seek a particular musician to play at a *bira* because he knows many *kutsinhira* styles and plays with a very power-ful bass line or because he is expert in playing the high-tone patterns in the *kushaura* style.

The art of variation and improvisation is an important aspect of general musicianship. In this, players of *mbira dzavadzimu* often focus on the ability of the musician to create different kinds of melodies in the right-hand part, utilizing the entire upper range of the instrument. I have heard musicians criticize others as beginners for their inability to use high-tones effec-tively while playing a piece. When mbira players asked me to perform for them I often felt that they reserved judgment until I had developed a piece sufficiently to include high-tone varia-tions. Only then did they express approval. Another aspect of improvisation has to do with the relationship among the differ-ent parts of mbira pieces. Great musicians have the skill, upon hearing a *kushaura* part of a piece for the first time, to impro-vise an interwoven *kutsinhira* part, successfully accompanying the first player.

As noted above, a good musician can interact well with oth-ers in an mbira ensemble. Kunaka criticized one mbira player in a group for "not doing his job" while playing *kutsinhira*. In-stead of meshing his part neatly with that of the first player, the musician's playing overlapped and clashed with that of the *kushaura* part. An expert player must be able to perform *ku-shaura* and *kutsinhira* parts which complement those of the other musicians around him.

The greatest mbira players develop their own styles of per-formance.[b] In this respect the playing of individual musicians is distinguishable on the basis of a number of factors ranging from the personal variations they create and the ways in which they interpret traditional versions of mbira pieces to the overall sound they produce with their instruments. Mubayiwa Banda-

[b] Aspiring musicians frequently adopt such styles as models. The styles can also become the basis for musical parody on the part of more profi-cient players. For example, Andrew Tracey ("Jege A. Tapera," p. 45) reports that Tapera's performances incorporated elements of other mbira players' styles which he frequently mimicked humorously.

mbira's grandfather, a great mbira virtuoso, originally received the nickname Bandambira (from the verb *kubanda*, meaning "to crush") because of the tremendous force with which he hit his mbira keys, especially the bass keys. Some mbira players vary dynamics and accents in their playing. Simon Mashoko and John Kunaka, for example, sometimes introduce unexpected bursts of sound into their performances. Another excellent musician, Erick Muchena, receives praise for the evenness and precision of his playing style, "slow but sure." [c]

Musicians express great admiration for mbira players who can demonstrate thorough control of their instruments by performing with extraordinary skill, distinguishing themselves by the complexity of their music. As mentioned in the previous chapter, they have the ability, when performing alone, to sound like two or more players. Other musicians demonstrate their mastery of mbira music by playing the mbira while they are participating in other musical activities. Simon Mashoko is a master of the remarkable physical coordination and musical concentration such feats require. For his ability to play the mbira, sing, and dance at the same time, he has become a legend among his followers (Plate 36).[d]

While mbira players consider as important all the criteria mentioned previously, they recognize that only in the hands of champions are all standards met to perfection. More often musicians acknowledge both strengths and weaknesses in performers and balance these factors against each other in assessing their own abilities or in comparing themselves to others. For instance, one musician raised his right index finger and in-

[c] Side I, band 2, of *The Soul of Mbira* illustrates this style of performance by Erick Muchena and his brother Mondrek.

[d] A musician from the Salisbury area has amazed other performers with his ability to accompany his own mbira playing with *hosho* attached to his feet (Ephat Mujuru, personal communication, 1975). John Kaemmer has reported mbira players exhibiting their skills in the Madziwa area by walking or dancing while playing the mbira. He has also observed that a couple of musicians sometimes played with "the instrument turned upside down with one edge of the calabash resonator on the head" ("Dynamics of a Changing Music System," p. 123). Musicians also apparently enjoyed such displays of virtuosity in the past. A sketch made by Thomas Baines in the mid-nineteenth century depicts a group of mbira players, one of whom is not only performing while standing but appears to be playing a wind instrument such as a whistle or panpipe strapped to his chest as well (the drawing is the property of the National Archives of Rhodesia).

153

formed me that he was a "terrible man with this," indicating his formidable skill at high-tone variations. He suggested, however, that yet another musician had overtaken him "for tunes" (that is, for the size of his mbira repertory). After one mbira performance at which I was present, the friends of a young musician who was not performing at the time teased him. They said that the mbira player made the young musician "to be short" (that is, to feel inferior). The musician, visibly embarrassed, denied the challenge but later admitted that the mbira player could "put more" into the *kutsinhira* parts than he could. However, he maintained that he could match him in playing *kushaura*.

Mbira players' judgments concerning other aspects of mbira music point to differences in personal and regional taste. These include such considerations as the musician's basic equipment, *chuning*, the optimum number of mbira within an ensemble, the nature of the mbira repertory, and playing styles.

The basic equipment used by mbira players differs. For example, the number of keys on different mbira of the same type can vary. In modern versions of *mbira dzavadzimu* there is a certain amount of variation upon the standard model of twenty-two keys. Some players add one or two extra keys to enable them to extend the range of their instruments and to facilitate playing new variations. There appears to be a slightly greater variation in the number of keys among other mbira types: two *njari* made by Mashoko in Ft. Victoria and by Mambo in northeastern Zimbabwe have thirty-five and twenty-six keys, respectively. Extra keys on the large Shona mbira do not change the basic seven-pitch scale, but rather reinforce its sound through additional unison or octave pitches. John Kunaka plays an *mbira dzavadzimu* with twenty-four keys. He modelled his instrument upon a twenty-three key mbira his uncle had crafted. Originally, Kunaka added the other key because he felt it would be useful in performing the complex piece "Dangurangu." He now also uses the extra key for special high-tone variations on other tunes such as "Nhemamusasa" and "Nyamaropa huru."

Second, mbira players attach a varying number of vibrators such as shells or bottle-tops to the soundboards of their instruments and to their gourd resonators. While a certain amount of buzzing is deemed appropriate by musicians, the proportion of buzzing to the sound of the mbira is a matter of personal taste. Once when I played for some Zezuru people a Kwanongoma *karimba* with only two bottle-top vibrators on the soundboard, my audience said they enjoyed the music, but that more bottle tops added to the resonator would make the sound complete. On another occasion Hakurotwi Mude removed the shell vibrators from his gourd resonators and replaced them with new bottle-top rattles. He said that the former rattles were "too much" and that the mbira were not sounding right when resonated in the gourds. The new vibrators offered less vibration and therefore, according to Mude, a more appropriate balance to the mbira's voice. Musicians who are especially fond of the buzzing quality add several rows of bottle-tops to their resonators.

Related to the concern of mbira players for their basic equipment is the issue of mbira *chunings*. As noted in the previous chapter, in some parts of Zimbabwe, particularly where the *mbira dzavadzimu* predominates, there are a number of optional *chunings* available to performers. Mbira players may discuss objectively the merits or drawbacks of their own *chuning* preferences, but at other times musicians are considerably less charitable toward mbira with different *chunings*. They may judge an instrument to be "out of tune" even though it is internally consistent according to the basic tuning plan of the mbira. Musicians utilizing a relatively low *chuning* typically criticize mbira with higher *chunings* as having "too small" or faint a voice. One hears mbira players who favor relatively high *chunings* criticize the *chunings* of other musicians as being "too low" and "sounding like bees." Since the bass keys can produce a disproportionately great amount of response from the rattles, this refers partly to the amount of buzzing which results from low *chunings* and obscures the clarity of the bass pitches. As already mentioned, in areas where a choice of *chunings* is available to musicians it is not uncommon for performers over the course of their careers to adopt new *chunings* for a "change," thereby giving fresh character to the mbira pieces that they perform.

Musicians also have strong feelings about the optimum number of mbira played together and the function of each when more than two are involved. Some musicians feel that two or three is the optimum number for the musician to hear the *kushaura* and *kutsinhira* parts clearly. They say that when more than three musicians play at the same time, each cannot hear the others well enough to perform well together. Other musicians have taken issue with that judgment. It is true, they answer, that when one plays mbira in his gourd, he can hear his own mbira and those on either side of him best. However, if many musicians play together and each hears well the mbira on either side of him, then the whole should also be beautiful.

Since the basic performance of an mbira piece comprises a pair of *kushaura* and *kutsinhira* parts, the question arises of the function of more than two mbira players in an mbira ensemble. The answer is a matter of personal taste. Some mbira players maintain that when more than two musicians perform together they should support each other by doubling parts and adding more power or volume to the group. If three musicians play together, says John Kunaka, the third musician should double the part of the first and play *kushaura*. This is appropriate because the *kushaura* part contains the basic character of the piece and listeners easily recognize and appreciate it. The *kushaura* tends, moreover, to place more emphasis on the melody in the upper parts of the music, which, depending on the characteristics of the gourd resonator, do not always carry as well as the heavier bass of the *kutsinhira*. Doubling the *kushaura*, then, creates a better balance among the parts and increases the power of the group.

In Kunaka's view, if the ensemble adds new mbira players beyond the basic nucleus of three, each new player should reinforce a part already being performed by the musicians: if ten musicians play together, they should perform alternately the *kushaura* and *kutsinhira* with each man seated between two other musicians playing the part complementary to his own.

Ephat Mujuru and others criticize as redundant the practice of doubling parts. In the view of these musicians, each performer should play a different part in an mbira ensemble, regardless of the size of the group. In an ensemble organized around this principle, musicians simultaneously perform different *kushaura* and *kutsinhira* versions of one piece and when it is appropriate they add variations associated with other pieces sharing an underlying structure with the one being played. For instance, on a number of occasions when the group *Mhuri yekwaRwizi* performed with five mbira players, Mude told each musician to play a different part. One musician played the *kushaura* to "Kariga Mombe" while the second performed the *kushaura* to "Mahororo" and the third performed the *kushaura* to "Nyamaropa." The remaining two musicians added different *kutsinhira* parts. In justifying this practice, Cosmas Magaya ex-

156

plains, "One reason why there are so many different parts for mbira pieces is so that many musicians can play them together." The combination of particular versions of different mbira pieces, however, does not find unanimous approval among mbira players. John Kunaka disagrees vehemently with Mude's performance practice described here. Although he concedes that "Mahororo" and "Nyamaropa" would make a "nice song" together, he is adamant that "Kariga Mombe" could not be combined with "Nyamaropa." [e] "It is not good to me," he says. "It is forcing the mbira. If you play like that at Nyandoro [the place he regards as the birthplace of *mbira dzavadzimu*], they will stop your mbira and tell you to go away." Cosmas Magaya, the musician from Rwizi, replies, "But we did play like that at Nyandoro, and the people are still talking about us today; they loved us so much." The practice of simultaneous performance of different mbira pieces clearly remains a matter of taste and esthetic judgment among musicians.

The nature of the pieces within an individual's repertory is itself sometimes grounds for dispute among musicians. Within the repertories of some mbira players there are a number of pieces adapted from other types of mbira and from traditional vocal and drum compositions. Some musicians, especially older players, criticize those who have adapted music not originally intended for their type of mbira. Muchatera Mujuru laughed and shook his head with disapproval when he heard "Chemutengure" performed on the *mbira dzavadzimu*. "The *shangara* dance pieces are not meant for an mbira that is played for the spirits," he said to me. John Kunaka similarly expressed his disapproval of the mbira performance of traditional pieces for drums and chorus. To him, this was "sacrilegious." Ephat Mujuru, however, took issue with him: he had played such pieces at religious ceremonies for spirits who had appreciated them greatly.

Musicians also express concern over the tempo with which different performers play the mbira, sometimes criticizing those

[e] In Kunaka's view, "Nyamaropa" and "Mahororo" made a "nice song" together because "Mahororo" could, in fact, function as a *kutsinhira* part for "Nyamaropa," interlocking its pitches in the high-tone and bass melodic patterns of the pieces (see Example 4). On the other hand, he viewed a combination of "Kariga Mombe" and "Nyamaropa" as "forcing the mbira" because "Kariga Mombe" has pitches which, for the most part, duplicate those of "Nyamaropa" on the same pulses of the music.

who play too fast. Excessive speed draws three objections: first, it is not appropriate for the *mbira dzavadzimu* ("Old people won't like it; they will say you are playing it like a guitar"); second, players do not always have the skill to play consistently well at fast tempos (a performer will make mistakes or play poorly; his fingers "would be short to the keys" or "would jump keys"); and, third, people do not enjoy dancing to the music ("They become tired just from listening"). The appropriate tempo for mbira pieces varies with the context of the performance, however. When a person plays for himself outside a *bira*, he can choose any tempo that appeals to him. The demands of a *bira*, however, require him to perform in such a manner that "the mbira will shout and be heard." Often the pieces begin slowly, both to enable the musicians to warm up and, as Mude says, "to draw the interest of the people" (other participants). As the dancing gets underway at the *bira* the pieces accelerate considerably. In this context, consideration for the tastes of the possessed medium also influences the tempo of mbira pieces. The spirit medium sometimes directly instructs the players to increase or decrease their performing tempo.

I have sometimes heard musicians criticize others for changing variations too frequently within the performance of a piece, because as Hakurotwi Mude says, "People won't sing when the mbira player changes all the time." In other words, since the singers base their vocal lines in part on the resultant patterns of the mbira music, it is difficult for them to adapt an appropriate vocal part when the player changes the music too frequently. Although the amount and frequency of variation on a piece is primarily a function of such factors as the skill of the performer and character of the composition, the context of the performance also affects it. When playing for himself, a musician is freer of constraints than when he performs at a *bira*.

Mbira pieces consist of basic structures that support variations, but there are limits beyond which musicians should not go in their improvisation. Mbira players sharply criticize those who overstep the limits or who try to take short cuts which do not satisfactorily outline the basic structure of the piece. One performer was blamed for not playing mbira pieces properly because in his variations he sometimes became so carried away that he skipped sections of the piece or left out important pitches. Such practices are regarded as mistakes, distinguished from accidents that might be incorporated into a piece as a new variation.

158

Related to the issue of tasteful improvisation in mbira music is the concern among musicians regarding some of the styles that have evolved in recent years. One of the most controversial styles of playing, described in Chapter 4, is called *majimba* by some musicians. This style consists of variations that offer an abrupt departure from the traditional versions of a piece. Listeners enjoy them in part for their effect as "musical jokes" within a performance. Since attitudes toward *majimba* seem to reflect a generation gap among musicians, the younger players being most favorably disposed toward its use, it is possible that as time passes the most respectable of the *majimba* forms will begin to take their place among legitimate variations for the mbira.

Within the social circles of Shona musicians, then, critical evaluation of their colleagues by individual musicians reflects a sensitivity to many aspects of the art of mbira music, from general considerations implying a standard of musicianship to more personal ones. As young performers develop their skill they adopt the standards of musicianship from their teachers or indirectly from emulation of other advanced musicians. Eventually, as they become mature players, they too make personal judgments concerning the music, and these ultimately lead to the crystallization of their own unique styles of performance.

7.
The Poetry of the Mbira

Amid the flickering candlelight and the shadows, a dignified old man sat back against the wall of the thatched-roof brick round-house and watched the goings-on of the *bira*, an all-night ceremony for the ancestral spirits. His tattered overcoat kept the winter air from chilling him as he clapped energetically to the accompaniment of the mbira ensemble. The house was filled with villagers singing and clapping. Dancers passed before him. His face remained expressionless as he watched the proceedings. About every thirty seconds or more, however, he burst forth with a seemingly effortless line of poetry, a mixture of singing, talking, and sighing. So subtle was his participation that it was not clear from the reactions of others in the crowd whether or not they had even heard him, as they seemed involved in their own thoughts and their own roles as participants. Periodically, however, several of the younger villagers covered their mouths to keep from laughing outright at the statements of the old man. "You have killed the elephant, but the head is mine," he sang. "You have brought me butter, but I have no bread." A young man with fancy European clothes danced over in front of the singer and shortly thereafter the old man sang, "It is those young men with their tight pants who have brought the white man's ways upon us." The embarrassed youth danced away from the vocalist.

The next day a villager smiled, thinking back on the *bira*, and commented to me: "That clever old man; he really kept things going last night."

Poetic song texts are a central feature of Shona mbira music. As one mbira player reported to me, "Mbira music without singing is like *sadza* without *muriwo*" (grain porridge without vegetables). One Shona gas station attendant who often listened to the radio while working described the impact of a performance of mbira music on himself and his fellow workers: "When Hakurotwi Mude is singing, we stop everything we are doing and listen to his words."

The texts accompanying *mbira dzavadzimu* serve an important communicative function. For the researcher interested in understanding this aspect of mbira music, problems arise in collection and analysis of the texts, problems common to the study of oral poetry in many cultures.[a] As a metaphoric art form which often contains allusions to old proverbs and historical or cultural events, oral poetry is not easily interpreted by researchers who are not native Shona speakers with an intimate knowledge of Shona culture.[b] Second, because of the subtlety of the symbolism in the song texts, the same line of poetry can hold various meanings for different people. A third problem is that some of the idioms used in the poetry consist of "deep Shona," ancient words or expressions the rich mystical meaning of which only the old people understand. Some of the older villagers say that even when they first learned certain lines of poetry from their parents or grandparents, the meanings of some words were surrounded with mystery and never fully explained.

Despite the fact that some of the ancient poetic phrases may have lost their meaning, one can learn a great deal about the traditional function of the poetry by comparing recently composed song texts to older texts the meanings of which are still accessible. For example, there are numerous poetic lines which make their point in the form of traditional proverbs. If the most

[a] Merriam has enumerated the difficulties of translation and interpretation of song texts (*Anthropology of Music*, pp. 188–89).

[b] It has been my good fortune to be able to work closely with Shona translators, many of whom were themselves either performers of *kudeketera* or relatives of well-known singers.

I am especially indebted to the following individuals for their assistance in the transcription and translation of the material on which this chapter is based: George Fortune, chairman of the department of African languages, University of Rhodesia; Aaron Hodza, a poet, research assistant, and demonstrator at the University of Rhodesia; Cosmas Magaya, an mbira player formerly with *Mhuri yekwaRwizi*; Claudius Magaya; and Stanlake Samkange, the noted novelist and historian at Northeastern University.

ancient of these lines have lost their meaning, new lines have replaced them in response to recent historical and social changes in Shona culture. A line from the repertory of Mondrek Muchena, "To eat with a teacher is good luck," illustrates this. This proverb is a humorous barb directed at modern Shona teachers who have had a Christian-European upbringing. As a good Christian, even more devoted, perhaps, than his European counterpart, the Shona teacher always prays for some time before he eats. Thus the words suggest that it is good luck to eat with a teacher because one can get a head start on eating the food while the teacher prays; one is assured of a full stomach. While the content of such a proverb is modern, its function—making indirect social commentary through ridicule—and its spirit are certainly traditional. Singers today often alternate lines that reflect the changes in Shona culture with others which are traditional or archaic.

The mbira players with whom I worked in Zimbabwe use the word *kudeketera* for the sung poetry accompanying mbira music.[c] Several types of poetry are distinguishable on the basis of such factors as form, content, and performance practice. According to their basic characteristics, I call them the fixed-line type, the narrative type and the mosaic type. Briefly, the fixed-line type consists of a short set of composed lines (sometimes only the title of the piece itself) that are repeated throughout the performance of the composition. In contrast is the long and

[c] There are problems with the definitions of *kudeketera* that have appeared in the literature on Shona language and music. For example, Hannan's *Standard Shona Dictionary* defines *kudeketera* as "to speak in an entertaining way." Such a definition implies that *kudeketera* texts are spoken rather than sung. The musicians with whom I worked clearly considered *kudeketera* to be a form of singing (*kuimba*) rather than a form of talking (*kutaura*), although singers of *kudeketera* do occasionally switch into a talking mode when giving directions to others or when commenting on the performance. A second definition in the *Standard Shona Dictionary* refers to *kudeketera* as singing in a "monotone." This also gives the wrong impression, since the melodic contour of *kudeketera* lines can encompass a range of as much as an octave.

In his comprehensive work, "Multi-Part Relationships," Kauffman (p. 143) describes *kudeketera* in mbira music as "a spoken lamentation . . . used to express personal troubles." While Kauffman appropriately stresses the importance of song texts of lamentation, the expression of personal troubles is but one of many different themes forming the basis of the *kudeketera* accompanying mbira music. The song text examples in this chapter illustrate this point.

involved, rapidly sung, storytelling style that I call the narrative type: singers of this type of poetry follow a traditional, composed story line but have some freedom to vary their renditions from one performance to the next. The mosaic type is an improvisatory form of poetry in which singers combine personal views, traditional proverbs, historical references, and other matters in a general commentary on Shona life.

It should be noted that while many texts of *kudeketera* performances clearly belong to one of the three types discussed in this chapter, there is sometimes a certain amount of overlapping among them. For example, the performance of "Kuyadya Hove Kune Mazove" on *The Soul of Mbira* (side I, band 4) has the basic character of a fixed-line type of *kudeketera*. The singer continually returns to the title of the piece or to variations on it: "To go and eat fish," "For sure, we will go and eat fish," "Excuse us, we want to go," "Oh yes, to go and eat fish." In the same performance, however, other lines are improvised which have the character of the mosaic type: "I am a pure MuMaramba by birth," "What sort of marriage was that of Mr. Mandocha?" "I am the only one who remained, Sir [others of his family were dead]."

Similarly, although the mosaic type of *kudeketera* is highly improvisatory, there are some pieces for the *mbira dzavadzimu* which have fixed lines associated with them. For example, in the Mondoro area, the line "Tanga wabvunza mutupo" ("First ask the name of the totem") seems to go only with the piece "Kuzanga." While many different lines are improvised around this basic phrase, its inclusion helps to signal the identity of the piece for listeners.

The Fixed-Line Type

The fixed-line type of poetry accompanying mbira music usually provides entertainment in secular contexts. It is a repetitive style of poetry in which a few composed lines alternate during the performance of the mbira piece. Sometimes performers repeat one line several times before proceeding to the next. The title of the song is often one of the featured lines of the performance. The following translation and text of the first part of a recorded performance of the *karimba* piece "Ndabva kumakudo" ("I have come from the baboons") illustrates these points.[d]

[d] The full performance by Simon Mashoko, accompanying himself with a small *karimba*-type mbira, is on *The Soul of Mbira*, side II, band 5.

1. Ndabva kumakudo kwaMuneri.

2. Ndabva kumakudo.

3. Ndabva kumakudo kwaMuneri.

4. Rimuka rine ngoma kwaMuneri.

5. Haaha kwaMuneri.
6. Haaha kwaMuneri.
7. Ndabva kumakudo.

8. Rimuka rine ngoma kwaMuneri.

9. Rodanawo vamwe.

10. Ndoindawo navamwe hee.

11. Ndoindawo navamwe hee.

12. Ndoindawo navamwe kwaMuneri.
13. Ndabva kumakudo.

14. Ndabva kumakudo.

15. Ndabva kumakudo.

16. Ndabva kumakudo.

17. Ndabva kumakudo.

18. kwaMuneri.
19. hee kwaMuneri.
20. hee kwaMuneri.
21. Ndabva kumakudo.

22. Rimuka rine ngoma haa.

1. I have come from where the baboons are (i.e., where they live) at Muneri's place.

2. I have come from where the baboons are.

3. I have come from where the baboons are at Muneri's place.

4. The virgin land has drums (sounding) at Muneri's place.

5. Ha, at Muneri's.
6. Ha, at Muneri's.
7. I have come from where the baboons are.

8. The virgin land has drums (sounding) at Muneri's place.

9. It (the land) is inviting others also (to the dance).

10. I will go along with the others also.

11. I will go along with the others also.

12. I will go along with the others also to Muneri's.
13. I have come from where the baboons are.

14. I have come from where the baboons are.

15. I have come from where the baboons are.

16. I have come from where the baboons are.

17. I have come from where the baboons are.

18. At Muneri's.
19. Hey, at Muneri's
20. Hey, at Muneri's.
21. I have come from where the baboons are.

22. The virgin land has drums (which sound).

Simon Mashoko described the piece above as belonging to a genre of songs called *makwaira* that young people between the

ages of twelve and twenty traditionally sang.[e] They were especially popular several decades ago. According to Mashoko, the
song "Ndabva kumakudo" had its origin in the late arrival of
one singer who, when asked where he had been, replied, "I come
from the baboons at Muneri's place." By this he meant that he
had been working late as a guard in Muneri's fields, preventing
them from being pillaged by baboons. According to Mashoko,
Muneri was a former Afrikaans missionary from the Dutch Re-
formed Church who had a bad reputation among Africans because of the cruelty with which he treated his servants.

The second line of the song, "the virgin land has drums," refers to the acoustic properties of a forest in which the sound of
a drum in a village on one side of the land frequently reverber-
ates through the forest so that people on the other side hear the
sound as if the forest itself were producing it.

Mashoko reports that song texts of this kind are usually repe-
titious and sometimes have the effect of jokes. Other Shona listeners reported that unlike some of the deep Shona texts discussed later in this chapter, these fixed-line texts may include
playful words or statements, the melodic contour and rhythmic
patterns of which happen to fit the mbira piece. Their value as
communication, in other words, is limited.

The Narrative Type

Narrative poetic texts often accompany the *njari* in secular contexts and tell a complete story. They have their counterpart in
a form of traditional Shona oral literature called *ndyaringo*,
which "deal . . . with particular situations and individual experiences in a narrative mode" and aim at entertaining adult
audiences through "virtuosity of language," "invention . . .
[and a] personal flair for vivid description."[1] In fact, some of
the narrative poetic texts, such as the following example of
"Mbiriviri," may well have had their origin as *ndyaringo* before they were adapted to the mbira. Such stories are still told
today for entertainment without instrumental accompaniment.[f]

[e] Ordinarily in a full *makwaira* performing group the leader sings the
line, "I am from the baboons," and the followers answer, "At Muneri's
place," in a call and response fashion. In Mashoko's solo performance,
however, he sings both of the parts himself.
[f] One such version of "Mbiriviri," narrated to Aaron Hodza by his
uncle, appears in Hodza, *Ugo Hwamadzinza AvaShona*, p. 77, under the
title "Ndoda Kushereketa."

"Mbiriviri" is about a man who is a "champion and about whom news has travelled very far."[2] The story describes the man's journey and his encounters with different groups of people, each in need of one of his possessions. Each group destroys the required possession but makes reparation beyond the traveller's expectations. At my request, after one performance of "Mbiriviri," Simon Mashoko translated and explained what he had sung. Although his remarks represent an informal delineation of the narrative, they do reveal the subtlety of the imagery and symbolism sometimes found in narrative type *kudeketera*. The explanation illustrates a number of stylistic features associated with *ndyaringo* as a generic form of Shona literature: segmentation of the story into a succession of clear individual pictures, use of closely parallel or repetitive phrases to set off the sections of the story and to carry the narrative forward, and use of hyperbole and fantasy to meet the expectations of an audience wishing to be entertained.[3] A complete text and translation of one of Mashoko's recorded performances of "Mbiriviri" is in the Appendix.[g]

"Mbiriviri"

[Introduction]

Literal Meaning	*Intended Meaning*
1. In this modern life people aren't settled.	1. The lives of our ancestors were better and more settled.
2. My grandfather was a doctor who gave me a tattoo mark that will last forever.	2. My grandfather was not really a doctor: The tattoo stands for the mbira. The mbira was given to us by our forefathers and with it come things we cannot forget.
3. You are leaving the music.	3. "Deep Shona": part of our forefathers' words. It does not necessarily refer to someone leaving the music. Perhaps they are scolding someone for not listening carefully or for ignoring the ways of the forefathers.

[g] Mashoko performs this version of "Mbiriviri" on the *Soul of Mbira*, side II, band 1.

Literal Meaning

4. I am a wanderer, my family no longer loves me.
5. A playful man has arrived.
6. From his boyhood, he was passed by five generations of boys, then married.
7. You have left your letter unfinished.

Intended Meaning

4-7. "Deep Shona": the meaning is unclear. I was taught them by listening to the singing of my mother's and father's brothers.

[Main Story Line]

8. I was walking with a knobkerrie and saw a ditch ahead. I threw the knobkerrie to the other side but it fell short. When I went to fetch it, I found honey with it; I don't know where it got the honey.

8. The knobkerrie stands for the mbira. When it hit the ground on my side of the ditch I heard beautiful music arise from it. Then I took the music to the people.

9. When I started to go to Njanja, I found there old men worshipping their spirits while seated on the ground. I asked, "Why are you worshipping spirits on the ground?" I was told, "Because we have no mat to sit on." I said, "This is my mat; you can have my mat." They took it to use and returned it broken. I asked, "Why did you break my mat?" They replied, "No, don't cry; we will give you a gun." I said, "Thank you; I like the gun because I want to shoot the animal with the curved horns in the hills and eat it in a mouth without teeth."

9. The mat stands for the mbira. The old men were worshipping without an mbira.

The gun stands for a ladle for beer. The main character wants to join the people for beer (to "eat in a mouth without teeth").

10. I went to the hills and found people shooting an animal with a pop-gun. I asked, "Why are you shooting the animal with a pop-gun?" They said, "Because we

10. The hills are really homes, that is, where the beer has been brewed.

167

Literal Meaning

have no gun." I said, "Here is a gun." They used it and they broke it! "Why have you broken my gun?" I asked. "Don't worry," they replied. "We'll give you a cow." "Thank you; now I can get milk from it," I said.

11. I next came upon people sitting milking a frog. I asked, "Why are you milking a frog?" They replied, "We have no cow." I said, "This is a cow; you can get milk from this cow." But I found now they took the cow and cut off one of its teats. They said, "Sorry, but don't worry; people always repay you. We'll give you a wife."

12. So they gave me a wife with a long neck. That was nice for me for she had the same neck as mine. I said, "Thank you very much; you have given me a wife to brew beer for me." I said, "Let us go," and my wife began to walk ahead of me. I said, "You're walking so nicely for me, some one will try to kill me (jealous of such a beautiful wife)." She didn't reply. After walking like that, we found a big tree and sat and thought together. I told her, "You can cook beer for a few days while we're here!"

13. She cooked beer but it came out sour. I asked her angrily, "Why did you cook sour beer?" She said, "Oh, my husband, you're being stupid, now. My father told me,

Intended Meaning

Literally given a cow.

11. [Mr. Mashoko delights in surprising his listeners with such an absurd image, an unexpected turn in the story.]

12–13. Story proceeds literally.

[Here the wife follows the advice of her father and brews sour beer. The implication of her act is actually a good one. A number of Shona proverbs caution that

Literal Meaning

if you marry, cook sour beer and you'll know that place is yours." Those were good words. I said, "Give me my ax (ceremonial ax); I want to dance. You must go from me." As he dances, he finally slips and almost falls, but his wife catches him. "Why did you catch me?" he asks. "You almost fell down!" she replied. "No, you must go away or I may step on you and scratch you," the husband ordered. As the pleased husband dances by himself, the story ends.

Intended Meaning

a relationship between a man and a woman which begins too smoothly may ultimately be doomed to failure.]

When Mashoko sings "Mbiriviri" his performance takes on the dramatic qualities of traditional *ndyaringo*. His face comes alive with the portrayal of the characters in his story. In his narrative he shifts back and forth from third to first person, changing roles from narrator to main character, reliving the hero's adventures for the audience; and Mashoko's use of non-verbal vocal styles, deep with feeling, intensifies the emotional response of the audience to his narrative. He introduces the *mahon'era* and *huro* passages strategically in order to enhance the dramatic quality of the story. For example, they appear at certain points in between the major episodes, leaving the audience to dwell on the past encounters of the hero and eagerly to anticipate the next. At other times the *mahon'era* and *huro* passages enter in the middle of an episode, creating a feeling of prolonged expectation as the audience waits for the text to resume and for the plight of the main character to be resolved.

To heighten the imagery of his narrative Mashoko frequently uses onomatopoetic expressions in his performances. After the hero receives compensation for the loss of his gun, Mashoko helps the audience to visualize the main character's new wife walking so nicely before her husband with her backside swaying rhythmically, "ja . . . ja . . . ja . . . ja . . ." As this image crystallizes, Mashoko bursts out laughing with delight.[h]

[h] See *The Soul of Mbira*, side II, band 1, and just after line 59 in the transcription, p. 257.

In singing poetic texts of the narrative type, Mashoko recreates the episodes of the story for his audience, responding at times as if he were the main character himself; his audiences regard him as a great actor, mbira player, and singer.[i]

The transcription of "Mbiriviri" in the Appendix and a comparison of the basic story line of several versions of the piece show the kinds of variation found in performances of texts of the narrative type. First, as the transcribed rendition illustrates, Mashoko interjects parenthetic lines of poetry into the basic text as he gradually develops the story. Sometimes these statements are cryptic, as in the case of the "deep Shona texts" to which Mashoko referred. Other parenthetic lines include proverbs concerning serious themes such as aging and death: "The thing that grows old, wears out," as well as humorous lines that poke fun at some of the same serious issues: "I am old while my mother is still active. Isn't that unnatural, my good sir?"

Singers use such lines of poetry to depart from the established pattern of the narrated episodes, thereby surprising their listeners. In some cases the lines are intended to raise laughter; in others they serve as a dramatic device, increasing the audience's expectations before the story continues again. As Simon Mashoko reports, "When I am singing, you never know where I am going next." The parenthetic lines provide the singer with a means of embellishing the main story of the narrative differently each time it is told. In addition to this form of embellishment, performers can change the sequence of events of the main story line and vary the imagery of particular scenes from one performance to the next.

Finally, differences of an even greater magnitude occur in versions of narrative poetic texts if different singers perform them. For example, the story line of a version of "Mbiriviri" by Zakawa differs in two significant ways from one of Mashoko's versions.[j] First, there is an additional episode at the beginning of the story. The knobkerrie the main character throws across the river lands in a bee's nest. Thereafter he meets an old wo-

---

[i] For the past several years Simon Mashoko has worked as a catechist for the Roman Catholic Church in Zimbabwe and has received national recognition as a composer of liturgical music for the *njari*. The song texts that he sings today with his *njari* are for the most part his own compositions. They frequently tell stories from the Holy Scriptures rather than from Shona tradition (see biographical sketch of Mashoko, p. 223).

[j] Zakawa's version of "Mbiriviri" is on Columbia Records, AE48, Press-

man eating beeswax, and in characteristic fashion he offers her some of his honey. Unable to resist, the old woman devours all of his honey and then gives him a mat. This version explains the acquisition of both honey and mat. If the texts are taken literally, this episode fills a gap in Mashoko's version of "Mbiriviri." In Mashoko's version the main character throws his knobkerrie and "finds honey with it." No further explanation is given. Next he encounters old men worshipping without a mat and offers them his own. No explanation is made of how he acquired the mat. Since Zakawa's version was recorded in 1933, thirty-eight years before my own recording of Mashoko, the episode with the old woman would appear to have been an older part of the full story of "Mbiriviri." It is possible that Mashoko learned the song without this episode; on the other hand, it may have slipped from his memory over the years. It is interesting to note that Mashoko's symbolic view of the piece in which the knobkerrie and the mat both serve as symbols for the mbira explains the apparent gap between the first two episodes in his "Mbiriviri."

Second, Zakawa departs from Mashoko's version of the story at the point where the hero has lost his gun. Without compensating his character for the loss of the gun, Zakawa routes his audience through a series of humorous parenthetic lines ("Gutu and Rwodzi fought over a skunk [at the eating place of the chief]") to a description of the death of Chaminuka and then finally to a commentary on the singer's own poverty. Zakawa's rendition of "Mbiriviri" suggests that once a performer has followed enough of the traditional story line of a piece to establish its basic identity and character, he or she may develop the text in a personal way.

Because the primary function of the texts is entertainment, the singer is alert to audience response in the skillful development of the narrative. After the audience is fully involved in the performance the singer can embellish a scene by vivid description of an episode or by character portrayal. If audience attention begins to wane, he or she can cut a scene short and proceed with the main story. In this respect, singers of the narrative type of song texts are both actors and poets when they perform.

---

ing Number WEA 1907, recorded by Hugh Tracey. I am indebted to George Fortune for bringing this recording to my attention.

The Mosaic Type

Texts of the mosaic type are an interwoven pattern of improvised lines based on themes reflecting many different aspects of Shona life. Such texts are illustrated here by examples of the mosaic type of *kudeketera* sung with the *mbira dzavadzimu*, the instrument closely associated with religious ritual. One of the primary purposes of these texts is to facilitate meditation and religious devotion, although some lines entertain as well.

In the townships and villages where ensembles of *mbira dzavadzimu* participate in religious ceremonies or in secular performances, singers include texts of the mosaic type throughout the evening. Participants—old and young alike—when moved by the music, contribute their own poetic lines. Singers perform informally, alternating *kudeketera* texts with nonverbal vocalizations and other forms of musical participation like dancing, clapping, and playing *hosho*.

The Nature of a Kudeketera Performance

In the performance of the mosaic type of *kudeketera* singers both improvise new lines and select traditional lines from a storehouse of fairly standardized *kudeketera* expressions and themes. Additionally, singers include material in their performances which comes from other traditional forms of Shona oral literature, such as critical poetry (*nheketerwa*), proverbs (*tsumo*), and praise poetry (*nhetembo dzorudzi*). The *kudeketera* lines, like the ritual phrases reported elsewhere in Africa, often serve as symbols. "The singer does not have to labor his point. If he wishes to express joy, sorrow, anger, or some other emotion, he has only to select standard 'lines' which allude to them."[4]

During a performance of *kudeketera*, the Shona audience hears lines filled with associations for them, and dwells on a stream of images before the next line is sung. If the performer alludes to the "green trees of Chitungwiza," for instance, listeners may think of the legendary headquarters of Chaminuka, an ancient Shona spirit who performed miracles. For some it may evoke the image of the Shona empire before the coming of the Ndebele conquerors; for others, loss of freedom after the European invasion.

Performers have told me that when they are moved by the mbira music they have a vast repertory of *kudeketera* lines which they cannot always remember at other times. For example, Hakurotwi Mude once offered to teach me to sing *kudeketera*. He said he was unable to dictate a list of lines I could learn; instead, he suggested that I record his performances and learn the material from the tape. As Mude explained, "When I am singing, the words come out without my trying to say anything, when I am thinking deeply about the history of the Shona people," and he consciously thinks of what to say next as he performs only when he has personal troubles on his mind.[k]

Although performers often base their *kudeketera* texts on a common stock of traditional lines and themes, they alter them to reflect their own personalities and to suit the situation about which they wish to comment. For instance, one person may sing a traditional theme as "I have only four days left to live," while another alters it to reflect his or her bravado toward death: "There are four days remaining, but the seventh I shall snatch for myself." One individual sings the traditional line, "Do not laugh at the calamity of your friend, or tomorrow it will be yours," and another presents a more dramatic variation on the idea: "Laugh at the lame person only after you have died."

As one would expect, then, given the spontaneous nature of the mosaic type of *kudeketera* accompanying the *mbira dzavadzimu*, the texts differ greatly from one performance to another. Just as the *kudeketera* texts of an mbira piece differ from one singer to another, so they differ when an individual singer performs the same piece on different occasions. Moreover, *kudeketera* lines which appear in one piece can also appear in others.[1] Performers may also sing poetic lines originally improvised in some other context; lines which were originally a response to a large religious event such as a *bira* often occur outside this context. Similarly, participants in a *bira* may sing about events that took place outside the context of the performance. In these ways

[k] In addition to having a reputation as one of the greatest singers in Zimbabwe, Mude is well-known as a spirit medium (see Mude's biographical sketch, p. 226). When he is in a state of possession, listeners say that Mude sings especially "deeply." After the possession has run its course at a religious ceremony and the spirit has left him, Mude has no recollection of the events which have taken place or of the poetry he has sung with the mbira music.

[1] For example, on *The Soul of Mbira*, Mude repeats the line "*Mbudzirume namakudo tsvete*" during his performance of "*Nhemamusasa*," side I, band 1, and also uses the line during "*Nyamaropa*," side I, band 3 (see the transcriptions of these pieces in the Appendix).

173

kudeketera song texts are similar to song texts reported in other parts of Africa.[5]

There is a similarity between the nature of mbira music itself and the improvisatory style of the mosaic type of poetry accompanying it. As mentioned earlier, mbira music presents a complex of patterns to the ear. It consists of several interwoven lines interacting with each other throughout the performance of the piece, rather than being a continual development of a single melodic motive. Similarly, the *kudeketera* does not follow a continuous thematic development, but is a mosaic of texts, each group dealing with the life of the people in all its aspects and from every point of view. Included may be references to history, proverbs, social and political commentaries, activity of participants in the *bira*, praise of family members or ancestors, or other allusions to events in the experiences of those participating and to common troubles (often with humor to lighten the burden). Sometimes a singer slowly weaves his or her story through this mosaic of different themes. An idea is developed for a while and then dropped until later in the song. Sometimes different ideas develop at the same time. A singer does not always try to tell a story as such: he or she may let each statement stand by itself, having its own wisdom and creating a mood with the music. In some *kudeketera* performances the passages are sparsely interjected among those of *huro* and *mahon'era*; in others, consecutive lines occur in rapid succession. The *kudeketera* texts, like variations on the mbira piece, are performed as long as the artist remains in the mood and receives new ideas and images from the music: the number of lines in a particular performance of the mosaic type of *kudeketera* can range from as few as ten to a hundred or more.

The selection of lines sung during the performance of an mbira piece is the result of a combination of different factors, including the mood and personality of the performer, his or her knowledge of *kudeketera* phrases, the structure of the mbira piece, and the nature of the situation upon which the singer is commenting.

Developing Expertise as Singers

In a fashion similar to the way in which young musicians learn to play the mbira, singers learn *kudeketera* by imitating the styles of older performers whom they respect. Later they are able to add their own mark to the music. They practice to build up a storehouse of traditional *kudeketera* expressions and lines, never ceasing to expand their repertory of *kudeketera* lines by borrowing freely from each other's performances. For example, at one time Mondrek Muchena sang and played mbira regularly with Hakurotwi Mude's ensemble. Other members of Mude's group say that Mude's and Muchena's performances reflect these previous musical collaborations; Mude incorporates in his *kudeketera* performance lines he originally heard Muchena sing, and Muchena sings poetry he learned while playing mbira for Mude.

Beginning performers learn *kudeketera* lines not only by listening to the live performances of more experienced singers at religious and secular musical events, but also from radio broadcasts of traditional music and from a flourishing record industry featuring mbira ensembles. In this way young performers today are exposed to many singers from whom to select their models rather than depending only on singers in their own area, as beginners used to do. Such distinguished artists as Hakurotwi Mude and Simon Mashoko first developed their skills by imitating the singing styles of their relatives, but today young musicians in many different parts of the country listen to recordings and radio broadcasts from which they can imitate Mude's and Mashoko's styles.

Since *kudeketera* is an integral part of mbira music, young mbira players aspire to develop enough skill to be able to play their instruments and sing at the same time. Often players wait until they have some degree of mastery of their instruments before challenging themselves to add *kudeketera* lines to their music. In the process of learning to coordinate both skills, beginners sometimes make mistakes like "rushing the words to follow the music," "losing the rhythm of the mbira while concentrating on the words," or blurting out an incoherent sentence as a result of "trying to say too many things at once."[6]

By imitating more experienced performers, the young artist builds up a storehouse of traditional *kudeketera* themes and lines. Through diligent practice during formal musical events and sometimes at informal practice sessions with other musicians, performers acquire the skill to coordinate the vocal parts with the mbira music without faltering. Eventually, as they become more mature artists, they develop the ability to draw lines freely from their repertories to express a point and to improvise new lines at the time of the performance.

While many people in a village have some general knowledge of *kudeketera*, a few individuals are often found to be extraordinarily skillful. In an mbira ensemble, for example, there is often one member who is a specialist in singing. Some mbira players, such as Hakurotwi Mude, have developed such expertise as singers that they have shifted the emphasis of their careers to singing. At many formal events they delegate the major part of the responsibility for mbira playing to younger musicians. As in the case of *Mhuri yekwaRwizi*, an mbira group's reputation may derive as much from the performance of the featured singer as from the performances of the mbira players.

The following criteria of *kudeketera* performance result from ideas gathered through personal discussions with musicians and through conversations in which individuals passed judgment on the abilities of other singers. Two of the criteria have been discussed previously in Chapter 5, namely the skill of singers in hearing the inner parts of mbira music and in following the piece's underlying structure in their performances, and their sense of tasteful balance between vocal styles and mbira music.

A third criterion is the spontaneity of the singer in introducing new ideas into a performance of *kudeketera*. The mbira players of *Mhuri yekwaRwizi* criticized vocalists who repeated the same lines "too much." Lesser singers sometimes compose their lines beforehand and memorize them. While this practice is appropriate for beginners, it does not produce the spontaneous performance one associates with experts. The greatest singers achieve spontaneity both by improvising new lines during the performance and by freely selecting lines from their extensive repertory of expressions. A certain amount of repetition, however, is appropriate. Accomplished singers occasionally repeat their lines while thinking of what to say next or to emphasize a particular theme.

A fourth criterion is the ability of the singer to perform with "deep feeling." This implies that the performer sings with enough conviction to move the audience, who respond to the obvious sincerity of the singer's words. For example, after a performance of an mbira piece by the late Jege Tapera about suffering, the audience commented with satisfaction, "He is really crying, mourning."[7] The singer's ability to express things indirectly, "to be clever with words," is a fifth criterion. A singer is sometimes especially appreciated for his or her keen humor and ability to entertain audiences, evoking laughter while making a serious point. A sixth criterion is the singer's power, the sheer energy he or she puts into his performances. The seventh criterion is the singer's vocal quality.

Different people tend to emphasize different criteria when evaluating a *kudeketera* performance. For instance, one mbira player praised a well-known singer in a village in which I studied for his "cleverness" with words, although he thought the singer lacked "power." Another musician praised a popular singer for having a "beautiful voice," although some people remarked that other singers performed with "deeper" feeling. Thus, as they do in assessing the skill of mbira players, people usually acknowledge both the strengths and weaknesses of a singer and balance these factors against each other in making their judgment.

Listeners: The Challenge of Interpretation

An mbira player once suggested to me that one of the functions of mbira music is to attract the potential audience to the performer so that the words can be heard. Once the singing has begun, the musician reported, the audience's attention will not wane throughout the performance of the piece.[8] During a performance of mbira music, a rapport develops between the singers and the audience as the singers express their feelings and take the audience into their confidence. At the same time, the singers offer the listeners the challenge of interpreting their song texts.

Since subtlety is an important element in the art of *kudeketera*, performers strive to express themselves indirectly at times, and members of the audience must guess at the meaning of their words. It is not uncommon for individuals listening to a performance of mbira music to derive differing meanings from the singer's lines. There are a number of factors related to the performance of *kudeketera* which help to explain this.

Shona singers often express their feelings about personal, social, or political issues through allusion rather than through direct statement. According to general Shona mores, direct reference to personal feelings or troubles might embarrass the singer. Indirect ways of dealing with social problems seem to be more appropriate. Two anecdotes, typical of many, illustrate this point. A young man told me a story concerning the visit of a distant relative to his mother's house. During the course of the visit, the guest spat several times in the kitchen sink. The

177

mother, while offended, showed no outward concern. Later, however, she took her own son aside and asked him to spit in the sink the next time the guest entered the kitchen. When he followed his mother's instructions, she reprimanded him in a loud voice, "No, son, don't you know that that is rude?" From that time on the guest refrained from spitting in the house. On another occasion, at which I was present, a teacher invited a woman and her husband to dinner. Out of courtesy the woman offered to cook the rice, but because she lacked skill, she burnt it terribly. Too ashamed to face the dinner, she made excuses and left with her husband before the dinner was served. The teacher felt sorry for her but would not raise the subject with her directly. Instead, he invited her over the next afternoon while he was preparing rice. He courteously refused her offer of assistance and instead thought up topics of conversation to keep her there so she could watch rice being prepared properly.

Political issues are handled subtly in Shona song because it can be dangerous for Africans to express their political sentiments openly in Zimbabwe today. Singers use several techniques to make their points indirectly, thereby being "clever with words" and avoiding possible recrimination for things they have expressed publicly through song. They can incorporate into their lines abstract images that have meaning on more than one level. For example, a statement that appears to be a straightforward historical reference to Chitungwiza can have political meaning as well; Chaminuka has become a powerful political symbol among the Shona in recent years. Other lines, including humorous proverbs evoking laughter, make social commentary: "It is a pity to have only one child, for once bitten by a cockroach, he will surely die" (people should have large families).[m]

Maraire reports that in addition to proverbs, singers use such other forms of traditional Shona language in their texts as parables (*madimikira*) and secret language or obscure allusions (*chibhende*). The meaning of such lines is often elusive due to a "quality of the language" in which a word, phrase, or sentence may have many different interpretations. A sentence or phrase which in one context has a commonly understood meaning can in another context have the opposite meaning. For instance, the expression "*zvakakunakira wena*," meaning literally, "it is good for you," can also, in some contexts, mean "mocking you, laughing at you, making fun of you, fooling you."[9]

[m] Hamutyinei and Plangger's *Tsumo-Shumo* makes available an extensive collection of Shona proverbs.

Additionally, singers sometimes obscure their meaning by playing with words, exploiting nuances in the Shona language so as to create ambiguity for their audiences. For example, when a singer alludes to a person whose name has meaning as an independent word or phrase, it is not always clear whether the singer's remarks refer to the person, or to the word or phrase. Singers sometimes alternate lines that have underlying meaning with others that are intended to be taken literally, thus compounding the problem of interpretation. The audience can miss some of the implications of certain lines and can over-interpret others.[n]

Performers sometimes disguise their own point of view while singing *kudeketera* lines. A performer can sing in the first person when actually expressing an idea on behalf of someone else. This may express compassion for the situation of others. I once heard a young mbira player sing the line, "I am now too old to play the mbira." The line was sung for his grandfather who had taught him to play the mbira and was listening nearby at the time. This technique can, less sympathetically, expose the thoughts of others, subjecting them to ridicule. For example, the old man in the *bira* described at the beginning of this chapter sang the line, "You have killed the elephant, but the head is mine." While singing in the first person, he was actually exposing the point of view of Europeans. In his statement the singer distinguished between those who have done all the work (the hunters) and those who walk away with the profit (those who claim the head with its tusks have the most valuable part of the elephant). These words have a clear political connotation in Zimbabwe where Africans spend their days "killing the elephant" and the Europeans invariably claim possession of the "head." Sometimes days later, participants of the *bira*, reflecting on the singer's performance, may shake with laughter at remembered lines and say, "Ahh, but that clever old man is a terrible one, that one."

Using an alternative technique for disguising their point of view, performers can sing in the second or third person and be referring to themselves. They thereby avoid admission of direct involvement in the situation described or the attitude expressed. "The trouble is mainly yours," sang an old man to his audience on one occasion when he was actually expressing the feeling that only he shouldered the burden of the problem to which he

[n] For elaboration see Berliner, "Poetic Song Texts," pp. 462–63.

alluded. A singer sometimes shifts back and forth elusively from first to third person during the performance of an mbira piece, maneuvering behind his or her statements as if playing different roles. Faced with these aspects of the *kudeketera* performance, the listener must "work fast to keep up with the meaning of what the mbira player is saying [or] he may end up with a different meaning altogether."[10]

Contributing to the differing interpretations of *kudeketera* lines is the fact that listeners sometimes mishear the words among the competing musical elements of an mbira performance. For instance, on one occasion a discussion began over a statement a well-respected performer had sung. One listener had heard the line as *"Muna Mupfure mune mhangura"* ("There is iron ore in the Mupfure River") and another heard it as *"Muna Mupfure mune mhakure"* ("There is a poisonous snake in the Mupfure River"). What was interesting about the exchange was that each man derived an intended message or lesson from the singer's words as he had heard them. The first listener thought the singer was telling everyone that there was iron ore in the river so that they would be encouraged to fetch some and make mbira keys in the traditional way instead of using scrap materials. The second listener felt sure that the singer had recently come from the Mupfure River and was warning everyone to be careful when travelling there because he had seen a dangerous snake.

The difficulty of understanding the *kudeketera* texts increases when, in the excitement of the mbira music, ideas come to the performer "faster than his tongue can move"[11] and he resorts to the use of contractions or abbreviated expressions. At such times singers sometimes sing one of two *kudeketera* lines that were meant to be sung in pairs. Often the first of the two lines establishes the basic idea and the second serves in a sense as a punch line completing the meaning of the first; for example, "Do not laugh at the calamity of your friend/ Tomorrow it may be yours." Separately the lines are sometimes cryptic to the listeners, who must fill in the meaning for themselves.°

A final factor contributing to differing interpretations of *kudeketera* lines is that listeners sometimes hear the poetry outside its original context. For example, a line traditional in the Mondoro tribal trust land under the jurisdiction of Chief

180 ° See the translation of "Nhemamusasa," Appendix, p. 261 n.

Rwizi is *"Mbudzirume namakudo tsvete."* *Mbudzirume* ("he-goat" or male goat) is the name of a large hill in Mondoro, thus to the Rwizi people the line has the significance of passing on the news that baboons (*namakudo*) populate the hill, *Mbudzirume*. However, some listeners outside of the Rwizi area interpreted the line humorously. To them, *Mbudzirume* literally meant "he-goat," and to complete the line's meaning listeners inferred that the *namakudo* in question were female. The text conveyed the absurd image, typical of those some singers delight in creating, of the he-goat running off through the fields in pursuit of the female baboons. Listeners laughed at the improbable image, "Why, such a thing could never happen!"

This punning example also points out the ambiguity that sometimes results when a singer uses proper names, which in the Shona language generally have additional meaning as independent words or phrases. The ambiguity, as in the above example, is sometimes accidental; at other times it can be the result of a deliberate play on words by singers wishing to make their meaning more obscure. During a performance of mbira music, Shona singers take pride in being clever and elusive in improvising their song texts, and they challenge the audience to keep up with them. In the light of the factors discussed here, it is not surprising that numerous interpretations of the same line can occur.

Content and Social Function of Kudeketera Texts

The lines of the mosaic type of *kudeketera* comprise a wide range of traditional themes related to different facets of Shona life. The following categories and illustrations of these *kudeketera* themes come from singers' recorded performances of traditional pieces for the *mbira dzavadzimu*.[p] The examples demonstrate the diversity of subject matter in *kudeketera* of the mosaic type.

[p] The Appendix provides transcriptions and translations of three texts from *The Soul of Mbira* album illustrating the improvisatory nature of this type of *kudeketera* and the manner in which singers, during performance, interweave lines from the various categories below. Example B in the Appendix contains one of Hakurotwi Mude's versions of "Nyamaropa," and Example C contains one of Muchatera Mujuru's. These examples also illustrate the degree to which *kudeketera* performances of the same piece can differ; the singers either select lines from their repertories or improvise with only occasional repetition for emphasis. The mood and character of Mude's and Mujuru's performances differ sub-

Category 1. *Mourning and appeasement of the spirits*

Amai vangu vakafirei?
Midzimu yekuno yakaendepi?

Why did my mother die?
Where are the ancestral spirits of this land? (Why aren't they helping the people who live here?)

Category 2. *Historical references*

Ndiro gwenzi rakaviga mambo (quoted from a traditional praise poem).

It is the shrub which hid the chief. (Reference to the traditional story of a chief who eluded his would-be assassins by hiding behind a shrub.)

Zita guru haribve mudongo.

The famous name does not leave a deserted village. (Reference to the memory of the great Shona spirit Chaminuka.)

Category 3. *Passing on general news*

Muna Mupfure mune mhakure.

There is a poisonous snake in the Mupfure River.

Ona, Hurungwe kune mombe isingarime.

Look, in Hurungwe there is an ox which does not plow.

Category 4. *Commentary on events taking place at the time of the performance*

Waida mbira nhasi wanyara.

He who liked mbira has today been put to shame (the mbira players at the event have performed so well that they have shamed another mbira player who is present as a listener).

Tambai baba waDhori waro!

Dance, you father of Dhori! [a girl's name].

---

stantially as well. Mude, performing with his exciting ensemble, drives the group forward with his dynamic singing style, and his lines deal with a wide range of subjects. In contrast, Mujuru is heard singing and playing the mbira by himself in a very relaxed, introverted, and deeply moving personal manner. His texts frequently return to the theme of death. Example D, "Nhemamusasa," illustrates the spirit of a *kudeketera* performance in a traditional communal spirit possession ceremony. More elaborate texts of the mosaic type are in the appendix of an article by the author (Berliner, "Poetic Song Texts").

Category 5. Praising members of the singer's family

Amai vangu, VaKarupete, vakapeta zuva nepasi waro!

My mother, VaKarupete, who wrapped up the sun and the earth!

Asi chidawo chakanaka Mudyanevana!

The best sub-clan name is that of Mudyanevana!

Category 6. The singer's troubles

Nhamo yangu yatungamira, vakomana.
Seriya rakafane mombe.

Trouble has led me, boys, like that one (that is, the big lout) which resembles an ox (the singer is led by troubles like an ox pulled by a ringleader).

Ko, nyama ndoiwanepi zvangu nherera?

Where can I find meat, orphan that I am?

Category 7. Death and afterlife

Kufa kwandiona.
Kudenga kune mare.

Death is watching me all over.
There are wonders in heaven.

Category 8. Social and political commentary

Munokanga mhandire sadza mambodya?

You roast maize when you have eaten sadza? (ridiculing others for their greed).

Kungangondidzvokora pasi ndepangu.

Even though you glare at me angrily, I am still the owner of this country (addressed to the whites of Zimbabwe).

Category 9. Humor as an end in itself

Amai nomwana mudzvokoranua. Runenge rutsindi rwakarume hacha.

The mother and the child glare angrily at each other. When they are in that state, they look like squirrels whose mouths are bulging with *hacha* fruit.

Ndanga ndaerera mvura musinaka.

I was nearly drowned in a dried-out river bank (literally, I was nearly carried away by a waterless river).

Category 10. Proverbs

Asi kurima zvinonetsa asi kudya inyore.

To plow is difficult but to eat is easy.

Guya kutsvuka mukati mune honye.

The fig is brown (ripe and attractive) outside, but inside it is filled with worms (don't ever judge the substance of things by their appearance).

183

Category 11. Deep Shona (Lines whose meanings have been lost)

Wosiye ngoma.	You are leaving the music. (At one time possibly an admonition directed at people who were leaving the performance of music at a *bira*, a ceremony for the ancestral spirits, or perhaps it refers more broadly to people who are forgetting the righteous ways of the ancestors.)

In summary, the poetic song texts perform a number of social functions for the listeners, functions related to the alternating themes and meanings of *kudeketera* during each of the mbira pieces. Texts that refer to the spirit world serve as communications to the ancestors. Performers mourn for their departed relatives, showing that they still respect them in memory, and ask for assistance in the struggles of life. *Kudeketera* phrases of an historical nature remind the participants of their common historical roots and help to promote a feeling of solidarity among the listeners. Lines that pass on general information to the participants serve as local news outlets, informing listeners of events and sometimes referring to lessons the singer has learned through his or her experience with these events.

Through *kudeketera* texts of a different sort, participants offer commentary on events taking place at the time of the performance. These lines promote a feeling of rapport among the participants and provide an opportunity for occasional banter through song. By singing lines of self-praise or praise of members of one's own family, the singer shows respect for others and indulges in a form of respectable boasting. Texts on the subject of personal troubles allow the performer to express his or her sorrow over life's difficulties as well as compassion for the problems of others. *Kudeketera* phrases dealing with the theme of death and the afterlife perform a cathartic function for the participants, enabling them to express their apprehension. Through the performance of texts offering social and political commentary, the singers air their feelings about issues affecting people in the village or the Shona people as a whole. Singers can handle social themes to comment on the behavior of individuals who have strayed too far from the respected norms of society, with the ultimate goal of modifying that behavior. Humorous texts allow performers to express certain attitudes openly which they might not feel free to express otherwise. Some outstanding singers of *kudeketera* have a reputation for taking liberties in expressing irreverent attitudes others might share, but would never say aloud. On one occasion, for example, I heard a performer sing the line: "A short girl, when she is sitting, can't cook sadza," making light of the image of a short stout girl, seated, attempting to reach up and over into the large Shona cooking pots without rising. On this occasion, people shook their heads with laughter and said of the singer, "He's too proud!" Humor also serves as a release mechanism for the anxiety people feel over the serious themes heard throughout the evening.

Singers include deep Shona texts with meanings inaccessible to the participants for the sake of tradition; they serve to establish a link with the past. Didactic or moral proverbs and religious themes perpetuate respect for the traditional values of the Shona culture and intensify the effect of the music as a social force within the community. Mbira players and singers are quite conscious of their role in this respect. In the words of Simon Mashoko, "When I perform our traditional songs, I feel like a man who wants to show the greatness of our forefathers, . . . like a man who doesn't want to break with our past laws and traditions."

Throughout the evening at both religious and secular events where musicians play the *mbira dzavadzimu*, those participants moved by the music can contribute their own lines as performers or composers of the poetic song texts of *kudeketera*. Through the themes of the poetry individuals can express not only their own feelings and thoughts, but also those of other participants. *Kudeketera* texts about real people everyone knows and about common plights enhance the cathartic effect of the music. At a *bira*, the performance of *kudeketera* does much to bring about and to sustain a mood of pathos.

8.
Music and Spirit Possession at a Shona Bira

It is a basic tenet of traditional Shona religion that after people die, their spirits continue to affect the lives of their progeny. In other words, the world of the living is a function of the workings of the spirit world. In the traditional Shona view, then, a person's fortune and fate in the world are to some extent the result of an interplay of forces outside of the person's own control. If, for instance, individuals within a family remember their ancestors and honor their moral values, the spirits will look after the family and offer protection. If, however, a person forgets or dishonors departed ancestors, the spirits can either punish their progeny directly, or by withdrawing their support leave him or her vulnerable to the forces of mischievous and belligerent spirits and witches.[1] A traditionalist's first reaction in the face of misfortune (failure of crops, prolonged illness, sudden death in the family) is to ask, "What have I done to offend my ancestral spirits?"[a]

Once such trouble as illness occurs, an individual either privately consults the spirits of his or her ancestors in prayer or goes to a *n'anga* (doctor) for treatment. If the herbs prescribed

[a] This chapter is primarily concerned with placing mbira music in the general context of traditional Shona religious ritual. Elaboration of the tenets of Shona religious belief and detailed descriptions of a variety of Shona rituals are in Gelfand (*Shona Ritual* and *Shona Religion*), Murphree (*Christianity and the Shona*), Daneel (*Old and New in Southern Shona Independent Churches*), Holleman ("Accommodating the Spirit"), and Garbett ("Spirit Mediums").

by the *n'anga* do not help the patient and his or her condition worsens, the *n'anga* frequently advises that the illness is not a natural one: it is caused by an ancestral spirit to call attention to some personal or social problem or to indicate that a spirit wishes to possess the patient's body as its host. In such a case, the patient's problem becomes the domain of the *svikiro* (spirit medium), and the *n'anga* advises that the family of the affected person arrange a traditional religious ceremony called a *bira* (plural *mapira*) for the ancestral spirits. (Note the similarity between the words *mbira* and *bira*. Whether they were both originally derived from the verb *kupira*, "to make a ritual offering," is a matter of speculation.)

Although the *mapira* described in this chapter provide the most common traditional religious context for mbira music in Zimbabwe today, the music also has an important function in other religious contexts as well. For example, mbira music is a regular part of the more recent development of the *dandaro* (plural *matandaro*), which has been growing in popularity in the townships. *Matandaro* are spirit possession ceremonies similar in some respects to the *bira* but modified for compatibility with urban African lifestyles. They often take place at the home of the spirit medium in the township and are on a smaller scale and less formal than the *bira*. At some of these ceremonies a ritual form of handclapping suffices to bring about the spirit possession, without any formal performance of mbira music. The event usually ends before sunrise so that participants can get some sleep before going to their jobs.

Mbira music also plays an important role at special rain-making ceremonies (*mukwerera*), post-mortem ceremonies, and, occasionally, funerals.[2] Finally, the mbira is also present at ceremonies for cults of followers of the *mashave* spirits, rather than the ancestral spirits (*vadzimu*). The *mashave* spirits are animal spirits or the wandering spirits of people who did not have proper burial rites at death. The ceremonies for the *mashave* spirits are in many ways similar to that of *mapira*, and at some religious rituals the mediums for *vadzimu* and *mashave* spirits become possessed and interact with each other, sharing in the evening's activities.

The Bira: Background and Context

The *bira* is a formal, all-night ceremony in which family members come together to call upon a common ancestor for help. During the ceremony a spirit medium discerns the cause of the illness or misfortune through consultation with the afflicted. The family serves ritual beer, especially brewed in honor of the ancestors, and sponsors an mbira ensemble to provide the evening's music.

All the spirit possession ceremonies I attended in the Mondoro and Salisbury areas were accompanied by ensembles of *mbira dzavadzimu*. At some ceremonies, however, especially in other parts of Zimbabwe, drums accompany or replace mbira, depending upon the musical practices of the region in which the ceremony takes place, the needs of the spirits for whom the *bira* is held, and the availability of musicians for the ceremony. For example, in parts of the country where the *njari* and *matepe* are popular, drums are often part of the mbira ensemble. As a general rule, however, ensembles consisting of the *mbira dzavadzimu* do not include drums in their performances. As John Kunaka explained to me, "Our mbira has a big voice and doesn't need the drums. However, the *njari* has a small voice and needs the drums' help."

A *bira* for the family spirits (*vadzimu*) can occur at any time during the year when there is cause. In addition, there are special ceremonies related to the changing seasons at regular intervals during the year. The participants direct these at the powerful *mhondoro* spirits who control the rainfall, the excess or absence of which will ruin a crop. For example, the initial prayer for rain before the planting season, and the sampling of various crops as they ripen in the fields, are occasions for *mapira*. The ceremonies for the *mhondoro* spirits differ from those for the family spirits in that it is the chief who is responsible for initiating the proceedings of the event and for providing the necessary ingredients for the ritual beer.[3]

Spirit possession ceremonies traditionally are held in the villages on the land previously inhabited by the ancestors. This is not always possible in recent times, however, since the white government has forced Shona groups to leave their traditional homes and to migrate to other areas to permit whites to take over the most fertile land for cultivation. Now, the *bira* takes place in the village of the Shona tribal trust lands (Plate 37) either in a *banya*, a specialized house built for the spirit and used only on religious occasions, or in a large village roundhouse converted for the event. The buildings are usually modest in size, with space for twenty to forty people (Plate 38). Some are large enough to hold one hundred or more; Muchatera Mujuru built one such *banya* at his home in Dambatsoko, Rusape. Before the *bira* takes place the villagers clear the area of furniture and cooking ware. They fill the fire pit with dirt to make it level (if fire is not needed for warmth) and remove the large clay cooking pots from the cement bench against the far wall of the building. The mbira players perform while seated on the bench and store their instruments and resonators there during rest periods.

The proceedings of the *bira* (Plates 39–42) usually begin after sundown inside the *banya* or round-house.[b] Kerosene "lanterns" (open cans of kerosene with a burning wick) provide a dim light as members of the immediate family, neighbors, and guests arrive. Participants sometimes remove their shoes and wrist watches before entering the place of the *bira*, since such symbols of modern life might offend spirits unfamiliar with the objects during their own existence in the world of the living. The men sit on one side and women and children on the other, and someone ladles millet beer (*doro*) out of large clay pots, each pot designated for one group. One is for the spirits and their mediums. Others are for the villagers and guests, and a special pot is for the mbira players. A sweet, non-alcoholic beer (*mahewu*) is also on hand for those who prefer it.

It is not uncommon for villagers to invite one or more professional mediums and their attendants (*vanechombo*) to participate in the *bira* (Plate 43). A medium may be associated with a particular spirit whom the participants would like to consult for advice, or the villagers may invite a medium in order to help to bring about the possession of the ailing person for whom the *bira* is held; they believe that the affected person will recover only after having submitted to possession by the spirit who has caused his or her illness.

On such occasions the professional medium assists the ailing prospective host by using his or her influence both in the spirit world, to encourage the new spirit to come down to earth to participate in the *bira*, and in the real world, to help guide the new medium after possession has taken place. The latter service is important, because a spirit sometimes becomes skittish and fearful during its first experience in returning to the world of the flesh in a human host, and the host may require counselling

[b] I am grateful to Hakurotwi Mude for his kind permission to take these photographs of the *bira* in his village and to reproduce them in this work. 189

to prevent it from leaving the scene of the *bira* before settling the matter at hand. In fact, I was told of one dramatic event at which a possessed professional medium actually tackled a frightened host, who was trying to run out of the *bira*, and wrestled him to the ground to prevent him from leaving the ceremony before he had performed his proper function.

At ceremonies to appeal to specific ancestors, the mediums associated with these spirits sit on reed mats in front of the mbira players. Early in the evening, when the mediums formally receive the ritual pot of beer reserved for the ancestors, the villagers openly tell their problems and ask the spirits to appear at the ceremony and to counsel them.[4]

At the beginning of the evening there is an air of casualness as people drink and chat together, listening to the mbira ensemble. Gradually they enter into the performance themselves, dancing, singing, and clapping. As the music becomes intense and more participants enter into the performance, the suspense mounts. No one knows just when the possession of the medium (or mediums) will occur, or, at times, whom the spirits will possess. The spirits sometimes choose unsuspecting participants as their hosts.

The Music of the Bira

In its many aspects the *bira* is a communal affair; its music is the sum total of the contributions of all the members of the village who choose to participate. The mbira usually provide the nucleus of the music. A well-known mbira player who performed for a powerful medium told me, "The mbira is not just an instrument to us. It is like your Bible. . . . It is the way in which we pray to God." In the context of the *bira*, the people believe the mbira to have the power to project its sound into the heavens, bridging the world of the living and the world of the spirits and thereby attracting the attention of the ancestors. In the hands of skillful musicians the mbira is able to draw spirits down to earth to possess mediums. At the *bira*, the members of the mbira ensemble are responsible for the possession of the spirit medium or mediums. Their music, moreover, places other villagers in a meditative state and inspires their tireless participation in the dancing, clapping, and singing which accompany the mbira music throughout the evening.

It is usual for mbira players to perform after sundown, beginning perhaps at eight o'clock and continuing until sunrise.

190

Even after the *bira* concludes the villagers are sometimes in the mood for mbira music as they relax and unwind. They will then ask other performers, either younger musicians in the area or other mbira players who were present at the ceremony as guests, to perform for their entertainment, continuing the mbira music through the morning and into the afternoon.

Around the nucleus of mbira music and the basic supporting rhythm of the *hosho*, participants at the *bira* engage in three forms of musical expression: singing, handclapping, and dancing.[c] In general, there is a great deal of freedom in the vocal parts (*huro*, *mahon'era*, and *kudeketera*) and participants join in the performance of singing at will. Performers may sing standardized phrases in unison or different phrases simultaneously. The traditional vocal styles range from very simple to very complex patterns so that each individual in the village can perform at his or her own level of proficiency. Participants often vary the standard parts and improvise new ones at the time of the performance.

Over the years villagers become intimately acquainted with each other's musical styles. Listening to the playback of recordings made at their *bira*, villagers are quick to recognize individuals from among the total complex of sound, even to the extent of distinguishing among the ululations of individual women. Clearly, the vocal parts individuals sing to the mbira music are often unique. A story told to me by an ethnomusicologist about his experience in learning the vocal parts to mbira music in a particular Shona village illustrates this. After memorizing a part from a recording he had made, he returned to the village and sang it for the villagers involved in the recording session. Upon hearing this the performers broke out laughing and declared, "Why, you're singing with [so and so's] voice!"[5]

Active participation in the music is characteristic of the *bira*, and reflects the communal nature of the music, in which highly talented or professional musicians can express themselves without restraint within the same context as beginners. To respond actively to music in Shona culture is so ingrained that I have often seen individuals who were listening through earphones to the playback of a recorded *bira* dance and sing new parts to the music as if they were present at the live event.

[c] The music of the *bira* is on *The Soul of Mbira*, side I, band 1, and on *Shona Mbira Music*, side II, band 1.

Singers participating in the *bira* frequently alternate vocal styles in the performance of an mbira piece. If their talents lie in one area, such as yodelling, they may concentrate on this style during a piece. People with specialized talents sometimes weave their parts together, some singing the low relaxed *mahon'era* phrases and others punctuating the music with high intense *huro* passages or singing out interjections of the rapid *kudeketera* texts to the music.

The non-verbal vocal styles have a number of important functions connected with the *kudeketera* lines. They provide villagers with a means of participating in the music that does not interfere with the performances of the individuals who are singing poetry. Also, the non-verbal styles are deeply emotional and thus can sustain or enhance the mood of the performance in between the poetic lines. As the many different vocal parts come together at the *bira* they overlap rhythmically and melodically, forming a beautiful, rich texture with the mbira music.

As mentioned in the previous chapter, the poetry sung at the *bira* serves as a vehicle for the expression of a wide range of themes. Many lines are melancholy in mood, as, for example, that of one participant who sang, "You may think that I am enjoying myself while singing here, but inside, my heart is filled with pain for those below the ground." Other traditional lines are devoted to mourning for departed relatives. The constant expression of sorrow for departed relatives is not merely a form of grieving, but also a means of showing that one remembers his or her departed relatives, and of petitioning them for assistance with troubles in life.

While both men and women sing in *mahon'era*, *huro*, and *kudeketera* style, a fourth vocal style, *kupururudza* (ululation), is exclusively the province of the women. It is an expression of approval or encouragement for all the performers and it adds to the excitement of the music. In response to the ululation, participants put more of themselves into whatever part they are playing in the total musical event. The counterpart of ululation for men, a powerful, rhythmic dental whistle called *mheterwa*, is also heard periodically throughout the evening.

At a *bira*, dance participation is as informal as vocal participation. Throughout the ceremony individuals rise to dance when they feel moved to do so, and for as long as they wish. Sometimes they dance in place where they have been sitting; at other times, looking for more space, they come forward into the center of the round-house and dance in front of the mbira players and the mediums. Although the participants often dance in place and in close proximity to each other, they move without bodily contact with the dancers around them. Many stare into space as if their minds are far away in their own world of expression, perhaps in deep thought about their departed ancestors.

The dance steps are diverse. They are similar to the singing parts in that they include both complex movements and simple patterns that are technically within the grasp of all the participants. Among the most basic steps is one in which the dancer hops twice on each foot (on two consecutive main beats of the *hosho* pattern), continually shifting his or her weight from one foot to the other. In a minor variation of this step, one leg is bent and extended forward while the other leg carries the weight of the body for two beats. A further development consists of kicking the bent leg straight out on the second stomping beat of each foot's pattern. In continuing this basic pattern the dancers frequently turn slightly from side to side as they kick the appropriate leg forward and shift their weight from one side to the other.

In another style, a person dances in a slightly crouched position with his or her arms and hands extended forward, palms upward. While the dancer bobs up and down to the pulse of the music, his or her arms are alternately extended forward and drawn back to the body. Other dance styles are more reminiscent of the gymnastics of ballet—great leaps in the air with arms outstretched and one leg extended in the air behind the dancer. Other styles include steps which repeatedly lift the dancer off the ground so that the person gives the effect of dancing almost in the air.

Mime can also be a part of Shona ritual dancing. For example, on one occasion at which I was present an elderly man launched into a dramatic recreation of the story of a lion hunt. As he danced, he mimed each stage of the episode from the initial sighting and stalking of the lion to the final kill.

Some performers occasionally add humor to the *bira* through what might be called dance "jokes," by introducing movements which appear to be incongruous in the situation of the *bira*. One man, while dancing in a standard style, suddenly dropped to his knees and hopped along the floor in perfect time to the music. As suddenly as he had fallen to his knees, he leaped back to his feet and danced normally again. Other participants 193 laughed aloud at his antics. Another dancer with a reputation for being something of a jester drew laughter by periodically swivelling his hips in an overtly sexual manner in the middle of his performance. While certain mbira pieces suggest particular styles of dance, most allow participants complete freedom to express their individuality. Highly talented dancers improvise, creating their own styles. At times, the fingers of the mbira players are themselves "dancing" on the mbira keys in movements and variations not unlike the movements of the dancers before them; the repetition of basic patterns gradually gives rise to new variations. Perhaps a similar view of the association of the two art forms was expressed by Simon Mashoko when he corrected a mistake I made while playing mbira, saying that I should "dance more times" on a particular key.

At a *bira* the participants join freely in two forms of rhythmic accompaniment to mbira music, expressed through handclapping and dancing.[d] In the first form, the participants clap interlocking rhythmic figures that fit the mbira music. As discussed in Chapter 5, the simplest patterns consist of clapping on each main beat of the three-pulse *hosho* rhythm. The handclapping patterns can be complex, with accents falling between the main beats of the music and different rhythms clapped against each other. Woodblock clappers may contribute an additional voice to the handclapping patterns, as may homemade percussion instruments of various timbres. One evening, for example, I heard an old man add a complex rhythmic accompaniment by throwing uncooked rice from side to side in an enamel bowl.

Participants perform the second style of rhythmic accompaniment with their feet. This is the *shangara* style (alluding to the formal *shangara* exhibition dance), "dancing with a voice." When employing this technique, dancers stomp out complex rhythmic patterns, using the earth's surface as the membrane of a drum. The *shangara* parts involve a great variety of patterns, some of which correspond to those of the handclapping rhythms. Sometimes performers attach small round gourds filled with seeds (*magavhu*) to their legs to amplify the rhythms. There are specialists in dancing in this style who know many patterns and can perform with great skill. Just as a group of in-

---

[d] These styles of performance in the *bira* ceremony are on *The Soul of Mbira*, side I, band 1, and on *Shona Mbira Music*, side II, band 1. The softer of the two styles is the one produced by the dancers' bare feet on the floor of the *banya*.

dividuals can sit together and clap out complex rhythmic figures, sometimes two or three people dance *shangara* styles together, drumming out to the music of the mbira interlocking
rhythmic patterns with their feet. The *shangara* style is physically very demanding and few dancers perform it for long
stretches of time. Dancers will often alternate this style with
others during their performance. At the *bira* participants enjoy
the challenge of carrying on more than one musical activity at
a time: singing and clapping, dancing and singing, playing
hosho and dancing or singing, and so on.

The physical surroundings of the performance reinforce this
involvement. As a result of such factors as the acoustic properties of the small round-house, the powerful, penetrating music
of the mbira ensemble, and the communal response from all
quarters of the *banya*, the sounds of the music surround the
participants in a "total musical environment." This atmosphere
intensifies the villagers' experience in the *bira*.

At the *bira* the roles of the villagers, the musicians, and the
mediums overlap. While the mbira music brings about the possession of professional mediums and other participants, the nature of the event permits the musicians the full range of audience participation at the *bira*, even to possession itself. As a
general rule, however, their own music does not cause the possession of the mbira players unless they themselves also happen
to be professional mediums. On occasions in which I have seen
an mbira player possessed during a *bira*, the other musicians in
the ensemble filled in his part until the possession had run
its course and he rejoined them. In the case of a *hosho* player
possessed, some member of the audience can take over his role
and perform with the mbira ensemble.

Hakurotwi Mude is a well-known medium. For a time his
ensemble also included another medium, Webster Pasipamire,
who played the *hosho*. At ceremonies where *Mhuri yekwaRwizi*
performed, both individuals often became possessed by their
respective spirits and interacted with the participants as mediums. Such groups are particularly popular at ceremonies, for
they are in a position to provide two overlapping professional
services: their outstanding mbira music helps to bring about the
possession of other mediums, and the musicians themselves can
become possessed and offer consultation, or help to guide the
new spirit for whom the *bira* is being held.

While the roles of musician and medium are often comple-   195

mentary, they sometimes conflict with each other. At one ceremony I attended, a participant became possessed and began
playing the *hosho* with a vengeance. As he played, his rattles
temporarily overpowered the sound of the mbira and everyone
present was swept away by his "spirit's" powerful performance.
As long as he was possessed, the participant's behavior followed
the same pattern: he stood dancing and playing *hosho* furious-
ly, expending every ounce of energy and strength until he fell
exhausted to the ground. After catching his breath again he
rose to his feet and, still gasping for air, he resumed his performance with the same intensity. It was interesting to note that
although the spirit's presence was exhilarating to the guests, the
musicians complained about him the next day. He was playing
hosho poorly; he was not following the rhythm of the mbira,
and he could not keep a steady tempo. His presence was offen-
sive and disruptive to their music. When I asked the musicians
if he was really to blame, they shrugged their shoulders: when
a man is possessed by the spirit, he must follow the spirit's
will—there was nothing he could do. This fact, however, did
not fully compensate for their annoyance regarding the evening's performance.

The musical proceedings of the *bira* are the result of the interplay among the participants, the mediums, and the musicians. The participants themselves influence the events of the
evening through their interaction with the musicians. They
sometimes call out for their favorite compositions and the mbira
ensemble honors their requests. Also, individual musicians or a
whole ensemble may appear at a *bira* without an official invi-
tation. On such occasions the villagers give each musician or
ensemble a chance to demonstrate their skill, and then they
select the best players to perform for the remainder of the evening. At one *bira* which I attended, a second mbira ensemble appeared halfway through the ceremony and, with the encouragement of the villagers, eased the first group out of its position,
even though the former had been hired for the evening. The
villagers handled this without ever directly confronting or em-
barrassing the first band. When the second group of musicians
first arrived outside of the *banya*, the villagers prevailed upon
them to perform, expressing their dissatisfaction with the first
group. The *chuning* of their mbira was not pleasing to them, the
musicians did not play with enough power to make people dance
well, and they took breaks for beer too frequently between

tunes. Thus encouraged by the participants, the second ensemble filled in for the first group when it took its next beer break, and then continued to play through the evening without ever giving the first group an opportunity to replace them.

The interaction between musicians and participants at a *bira* is sometimes very lively. When the mbira players are especially pleased with the music they sing out exclamations of praise for themselves and other participants. When they are dissatisfied with the music, they sometimes sing lines of poetry criticizing participants who are not performing well. The mbira players are, in return, the object of comment by members of the audience, who can voice either criticism or praise of the mbira players. It is not uncommon for a participant to drop a few coins into the musician's gourd resonators as a token of approval. This gesture is sometimes accompanied by the exclamation "Vasekuru!" (Grandfathers!), a call upon the ancestors to assist the musicians in their performance. Such gestures often evoke a response of ululation from the women. Just as the power of the mbira music moves members of the audience, so the audience's response in singing, dancing, and clapping affects the mbira players. The audience's participation comes as expressive response to the mbira music, and it is at the same time an integral part of the overall event.

In addition to the participants' influence on the musical proceedings of the *bira*, the mbira players themselves determine the course of events. During the *bira*, musicians play from ten to thirty or more different mbira pieces, depending on the length of the performance of each and the size of the performer's repertory. Skilled players often play as many tunes as possible. However, when younger or less experienced players perform at a *bira*, they sometimes repeat a limited selection of pieces throughout the evening. As long as the musicians perform with power and feeling, the other participants are satisfied with the evening's event.

Frequently during the ceremony mbira players take brief breaks between tunes, and they occasionally take breaks for as long as ten or fifteen minutes to drink beer with the other participants. The beer is not simply for refreshment. Playing the mbira becomes hard work as the evening progresses. Musicians sometimes play for as many as twelve hours, and the beer can serve as an anesthetic so that the players will not feel the pain of their swollen fingers and can continue to perform all night. It   197 also helps the villagers to resist their fatigue so that they can participate in the music throughout the evening.

Hakurotwi Mude once remarked that the mbira is not played "for pleasure," but rather to appeal to the ancestral spirits for assistance with troubles in life. The same comment might well be made of the general performance of music at a *bira*. Although the music and socializing that take place are pleasurable, there is a serious purpose behind the event and participants push themselves beyond what is physically comfortable in their performances.

This was demonstrated to me dramatically during a *bira* in which an ailing woman's spirit refused to possess her. At four o'clock in the morning, in a desperate effort to bring the spirit, all present began to dance with as much power as possible to force the spirit to come. Many villagers who had been dozing in seated positions against the walls of the *banya* suddenly rose with half-closed eyes and began to dance energetically again. The mbira players accelerated the tempo of their music and the villagers' clapping, singing, and dancing rose to a furious level of intensity. All participants concentrated every ounce of strength they could muster into dancing as hard and as fast as they could. At the height of the frenzied participation, the forlorn-looking prospective host leaped to her feet and danced as hard and intensely as everyone around her. Her spirit came and the air was filled with the ululation of the women. Afterward many people fell back to their seats, exhausted from the expenditure of energy.

Similarly, while mbira players can perform in a relaxed fashion for their own entertainment, at the *bira* their first responsibility is to the other participants and to the possessed mediums. Thus performers often have to play with great power long after their hands are tired and their fingers have become swollen. Even musicians who perform the mbira with the aid of metal rings for protection sometimes develop bruises or blood blisters as a result of their demanding performance at a *bira* and may abstain from playing the mbira for several days afterwards.

In order to bring about the initial possession of the medium, musicians perform the pieces which they say the medium's spirit favors. If the musicians are familiar with a particular spirit through having performed previously for the same medium, they know the spirit's musical preferences, and this enables them to bring about the possession of the medium with the least difficulty. As Cosmas Magaya reported regarding his group's performance for one spirit, "When we used to play 'Nyamamusango,' the spirit would come in just a few minutes; the spirit really wanted that tune."

If the villagers hire mbira players to play for a medium for the first time, the musicians experiment with different pieces until they discover the ones which will bring about possession by the anticipated spirit. Moreover, if a medium has more than one spirit, the players must learn which tunes bring out either of the spirits when his or her presence is called for. Theoretically the pieces that appeal to the spirit are those the spirit enjoyed years ago when he or she was a living being. For this reason mbira players must be familiar with the classics of the mbira repertory.

Occasionally at a *bira* musicians experience great difficulty in bringing about the possession of the medium for whom they are playing. Under such circumstances the participants may look elsewhere for mbira players who can attract the medium's spirit. This suggests that the spirits have preferences not only for particular mbira pieces but for a particular type of mbira, or even for the members of a particular mbira ensemble. It is not uncommon to hear of mbira players regularly travelling some distance from their homes to other villages to perform for mediums who have requested their services at ceremonies. These situations sometimes arise as emergencies, and mbira players find themselves awakened in the middle of the night and called upon to perform at a *bira* in which other musicians have been unsuccessful in bringing about the possession of the mediums.

Finally, as in the following story told by musicians about the virtuoso Mubayiwa Bandambira, it may be necessary to reschedule the *bira* because even the best mbira players have failed to bring about the possession of a medium. On one occasion, a village hired Bandambira to play for a *bira* in which a very stubborn spirit refused "to come" (possess the medium). It is said that Bandambira played through the night without sleeping and at sunrise asked that food be brought to him so that he could continue performing. Bandambira then played on for two days and two nights, taking only short breaks for food and naps, before he finally admitted defeat, and the *bira* concluded.[6] This story epitomizes the great strength and endurance of mbira players, as well as the extent of their devotion to the spirits for whom they play.

199

The Possession of the Medium

Spirit possession sometimes takes place early in the evening, shortly after the *bira* has begun, although in most of the events I have witnessed possession has taken place either after several hours of music or in the early hours of the morning. I have been told of some stubborn spirits who appeared only after twelve hours of almost continuous music. When possession does take place at the *bira*, it is often sudden and startling to the uninitiated. The prospective host may be sitting quietly with a glazed look in the eyes; without warning he or she is shaken as if by an epileptic fit, filling the *bira* with cries of anguish. Different spirit mediums have different styles of evidencing their possession by spirits. One medium I often observed shot from his seat with a loud exclamation and the dancers jumped out of his way as his body hit the ground. He rolled over and over on the ground, his entire body in a spasm and his teeth chattering loudly as his voice repeated a chilling cry in a falling melodic line: "ah dha . . . dha . . . dha . . . dha . . . dha . . . ahhhh dha . . . dha . . . dha dha dha dha dha. Ahhhh . . . dha dha dha dha dha." As he tossed and turned, participants continued to dance around him, careful to stay out of the way of his kicking feet. After fifteen minutes he ceased his cries and his body quieted. Eventually he rose and left the house. He returned shortly thereafter, wearing black cloth in place of his European clothes, and from that point on was the spirit who possessed him.

Another medium became possessed in a less violent manner. With a long groan he fell forward onto his knees. As he stooped forward with his hands behind his back and twisted his head from side to side, his attendant met him, stripped him of his shirt, and removed his socks and shoes. While the attendant went to fetch the medium's robes, the possessed man moaned and cocked his head as if trying to hear something far away. He sometimes turned toward the performing musicians and, putting his head between two gourd resonators, bobbed in time to the music. He periodically tucked his thumbs under his armpits and slapped his arms against his bare sides. They made a loud crack like the sound of a drum. His attendant returned shortly, rolled up the bottoms of the medium's pants, and fitted him with a skirt of black cloth, a black shawl, and a black feather headdress. As the medium rose from his knees he was handed a long steel staff. When he danced with the staff he moved with irregular bursts of intensity, sometimes strolling in place and at other times shaking with fury. When he sang his voice took on a low, hollow, raspy quality; at times he seemed almost to growl his phrases. The medium's movements, like his voice, were no longer his own but represented those of the spirit who possessed him.

Once the spirit seizes his or her host, the musical proceedings of the *bira* revolve around the medium. The possession of the medium has a great impact on the participants. As the spirit takes a person, the air fills with ululation. The participants respond to the possession by performing their parts with tremendous intensity and vigor, and the musicians play mbira with all the strength they can muster.

The mbira players' music is responsible for bringing about the initial possession of the medium, and for keeping the spirit at the *bira*. If the players relax the intensity of their performances after the medium is possessed, the spirit may drift away from the host and depart from the *bira* shortly after his or her arrival. Therefore, once the spirit arrives the mbira players must play especially hard, "giving the spirit power" to possess his or her host and to participate in the events of the evening.

In the drama of the *bira*, possessed mediums acknowledge the presence of other mediums and often interact with each other in well-defined roles reflecting their status in the hierarchy of the spirit world, the younger and lesser spirits deferring to the older and more powerful spirits. At one *bira* at which I asked a possessed medium for permission to record the music of the ceremony, he informed me that while this would be all right with him, he was a lesser family spirit who did not have the authority to give me permission to make the recording. He advised me to wait to consult the more powerful spirit who would be arriving later in the evening.

Mediums sometimes become accustomed to participating at rituals with certain other mediums. At one ceremony at which I was present, a possessed medium complained about the absence of "his friend" (another spirit with whom he frequently shared the events of the *bira*) and instructed the villagers to make sure that the spirit's medium was present at the next ceremony in their area. Finally, mediums are very sensitive regarding the issue of the authenticity of their spirits, and I have heard of possessed mediums "chasing from the *bira*" other individuals who they felt were only feigning possession. As one medium ex- 201 plained to me, "It is a dangerous thing to play with the spirit."

The possessed medium is also in a position to exercise license in his or her relationship with the members of the village. If angered, the medium can order a person to leave the *bira* without giving any reason for the order. Within certain limits almost anything is appropriate behavior from the possessed medium. On one occasion I saw a medium, without warning, punch an unsuspecting villager in the stomach, and then just as suddenly draw back passively as if the incident had not taken place. The medium's relationship with the mbira players also reflects the capriciousness and the unpredictability of the spirits. For example, the spirits are sometimes sharply critical of the music at the *bira*, and I have heard of one ceremony at which a possessed elderly woman actually seized the mbira of musicians who were playing poorly and threw their calabashes out of the *banya*. In a sense, this aspect of the interaction between the possessed mediums and the participants is a symbolic dramatization of the participants' relationship with the ancestral spirits: Shona traditionalists see their lives as subject to the will and whim of their departed relatives and other members of the spirit world.

The interaction between musicians and mediums at the *bira* is a significant one. While possessed, the mediums impose their musical tastes upon the mbira players, and the musicians follow the directions of the possessed medium, switching pieces whenever the medium expresses interest in another composition. Sometimes the medium abruptly orders them to begin a second piece before they have concluded the first. At other times he or she is more sympathetic, giving them advice about their performance and coaxing them on. The mbira players willingly submit to the demands and criticisms of the medium, both out of respect for the spirit's authority and because they consider the spirit who has heard many great musicians in his or her previous experience to be a shrewd judge of the quality of the mbira performance. There is some disagreement among musicians, however, regarding the degree to which they are responsible for following the spirit's orders. One musician argued emphatically that once the spirit comes they must follow his or her word completely. If the spirit likes a particular tune and requests it over and over, the musicians must play that tune the whole night to satisfy the spirit. Other musicians disagreed; they felt that they had some obligation to perform many different tunes during a *bira* and should ignore the spirit after he or she had possessed the medium, if the spirit kept asking for the same tune over and over again. Another musician explained that the spirit of a person who had been a great beer drinker when alive might behave in a rowdy and unreasonable manner when possessing his or her host, and a musician should not blindly follow the requests of such a spirit.

Some mbira players, such as Luken Pasipamire, express their appreciation for the criticism of mediums: "The spirit's words are good to us," reported Pasipamire. "It is the spirit who knows mbira music best and wants it to be played well. . . . Usually the spirit persuades us in a good way, not shouting, but says, 'Come my young brothers, you played so well before, why not tonight?' These words make us play better."

The very presence of the spirit, as well as the speed with which the possession of the medium comes about, is a credit to the mbira players and testifies to their ability as performers. The degree to which the Shona associate possession with the quality of an mbira performance is illustrated by several remarks recorded by an ethnologist. One villager said that "the music [at a particular ceremony] was so well done that the spirits were hovering about waiting to appear." A singer remarked that the music was so nice it made her want to become possessed, and one man said that on a certain occasion the music was so good that the spirits were even possessing children.[7] Critical interaction with the mbira players is also a way in which the medium demonstrates the presence of his or her spirit to the participants.

After the possessed medium has participated for a period of time with the other villagers in the musical activities of the *bira*, he or she calls for the music to stop and prepares for consultation. The mbira players discontinue their performance at this point, often leaving the *bira* for an hour or so. Their services are unnecessary during the formal discussion between the mediums and the participants, and if they are playing for villagers to whom they are not related the issues at stake do not always concern them. They remain in the general area, however, in case the spirit calls for them.

When the medium is ready to be consulted, he or she sits on the ground beside the attendant. The villagers then gather around them. The attendant frequently acts as an interpreter, since the medium's words can include a mixture of different   203

languages, dialects, or archaic forms of Shona not easily understood by the villagers. The discussion with the medium takes on
a democratic character in which everyone present has an opportunity to raise questions or to state his or her position on the
issues. Often it is not until after much deliberation that the
medium makes a final judgment in the matter at hand. In
this respect the medium serves as the "mouthpiece of the
community."[8]

The *bira*'s role as a means for villagers to impose the moral
values of the society on individuals who have strayed too far
from the community's accepted mores was clearly demonstrated at a spirit possession ceremony I attended. On this occasion,
after having made a token offering to the spirit, a worried
young couple confronted the possessed medium with their ailing infant daughter. The baby had been seriously ill for some
time and the *n'anga*'s medicine had failed to improve her condition. During consultation with the parents, the medium confirmed the *n'anga*'s former diagnosis that the illness was not a
natural one, but one which had been caused by gravely disturbed ancestors. He explained this in terms of other family
troubles which the parents revealed to him: shortly before the
child became ill her grandmother had died; and her grandfather, having become selfish in his old age, had refused to return his wife's possessions to her side of the family. This trans-
gression of the traditional Shona law of inheritance had angered
the ancestors, who then afflicted the granddaughter in order to
point out the seriousness of the offense and to demand rectification of the matter. The medium advised the worried parents to
convey his judgment to the child's grandfather, pressuring the
old man either to give up his departed wife's possessions or to
bear the responsibility for the prolonged illness, or even death,
of his granddaughter. The medium's clients expressed their
gratitude to the spirit as well as their resolve to follow his advice, and the consultation concluded.

In such instances the *bira* serves as a vehicle for imposing
constraints on the behavior of deviant members of the community, including even the elders, who normally command the
greatest amount of authority and respect in Shona society. This
is accomplished through the medium who, when possessed, represents the ultimate authority of the oldest members of the society, the ancestral spirits, who are considered legitimately to

govern its affairs. As in the example above, the implicit or explicit threat of the invocation of "mystical sanctions" against the parties involved can reinforce the authority of the medium.[9]

After the medium has finished deliberating his or her judgment at the *bira*, the villagers resume their participation in the evening's music. The medium may continue to interact with the villagers in a state of possession, sharing in the musical activities, or at the conclusion of the consultation he or she may call for a particular composition the spirit requires in order to depart from the *bira*. The medium then leaves the building, returning a few minutes later dressed in street clothes and with his or her normal personality, ready to participate in the music with the villagers until sunrise, when the *bira* officially ends. If the occasion warrants, the *bira* concludes with a short procession led by the mediums and accompanied by the mbira players, to a place at which the villagers sacrifice a ritual ox in honor of the spirit. The participants divide the meat among themselves. At a *bira*, then, there is lively interaction among the audience, the musicians, and the medium, all of whom can influence the evening's proceedings. Because the interplay among them is never exactly the same, each *bira* is unique.

Shona religious ritual, rather than seeking to analyze statements of ideology, acts them out. The dramatization provides "each member of the ritual group an opportunity to take part."[10] It is through the music and dancing that all members have the opportunity to take part in the drama of the Shona *bira*. Their vigorous participation in singing, dancing, and clapping supports the role of the mbira players in bringing about the possession of spirit mediums, who, as honored guests at the *bira*, bridge the world of the living and that of the ancestors.

While the primary purpose of the *bira* is of course religious, the event affects participants deeply in other ways as well. Throughout the evening people dwell on the strong cultural associations of the music. These are largely involved with the past: the ways of the ancestors, traditional Shona values, historical events, and so on. A feeling of solidarity emerges in the community as villagers ritually unite with their ancestors through their common participation in the musical activities of the *bira*. In this respect, the *bira* is like a long communal journey through the night. When the music stops, the mediums convey their messages as official representatives of the spirit world, 205 explaining the troubles that have plagued the village and suggesting some means of rectification. After the consultation, the villagers and the spirits continue their joint participation in the music until sunrise. Throughout, the music of the mbira ensemble has provided the villagers with the inspiration and the energy to travel together through the night.

9.
The Law of Mbira: Mbira in the Lives of Performers and the Changing Status of Mbira Music

The mbira plays a central role in the lives of the musicians who specialize in its performance. The close identity of these musicians with their art and the significance the mbira has for them reflect the deep meaning of the mbira among Shona traditionalists in general.

Biographical sketches of a number of well-known mbira players provide further insight into the meaning of the mbira for the Shona people. The biographies are derived from interviews in which musicians discussed their personal histories with respect to the mbira. These biographical sketches demonstrate the interrelationship of the various aspects of the music dealt with in previous chapters. This section concludes with a discussion of some features common to the lives of mbira players and of the changing status of mbira music among the Shona people.

Biographical Sketches of Mbira Players

Cosmas Magaya: born 1949, Mondoro;
veteran of mbira ensemble Mhuri yekwaRwizi
Cosmas Magaya (Plate 44) first became interested in the mbira   207

when he was about eight years old.[a] At the time his closest musician-relative was his cousin Ernest Chivanga. Chivanga, over ten years Magaya's senior, was at first very reluctant to teach him how to play the mbira. In fact, he refused to allow Magaya near his instruments, fearing that such a young child would not take them seriously and would knock them out of tune. Magaya was determined to learn, however, so each time Chivanga left the house he surreptitiously borrowed one of his cousin's instruments in order to practice. During these sessions Magaya attempted to reproduce a specific mbira piece from memory, one which he had heard Chivanga play many times. He concluded each practice session before Chivanga entered the house again, and returned the mbira unnoticed. Struggling on his own, Magaya ultimately succeeded in learning the *kushaura* part to "Kariga Mombe."

One afternoon when several members of his family were listening to Chivanga perform, Magaya asked to hold the mbira, and surprised everyone by playing the piece he had taught himself. Chivanga's attitude changed toward Magaya when he heard him play "Kariga Mombe," and he agreed to teach Magaya the basic patterns for two other pieces, "Nyamaropa" and "Mahororo." Since Magaya continued to be a quick and serious student, Chivanga consented to teach him additional pieces, and it was not long before the two of them were performing in public together, playing the *kushaura* and *kutsinhira* parts of mbira pieces simultaneously.

By the time Magaya was twelve, he and Chivanga had established a reputation for their music throughout their part of the Mondoro tribal trust land. Villages frequently hired them, for about twelve dollars apiece, to perform for *mapira*.[b] Since they often performed as many as four times a month, Magaya's father could depend on Magaya to pay for his own secondary schooling.

As a young performer Magaya created an image that delighted many people. He was very small for his age and played the mbira inside a huge calabash. Since Magaya was self-conscious about his playing, he used to perform with his head in the

---

[a] Cosmas Magaya's performance of mbira music is on *The Soul of Mbira*, side I, band 3, and on *Shona Mbira Music*. Magaya sometimes uses his grandfather's name, Kanengoni, in addition to his regular surname.

[b] All fees mentioned in this book are in American currency.

gourd, watching the keys carefully so that he would not make any mistakes. When the mbira rested on his lap while he played, all the audience could see was a large gourd with two little legs protruding out from underneath. People listening or passing by would laugh at the sight of him and call out *"Musoro mudeme"* ("The head in the gourd").

Eventually Magaya's reputation grew to the point that whenever Chivanga performed alone, his listeners called for Magaya to come and play the second part. At one point Chivanga became so jealous that he refused to let Magaya play his mbira, but Magaya's father bought one of Chivanga's mbira and presented it as a gift to Magaya on his fourteenth birthday. Magaya recalled that on one dramatic occasion when he was a very young musician, a great family argument ensued over his mbira playing. Magaya had contracted chicken pox. Prior to the outbreak of his illness, his father had made arrangements for him to perform at a *bira* several miles away. On the evening of the performance his mother argued that Magaya was too ill to make the trip and insisted that he stay in bed. His father, however, maintained that he should not break a contract and that Magaya needed the extra money for school fees. Since Magaya's father prevailed in the argument, an older brother put Magaya, who was too weak to walk, in the basket of his bike and pedalled him to the village where he was to perform. The evening remains in Magaya's mind as an agonizing one, for his body itched all night long and his mbira playing left no hand free for scratching. He remembers the occasion with great pride as well, because he played with all the strength that he could muster and the spirit came after only one song.

When he was fifteen his parents enrolled him in a Roman Catholic boarding school in another part of the reserves, and a period of great tribulation in connection with the mbira began for Magaya. Students who had studied there previously had warned him, "If you play the mbira, you'll be chased from school." Many Christians, European headmasters and Shona converts alike, looked with great disdain on the traditional Shona religious practices and everything associated with them. Heeding the warnings of friends, Magaya reluctantly left his mbira at home when he began school.

The year was a disastrous one for him. He could not study, for the mbira was always on his mind. At night he had dreams about the mbira in which he heard new compositions being 209 played and saw himself playing at *mapira*. He was always very close to running away from school. After the first academic year ended, he returned home and played the mbira all summer long.

During the following school year Magaya's problems mounted. He left his mbira at home once again and continued to hide his musical ability from the authorities at school. In spite of this, several students discovered that Magaya was an mbira player and spread rumors which eventually reached one of the African teachers who taught carpentry. As it happened, the teacher was fond of mbira music and asked Magaya to teach him how to play the instrument. Magaya, still fearing expulsion from the school, denied that he knew anything about the mbira. The carpenter did not believe Magaya and from that day on bore a grudge against him. On one occasion he beat Magaya for refusing to teach him mbira music. For several weeks after this incident Magaya avoided his carpentry classes, and the tension between Magaya and the carpentry teacher became so great that the higher authorities intervened. As it turned out, they allayed Magaya's fears. While in the past headmasters had been intolerant of traditional aspects of African culture, the Catholic Church had begun to change its policies. Some priests were experimenting with the inclusion of traditional elements of African music at masses. In fact, a well-known mbira player and convert to Catholicism, Simon Mashoko, was composing liturgical music for the mbira with the encouragement of the church leaders. The new headmaster of Magaya's school, sympathetic to this movement, invited Magaya to perform mbira for the school and made arrangements for him to meet and study with Simon Mashoko.

Once Magaya was allowed to play the mbira openly at school his attitude toward studying changed substantially. It was not long before he excelled as a student, and by the time he had finished the seventh grade he was serving Mass. Impressed by his potential, Magaya's teachers and the school authorities asked him to consider continuing his studies in order to become a priest. This created a crisis at home. Although Magaya's parents were pleased that he was receiving a European education, they feared the effect of prolonged Christian indoctrination. After some deliberation, they removed Magaya from Catholic boarding school and sent him to live with his brother in Bulawayo, where he could continue his education at a day school.

During the next two years in Bulawayo Magaya gave a number of solo performances of mbira music. His brother Simon accompanied him with *hosho* and they often played together at private parties for Ndebele people, the majority group in that part of Zimbabwe. Since the mbira was not part of the musical tradition of the Ndebele and other players were scarce in Bulawayo, Magaya found a great deal of interest in his musicianship. People sometimes came to his home to hear a sample of his music and threw coins into his calabash to show their appreciation. During this period Magaya had no mbira teacher, but he continued to practice regularly after school, perfecting his style and teaching himself new pieces.

After several years in Bulawayo Magaya moved to Salisbury to live with his uncle Claudius Magaya and to study for a diploma in salesmanship at the Community College Business School. Cosmas Magaya's father, who had become a successful master farmer, offered to assist in financing this schooling. In Salisbury Magaya met a relative, Erick Muchena (Plate 32), then in his late twenties, who had been playing the mbira for three years. At one time Muchena had been afraid of Magaya's playing. However, while Magaya was in Bulawayo Muchena had been studying with John Kunaka, a very accomplished player, and had been performing in public regularly, and now Muchena surpassed Magaya as a musician.

Magaya "forced" Muchena to teach him, often diverting him from the beer halls where he liked to spend his free time. At the same time, Justin Magaya (Plate 31) appeared in Salisbury. He was a relative of Cosmas' who had grown up with him in the villages of Mondoro. Originally both Chivanga and Cosmas had taught Justin how to play the mbira. Since then Justin had been trying hard to beat Magaya at mbira playing, and a friendly rivalry developed between them. Justin's competitive spirit made Magaya angry, so he practiced harder than he ever had before, studying as much as possible with Muchena, and eventually managing to surpass Justin and to stay ahead of him.

In recent years Cosmas Magaya has been working for the sales and promotion division of the Dairy Marketing Board. He is now a sales representative in charge of the African townships and the Matebeleland country stores. Magaya remains an active professional mbira player, performing at *mapira* and at their urban counterparts, *matandaro*, with Hakurotwi Mude's ensemble, *Mhuri yekwaRwizi*. Magaya also has developed a   211 reputation with his own mbira group, *Mhuri yekwaMagaya*, which appears on programs of the Rhodesia Broadcasting Corporation and has produced several 45 rpm records of their renditions of traditional mbira pieces.

Reminiscing about his personal history, Magaya attributed his early interest in the mbira to his father's spirit, who favored mbira music (his father is a practicing *n'anga* as well as a farmer). "I think that the spirit who possessed my father did not want him to waste the money on . . . mbira players [outside the family]," concluded Magaya, "and it was my father's spirit who caused me to learn the mbira."

Luken Pasipamire: born 1950, Mondoro;
veteran of mbira ensemble Mhuri yekwaRwizi
When Luken Pasipamire (Plate 45) was very young he saw the mbira that his grandfather, Kwari, is supposed to have played for the spirit of Chaminuka at his renowned headquarters, Chitungwiza.[c] The mbira had passed from father to son in his household for generations. When he first saw the instrument Pasipamire did not show any interest in it; he thought it was a toy and his father would not let him handle the mbira by himself.

It was not until he was twelve that Pasipamire became fascinated by mbira music. During that year his older brother, Webster (Plate 22), then about twenty-one, became seriously ill. When Webster's condition continued to deteriorate steadily, he was taken to a *n'anga*, who diagnosed his illness as having been caused by a spirit who wanted to possess him. The *n'anga* advised Webster to buy cloth for the spirit of his grandfather who had played mbira for Chaminuka. After consulting a number of different *n'anga*, each of whom confirmed the first *n'anga*'s diagnosis, Pasipamire's father made arrangements for a *bira* to be held in his village for the spirit causing Webster's illness.

On the evening of the *bira*, Banibus, Pasipamire's cousin, arrived with several other musicians to play for the spirit. That evening, mesmerized by the intensity of the music and the drama of the *bira*, Pasipamire watched his older brother become possessed by the spirit and interact with the participants,

---

[c] Luken Pasipamire's performances of mbira music are on *The Soul of Mbira*, side I, band 1, and on *Shona Mbira Music*.

displaying a personality Pasipamire had never before associated
with him. When the *bira* ended the following morning, Pasipamire's mother killed a chicken for the guests. Banibus and his
brother removed their mbira from the calabashes. After break-
fast, Pasipamire became curious and asked them to play their
mbira so he could watch their fingers. Pasipamire showed great
enthusiasm and Banibus taught him the *kushaura* part to "Nhemamusasa." Pasipamire was quick to learn it, but Banibus refused to teach him more, saying, "When I have a store, are you
going to collect shirts and groceries for me for free?"

The next day Pasipamire complained about this to his family.
His mother was very sympathetic and encouraged him, saying,
"Take a goat to give Banibus; then he'll teach you more." At
about the same time, Pasipamire had an important dream in
which his departed grandfather, Kwari, appeared and told Pasipamire that he wanted him to learn to play the mbira just as he
had once performed for Chaminuka. With this reinforcement,
Pasipamire travelled to Banibus' home with a goat from his parents, and Banibus taught him the *kutsinhira* part to "Nhemamusasa" as well as two new pieces, "Kariga Mombe" and "Mahororo." Banibus required some form of payment for mbira lessons because he did not consider himself closely enough related
to Pasipamire to teach him without remuneration.

Pasipamire learned to play his grandfather's mbira and his
parents were very pleased. He also made an mbira of his own,
modelled after his grandfather's instrument, using his father's
tools and forging the keys from old bicycle springs.

After a few formal lessons with Banibus Pasipamire continued to learn mbira music by listening to other musicians and by
copying their styles. He travelled to mbira players' villages and
sat close to musicians when they performed at rituals. "You
have to be very clever pinching songs," he explained, "for
many musicians will turn their gourds away when they see you
watching." However, Pasipamire spoke especially warmly of
several musicians—including his relative, Selistino—who always used to let him watch over their shoulders when they
performed.

In his early teens, Luken Pasipamire began to teach his older
brothers Jealous and Felix how to play the mbira. Both by this
time had learned to make mbira. Jealous had cried because he
could not have his grandfather's mbira. His father had teased
him about it: "Why did you let your younger brother overtake 213

you? You can't have the mbira because you aren't able to play it." This challenge was too much for Jealous to ignore. He built an mbira himself and practiced so hard for a year that he ended up more skilled than Luken. With the tables turned, Jealous began teaching Luken and Felix. At fourteen, however, Luken took the lead in playing the mbira once again and maintains that he has kept it ever since.

When Luken was fourteen, he and his brothers played together professionally at ceremonies. As teenagers they travelled all over Zimbabwe, performing in Marandellas, Nyamweda, Njanja, Engledorn, Bohera, Dorova, Chipinga, and elsewhere. They took buses to other parts of the country where villages had hired them. Often the bus drivers waived their fare for them in return for mbira performances during their trips. The travelling sometimes taxed their strength; they often left early in the morning and arrived at their destination only after sundown. They then played through the night until sunrise. During many periods the Pasipamire brothers had an engagement every weekend, and sometimes they performed for a different *bira* on several consecutive evenings. Payment could be as much as twelve dollars for each mbira player.

At an early age Luken Pasipamire decided that he preferred the mbira to school. His teachers at the Roman Catholic school at which he was enrolled were sympathetic to his interest and encouraged him to bring his mbira to school. He was often asked to perform for Shona history class, providing a musical background for his teacher's lectures. The gardening and carpentry teachers also encouraged him to play for their classes while the other students worked. When he was in his mid-teens he transferred from the Catholic school to a community school near his home. By this time, however, he had no interest at all in school. He often walked to school with the mbira under his arm and stood outside the schoolhouse trying to decide whether or not to enter. The teacher and other students beckoned him to come in; but he invariably shook his head, and returned home to play the mbira. Pasipamire stopped going to school altogether when he was sixteen.

Pasipamire's home was in a village in Mondoro, but he moved back and forth between there and Salisbury, living for periods of time with relatives who worked in the city. While in Salisbury he played with other musicians at *matandaro* in the African townships, as well as for *mapira* in outlying tribal trust lands. Since a *dandaro* did not generally go much beyond midnight, he was usually paid half as much as for a *bira*. Pasipamire's father was very proud of his son's ability to play the mbira and was also pleased that he could earn money. He could count on Pasipamire to help pay for his own clothes and food. It was while living in the townships that Pasipamire began performing with *Mhuri yekwaRwizi*. Still an active mbira player, Pasipamire is now in Gwelo, apprenticed to his brother Felix in the upholstery trade.

Thinking of his first interest in the mbira, Pasipamire emphasizes the dramatic effect his brother's spirit possession ceremony had on him. It was at the *bira* for Webster that Pasipamire first listened carefully to the mbira players. It was that ceremony which sparked his ambition to become an mbira player.

Ephat Mujuru: born 1950; performer and recording artist with his own ensemble, Mhuri yekwaChaminuka

Ephat Mujuru (Plate 46) was born in the village of his grandfather, Muchatera (Plate 43), an mbira player and distinguished spirit medium whose following accepts him as the present-day medium for Chaminuka.[d] As Mujuru recalls, he was raised in an environment in which "mbira was everywhere." Mujuru's first interest in the mbira stemmed from an elaborate ceremony held for the spirit of Chaminuka in Muchatera's village when Mujuru was a very young child. He remembers his first impressions vaguely: the all-night dancing, a large procession of mbira players (more than fifteen), and the sacrifice of many oxen for the spirit. Mujuru tried at the time to imitate the dancing of the older participants and tagged along after the mbira players with wide eyes and open ears. He remembers the dramatic possession of one of the members of the village by the spirit of a lion: the medium danced in lion skins. Mujuru decided when very young that he wanted to be an mbira player.

Mujuru remembers as a small child being too young to be permitted alone in the *banya* where the ceremonies were held. On occasions when his mother was unable to accompany him, he would sometimes sneak away by himself to the *bira*, fasci-

[d] Ephat Mujuru and his grandfather Muchatera appear in two films available through Pennsylvania State University (see p. 270, items 1 and 4).

215

nated by the music. His grandfather, who was in large part responsible for his upbringing, encouraged him to attend the ceremonies. Mujuru recalls one *bira* at which he watched the performance of an old *njari* player with immense satisfaction. The musician recognized his interest and allowed him to hold his mbira. As Mujuru sat down, delighted to have an instrument on his lap, others gathered and watched him play a single key over and over. "This boy will be a musician," proclaimed the *njari* player, and Mujuru glowed with pride. Mujuru's grandfather, Muchatera, was very pleased with his grandson's interest in the mbira and told other adults, "Look, now he's doing my work!" Each evening Mujuru sat beside Muchatera as he played, watching his fingers and longing to be able to play as well as his grandfather.

When Mujuru was about eight years old Muchatera gave him his first formal lesson, teaching him the *kushaura* part to "Ndaona Buka Nhemawara." After Mujuru had learned the *kushaura*, his grandfather accompanied him, playing the *kutsinhira* part. Thereafter, whenever his grandfather was not busy he sat with Mujuru, teaching him new songs, and then practicing the performance of the *kushaura* and *kutsinhira* parts together. Mujuru remembers his grandfather's kindness and patience as a teacher. He always encouraged him. He would never say, "That's a mistake." Instead, he advised him in a gentle manner, "That is all right, *but* you should play it *this way*," and demonstrated the correct version.

Mujuru played for his first spirit possession ceremony when he was ten years old. With hands shaking from nervousness, he joined the other mbira players hesitatingly. They were happy to see him and referred to him with amusement and affection as "Bandambira." Mujuru was amazed during the performance to notice how easily some musicians could sing and play the mbira at the same time. Whenever he tried to sing he would "forget the mbira" and lose his place in the piece. After his initial performance at the *bira*, Mujuru often played at ceremonies held in his village. He performed the pieces his grandfather had taught him and either listened to other musicians or slept during the performance of pieces with which he was not familiar. Over the next four years, Mujuru devoted most of his free time to playing the mbira, learning as many pieces as he could from Muchatera's vast repertory. By the time he was fourteen other musicians recognized Mujuru as an mbira prodigy. In addition to his performance at ceremonies, Mujuru began instructing others in mbira music, even mbira players who were older than himself.

Since he grew up in tribal trust lands, Mujuru dutifully went to a Roman Catholic school during the day. This was not a positive experience for him. His African teachers, Christian converts, were antagonistic toward traditional Shona religion and fought with Mujuru over his mbira playing. One teacher frequently charged that "to play mbira is a sin against God." Mujuru fought back, retorting, "Then why was the mbira created? Why doesn't God punish the man who gave us knowledge of the mbira?" Mujuru's teacher became cross when Mujuru met his pronouncements with such "insolence" and he made his dislike of Mujuru quite clear. Mujuru felt that his teacher was irritated with him particularly because he did so well in his classes.

Although he excelled in school, Mujuru's mind was always on the mbira. Mujuru's grandfather encouraged him to continue his studies of mbira music and supported Mujuru against his teacher. When ceremonies were held at his village, Muchatera encouraged Mujuru to skip school so that he could participate at home. Eventually, angered at the stories Mujuru told him of his teacher's slurs against traditional Shona religion, Muchatera removed him from the Catholic school and sent him to another school in Harare, an African township outside of Salisbury, where Mujuru lived with his father and his stepmother. The months that followed were difficult for Mujuru. Outside of the supportive atmosphere of his grandfather's village, he struggled to adjust himself to a new family situation and to acclimatize himself to urban life. Not the least of his troubles was that he did not have an mbira of his own on which to play.

Mujuru went without performing the mbira for half a year and then he had an important dream. In the dream, he saw near a river bank an old man whom he believed to be one of his relatives, Zhanje, of whom he had heard many stories. Zhanje had played the mbira for Chaminuka at Chitungwiza. The old man in the dream encouraged Mujuru, telling him that he must continue to play the mbira. In the dream he gave Mujuru a lesson and taught him a song. He said, "Play like this," and Mujuru could see the old man's fingers playing on an mbira. The dream went by very fast and was over before Mujuru could

217

question the old man. When he awoke the next morning, he had a renewed enthusiasm for playing the mbira. "Now I must go all over and watch those who play the mbira!" he resolved.

Mujuru then travelled to the homes of spirit mediums in the townships and borrowed mbira on which to perform. Many people were impressed. He played difficult pieces, including the version of "Nyamaropa" he had been taught by Zhanje in the dream, and his reputation spread quickly in the townships. At the same time, however, he was very poor and sometimes went hungry. Mujuru took odd jobs such as gardening in order to support himself. He also made a little money playing at *matandaro* around the townships. During his travels Mujuru mastered many songs from different parts of the country, and people began to come to his home to hear him play. By the time he was nineteen Mujuru supported himself by performing the mbira and by taking odd jobs in the outlying tribal trust lands. He charged twelve dollars for playing at a *bira* and sometimes received as much as ten dollars for playing at a *dandaro*.

When he was twenty Mujuru formed a group, *Mhuri yekwa-Chaminuka*, with another mbira-playing friend, Charles Mutwida. After several years' experience performing together, the ensemble made a number of commercial records. These were aired by the African sector of the Rhodesia Broadcasting Corporation and have helped to spread the group's reputation, which in turn has brought invitations to perform at *mapira* in many parts of Zimbabwe.

For a year Mujuru's group performed for the spirit of Hakurotwi Mude, the leader of *Mhuri yekwaRwizi*. During this period they often travelled with Mude to different villages, performing at rituals where Mude's spirit was invited to participate in the evening's events. Mujuru felt that he learned a great deal about mbira music by playing at these ceremonies, benefiting both from the model of Mude's inspired singing and from the critical evaluation of his ensemble's performance given by Mude's spirit.

Mbira playing has been the central activity of Mujuru's life, but he has found it necessary to become involved with other vocations in order to support himself. Over the years Mujuru has held numerous jobs, including those of lecturer at an African crafts village and salesman in a variety store. Today he is a professional mbira player, performing not only for Africans, but when opportunities arise, for Europeans as well. Mujuru feels strongly that it is necessary to educate all people of his country, black and white, regarding the importance of mbira music. Additionally, Mujuru is encouraged about the development of his mbira playing. He feels that his own style is now emerging as "music coming from my heart."

John Kunaka ("Maridzambira"): born 1929, Nyandoro; skilled blacksmith, carpenter, mbira maker, and mbira player
John Kunaka (Plate 47) first developed an interest in the mbira when, at an early age, he heard the music played in his village.[e] His father, who died when he was sixteen, was an *njari* player and his mother's father played the *mbira dzavadzimu*. Kunaka went to a Roman Catholic school until he was eighteen, and studied, among other subjects, European music. He learned the "sol-fa" system and was known as a very talented singer in the school choir. When he was eighteen his uncle hired him as a plaster boy for a contracted construction job. Working during the summer, Kunaka met some laborers from Fort Victoria who played a small, fourteen-key *karimba* from their home. He received his first mbira lessons from them, learning some of the standard tunes played for the *shangara* dances: "Chemutengure viri rengoro," "Kana ndoda kuramba murume ndoshereketa," and "Tsoro."

When Kunaka returned to his home at the end of the summer, he surprised the people of his village by building a replica of the small mbira, using wire for the keys. They had never seen that type of mbira before. Kunaka played this mbira for several years, usually at his mother's house and for his own pleasure. People who had heard of his talent used to visit his village and request him to perform, but he only gave them a sample of his music.

When he was twenty Kunaka temporarily lost interest in the mbira. He built a banjo from a length of branch, a round tin can, a goat skin, and wires, and practiced for six months, teaching himself traditional Shona songs. At the same time, he worked on farms in the Beatrice area and eventually saved enough money to buy a guitar. Upon acquiring the new instrument, he gave his homemade banjo to a small boy in the area. Kunaka progressed rapidly as a guitarist, and before long he

---

[e] John Kunaka (Maridzambira) performs on *The Soul of Mbira*, side II, band 2.

was supplementing his income from farm labor by performing professionally on the guitar in beer halls and clubs. To increase the appeal of his music he added Ndebele songs to his repertory of Shona songs. Kunaka played all over Beatrice for evening dances, accompanied by a *hosho* player. They usually made about five dollars apiece. At the peak of their popularity, during the period of the federation of Northern and Southern Rhodesia and Nyasaland, engineers from Lusaka recorded them.

When Kunaka was twenty-three some Italian carpenters in Harare hired him as their assistant. He learned a great deal about the trade and saved enough money to buy his own tools. Once he had acquired the technique for putting roofing on buildings and doing interior carpentry he began to accept commissioned jobs on his own. When Kunaka was twenty-five and working on a construction site near his home in Nyandoro, he met the leader and saxophone player of the Temba Jazz Band, which was playing at a local beer hall. He auditioned as a guitarist and joined the group, accepting the position in order "to shine" in town. The Temba Jazz Band played at parties for workers on local farms on Saturday evenings and performed in the beer halls on Tuesday, Friday, and Sunday evenings and on Sunday afternoons. Playing for farm dances usually paid four dollars. The beer halls paid less—only one dollar and fifty cents apiece—but they divided the door money among the band members. Kunaka played guitar with the jazz band for six months and then began to study saxophone with the leader of the group. After that period, however, the group went on the road, and Kunaka, not willing to leave his elderly mother by herself, would not go with them.

Eventually Kunaka sold his guitar and returned to Beatrice to accept new building contracts and to devote all his time to carpentry. Other musicians asked him to play the guitar again professionally, but he politely refused. "I was a man, then," he explained to me. "I had a wife and child and was too busy with work. That [guitar and jazz band] was a game for younger chaps." For the next few years he lived in Salisbury, where he divided his time between a construction contract for a new federal building and work for a timber company. By the time Kunaka was thirty his reputation as a carpenter had spread widely, and a European contractor invited him to return to Beatrice to work on a six-room farmhouse that needed roofing and interior work.

Since it was a large undertaking for one man, Kunaka invited Matimba, another relative and carpenter, to join him on the job. Matimba appeared in Beatrice with his tools and an *mbira dzavadzimu*, on which he was a very accomplished player. As soon as Kunaka heard the instrument played by Matimba, he wanted to learn to perform it. Matimba taught Kunaka the fundamentals of mbira playing while he was in Beatrice. After Matimba returned home, Kunaka tried to build an *mbira dzavadzimu* from memory. He remembers it as a very crude one, but adds with pride, "It was well in tune."

It was not long after Matimba's departure that Kunaka was visited by another relative, Mutinhima. Mutinhima was an older man and a revered player of *mbira dzavadzimu*, who performed for a very important spirit medium in Nyandoro. Kunaka respectfully referred to him as the "Professor for Mbira." Mutinhima was also a builder, and came to live with Kunaka in the hope of finding work in the Beatrice area. His relative stayed with Kunaka for a month and in that period of time taught him from his vast repertory of mbira compositions such standards as "Nyamaropa," "Nhemamusasa," "Chipembere," and "Kuzanga."

At the age of thirty-one Kunaka returned with his family to his home in Nyandoro and built a house. When he had settled his wife, he travelled once again to Beatrice to find work as a carpenter. At this point he still did not consider himself an mbira player. He did not have the strength to play well and performed only in his house. "I played the mbira then like a game," he said, "not in the *bira*." After working for another year in Beatrice, Kunaka learned to his dismay that the land at his home had been reapportioned by order of the government. Since the best land had already been spoken for by others, Kunaka decided to buy new property and to resettle his family in Nyamweda in the Mondoro tribal trust land.

After moving to Nyamweda, he discovered that the people there "knew nothing of mbira." A relative of his, Tembedza, who himself had a spirit and lived nearby, had been "suffering for [lack of] mbira." Tembedza often used to send his son a great distance from his village to ask Mubayiwa Bandambira to come to play for his spirit, but his child usually found Bandambira, who was in great demand in Mondoro, away at another *bira*. Tembedza was very happy to have an mbira player in his area, and he sent his children to Kunaka for instruction in 221 mbira music. Over the next few years, Kunaka's reputation as an mbira player spread throughout his part of Mondoro. Many people visited him, "coming in cars and buses" to listen to his music and to take him to their homes to perform for their *mapira*. In those days, Kunaka played the mbira alone throughout entire ceremonies. He was usually paid about eight dollars for his performance at a *bira*.

While in his early thirties, Kunaka travelled to Nyandoro and invited an uncle, Mutinhima ("The Professor for Mbira"), to return to Nyamweda to live with him. Mutinhima consented, and during the next six months they worked together on carpentry jobs and spent all their free time playing mbira music. They performed regularly at *mapira*, and Kunaka learned from Mutinhima several of the most difficult pieces for the mbira, such as "Dangurangu," "Nyuchi," and "Bangiza." By the time Mutinhima left him, Kunaka had begun to play "real mbira."

After Mutinhima's departure Kunaka was hired to play for several ceremonies at the village of relatives of his, Erick and Mondrek Muchena.[f] Both brothers were captivated by Kunaka's performance at these events and shortly thereafter became his most serious mbira students. He taught them without charge because they were relatives, and they in turn played at ceremonies in his village without expecting payment. In the years that followed, Mondrek and Kunaka became especially close friends and together formed an mbira ensemble that performed regularly at *mapira* on weekends.

Kunaka first began serious experimentation with making mbira when he was thirty-three years old. After struggling on his own for a period of time, his mother's brother, Mukwenha, also a skilled mbira player, instructed him in the art of mbira making. Over the years Kunaka developed his own style of mbira construction. He experimented with different materials for making the keys, first using five- and six-inch iron nails, then steel wire, and finally trying the type of steel rods used to reinforce concrete. He settled on the latter material not only for its sound quality but for its durability. As a powerful player himself, he used to break mbira keys made of other materials. Kunaka's mbira, distributed with the assistance of Mondrek Muchena as salesman, have become increasingly popular in the

---

[f] Erick and Mondrek Muchena perform on *The Soul of Mbira*, side I, band 2.

Mondoro and Salisbury areas for their craftsmanship and their *chuning*. Today, Kunaka leads an active and varied life as an expert mbira player, teacher, carpenter, blacksmith, and farmer.

Simon Mashoko ("Gwenyambira"): born 1918, Fort Victoria;
mbira player, composer, njari maker, recording artist,
catechist for the Roman Catholic Church

Simon Mashoko (Plates 36, 48) was born into a musical family: both his mother's brother and his fathers' brother played the *njari*.[g] Mashoko's interest in the music surfaced when he was fourteen years old, and both his uncles served as his tutors. After he had demonstrated his musical interest and talent, his father's brother built an mbira for him. From that day on Mashoko was allowed to play with his uncles, and they performed together at *mapira* "being three." They were not usually paid in cash for their performances but were given gifts of beer and of meat from the animals sacrificed at the ceremonies. Mashoko was a devoted student and practiced whenever he had the chance. During this period his mbira "travelled everywhere" with him, even into the fields where he played during work breaks. Like a "best friend," the mbira was always within reach, nearby even when he slept at night. "If a student wants to learn seriously," says Mashoko, "he must practice all the time." Mashoko went to a community school for secondary school education, but the most significant part of his youth, as he remembers it, was devoted to studying the mbira with his uncles.

When I asked Mashoko if he had ever learned mbira music from dreams, he replied that he had been told by older musicians, and assumed it to be true, that the forefathers of the Shona people had dreamed mbira compositions, but that he had never dreamed "that way" himself. Dreams did play an important part in shaping his career, however. Sometime after the age of twenty, when he was working an office job in Mashava, he had a series of strange and wondrous dreams. In the first dream, he woke in the middle of the night, hearing a voice calling, "Simon Mashoko, come here." He put on his short trousers and left his bed to go to the door of his home. He opened the

---

[g] Simon Mashoko (Gwenyambira) performs on *The Soul of Mbira*, side II, bands 1 and 5. A film available through Pennsylvania State University features his music (see p. 270, item 5).

door to look out and stood still as if frozen. There was a man in a long white robe standing in the air a short distance away, and two lions stood on the ground between them. The man beckoned Mashoko to come to him, but he refused, afraid he would be attacked by the lions. The man said many things to him, much of which he could not understand clearly—partly because in the background there was loud and strangely beautiful music that sounded like mbira music. "Now will you please come here?" asked the figure in the air. Mashoko replied, "No, I am afraid to come out of my house, for these two animals will eat me." Ignoring Mashoko's expressed fear, the man continued to speak in somewhat cryptic terms as the music sounded in the background. Suddenly he stopped his monologue and he and the lions disappeared. Mashoko shook his head in order to wake himself and then returned to sleep. Rising the next morning, he put the dream out of his mind.

It was not long afterward, however, that he had a similar dream. This time three men with wings appeared outside his house, calling to him in the same way. One was holding a sword which was engulfed by flames. "But I can't come to you," Mashoko protested in the dream. "You want to cut my head off." As in the first dream, beautiful and strange mbira-like music sounded throughout. One of the men made reference to his earlier dream: "Well, if you won't come here, remember another man who came to you and called you. You were afraid because you saw wild animals." "Yes," Mashoko replied, "but who was that man?" "You shall know him," they answered, and with that the figures disappeared.

Mashoko again did not pay any attention to the dream. Three months later, however, he came upon several Christian teachers discussing their religious experiences in a beer hall. They spoke of the Bible and Jesus. After the discussion broke up, Mashoko spoke with one of the teachers, a Roman Catholic. "Tell me, Father, can you interpret dreams?" he asked. After a long discussion the teacher advised Mashoko that the figure in the first dream, the one standing in the air, was Jesus Christ calling him to his side. Mashoko thought also of the words of the figure in the second dream, "You shall know him," and the teacher's interpretation rang true.

The Christian teacher had a strong effect on Mashoko, and as a consequence of their friendship Mashoko joined the congregation of a Catholic church in Gwelo. Upon completion of his religious training, he was baptized, although he continued to play the mbira for his ancestral spirits. He frequently returned home to visit his mother's brother, and they performed mbira music together. At twenty-one, Mashoko felt that he had mastered the mbira sufficiently to begin adding vocal parts. He developed his skill in singing by imitating his uncles, memorizing the lines of poetry they sang with the mbira music and learning the yodelling phrases they interjected among the poetic lines.

As Mashoko became increasingly religious, he thought deeply about his dreams again, particularly about the strange mbira-like music that had accompanied them. Finally, he concluded that "it was Jesus Christ or the angels who were playing the mbira in the dreams," and interpreted this as a sign that his special calling was both to the church and to the mbira. With this insight into his dreams Mashoko decided that henceforth it was his duty to play his mbira in the church and to compose liturgical music for the mbira.

Some time passed before Mashoko was able to realize his ambition, however, because he faced a great deal of resistance in the church. Other Africans told the European priest that Mashoko was an mbira player, and the priest, believing that the mbira was an instrument of evil spirits and of the devil, demanded that he give up the mbira if he wanted to remain a Christian. Mashoko refused. "I cannot leave the mbira," he told him. "If I want God, I must keep my mbira and play songs for Him." "But the mbira belongs to bad spirits," argued the priest. "No," retorted Mashoko, "I have been playing the mbira for many years and I have never seen any bad spirits. I must go forward with my mbira." While many members of the church accused him of not being a real Christian, Mashoko was convinced that the mbira and Christianity were not antithetical. He strongly believed that God wanted him to play the mbira for his people to remind them of the good ways of their forefathers.

While in the Gwelo area Mashoko had opportunities to play mbira commercially. In one instance he was hired along with other African musicians to perform traditional music during the intermissions at African sports events. The musicians each received about nine dollars for a day's participation. At the age of thirty-six he won first prize in a municipal contest for musicians performing traditional music of many different groups, and he received a trophy cup award for his talents.

It was after this event that Mashoko began devoting more of 225 his energies to the church. He learned the gospel stories and experimented with setting Shona translations of the gospel texts to mbira music. As the church began to loosen its restrictions regarding African music, a number of priests encouraged Mashoko to perform his liturgical music for the mbira. Subsequently he produced several records of his music, and his reputation as a performer and composer for the church grew rapidly. During this period, while he was working as a meter reader in Gwelo, a number of church officials took a special interest in Mashoko and created a position for him at several Catholic missions. Mashoko had the opportunity to teach his religious music to students and to study to become a catechist.

After thirteen years of carrying out partial duties as a catechist, Mashoko earned an official diploma for his work in 1966. Since receiving these credentials he has worked fulltime as a catechist for the Catholic church, in return for which he earns a subsistence income. Today Simon Mashoko is well-known throughout Zimbabwe, not only for his excellence as a performer of traditional *njari* music but also as the first composer of liturgical music for the *njari*.

John Hakurotwi Mude: born 1936, Mondoro
(district of Chief Rwizi); leader and
featured singer of mbira ensemble Mhuri yekwaRwizi

John Hakurotwi Mude (Plate 49) developed an interest in mbira music when he was very young.[h] In his village his grandfather played the *njari* and a number of relatives in his extended family (Dumba, Rwodzi, and Dandara) performed the *mbira dzavadzimu*. Mude's grandmother was a medium for a very important spirit, Marumbi, for whom there were frequent *mapira* in his area. It was in this context that Mude developed his immense fascination with mbira music.

When Mude was six he used to sneak into the *banya* during ceremonies, until the adults chased him out. Mude reports that when he was growing up, there were restrictions on the participants at such religious events. Only men and women who had passed their childbearing years could attend. The only excep-

---

[h] John Hakurotwi Mude and his ensemble *Mhuri yekwaRwizi* perform on *The Soul of Mbira*, side I, band 1, and on *Shona Mbira Music*. A film available through Pennsylvania State University features his performance (see p. 270, item 4).

tion to this rule was when a younger woman became possessed while listening to the mbira music from outside the *banya*.

At six, also, Mude began experimenting informally with the mbira. On one occasion that remains vivid in his memory, he stole an instrument that was within his reach and spent the afternoon playing with it. When his father found Mude and the mbira, he spanked him severely and reprimanded him for jeopardizing the safety of the gourd resonators. His grandmother overheard Mude's father scolding him and intervened. Because of her spirit, she was very sympathetic to Mude's interest and was in a position to exercise greater authority than most women in the village. After this incident Mude frequently visited his grandmother at her house, carrying an mbira with him. While his grandmother sat in a special stone chair from Chitungwiza, "a gift to her from the spirits," Mude sat at her feet randomly plucking mbira keys and periodically looking up at her approving smile for encouragement.

When Mude was of school age he enrolled in a local Roman Catholic school in Mondoro. Unfortunately, this precipitated a period of great difficulty for him. Mbira music always preoccupied Mude. Although he was not able to play the mbira himself, he often refused to go to school so that he could stay home and listen to his relatives perform. At this time Mude developed a pattern of illness. When he entered his classroom, he often became sick and recuperated only when his teachers brought him outside again. Because of this pattern Mude's parents consulted Cosmas Magaya's father, who was a *n'anga*, and were told that their son's illness was being caused by the *shave* spirit of one of Mude's ancestors who had been a hunter. The *n'anga* prayed to Mude's ancestors to enlist their assistance in preventing the recurrence of the illness, which then disappeared.

At fifteen Mude left school and travelled to Wankie to work for his uncle on a construction site. Over the following five years in Wankie, Mude was promoted from plaster boy to supervisor and caretaker of one of the compounds housing African workers. During this period Mude did not often hear the mbira, although some of the laborers played small *karimba*. However, Mude's memory of mbira music from his home "filled his heart" and "rang in his ears" all the time. At this time Mude's career as a singer began. Deprived of live mbira music, Mude tried to recreate the music with his voice, remembering mbira performances at former rituals and imitating the beautiful vocal styles 227 of his grandfather and grandmother. Mude and his uncle often sang together with *hosho* accompaniment, taking time off from work to "remember home."

In his early twenties Mude left Wankie and travelled to Salisbury to be with an older brother who had become critically ill. After his brother died, Mude decided to settle in Harare, an African township outside of Salisbury, where he found employment pedalling a tricycle through the city, selling bread and other food products. Later, Leonard Gutsa taught him the upholstery trade and he earned a more substantial living as an upholsterer. Although he worked weekdays in the city, Mude bicycled home to Mondoro each weekend. Since the trip took the better part of a day each way, Mude began singing mbira music to pass the time on his journey. Since Mude had last lived at home, the restrictions on young participants at the *mapira* had been relaxed, so he regularly participated in the singing at ceremonies in his area during his visits.

When Mude first moved to Salisbury he was plagued with periodic attacks of illness for the first time since his early childhood episodes at school. Mude consulted a *n'anga* and was told that his condition was caused by an unidentified spirit who wished to possess him. Upon the advice of the *n'anga* Mude's father prayed to the ancestral spirits on behalf of his son and Mude felt better once again.

Several years later, after he began his new trade of upholstery, Mude became the victim of an unfortunate political incident. Returning from work one evening, he was caught in a political disturbance in which members of the National Democratic Party dramatized their advocacy of a widespread strike against Europeans. Together with 400 other Africans, Mude went to prison for a month. After serving his term Mude returned to the *n'anga* and sought an explanation for why this had happened to him. Once again the *n'anga* interpreted his misfortune as the interference of a spirit who desired to possess him. Upon the advice of the *n'anga*, Mude then consulted a medium who was possessed by the spirit of one of his departed grandfathers. The medium advised him that he should return to his place of work in Salisbury and that the spirit who was causing this difficulty in his life would come to him sometime in the future. He further instructed Mude to go frequently to ceremonies so that the spirit could possess him.

228   Mude took the medium's advice and spent more time in the

Mondoro area going to different *mapira*. It was during this period that Mude first began to perform mbira music. A dream in which he saw himself playing the mbira kindled his interest. After waking the next morning he approached his relative Dumba, who played the *mbira dzavadzimu*, and expressed his desire to learn the instrument. Dumba was delighted to teach Mude, since there were few mbira players in the area; he and Rwodzi had too much work "on their shoulders," being in constant demand at ceremonies. Dumba agreed to take on Mude as a student in return for Mude's assistance performing at *mapira*. Dumba first taught Mude "Nyamaropa" by showing him the correct fingerings for the mbira and by pointing to the keys that he wanted Mude to play in a designated order. Mude reports that his first lesson was an easy one because both the piece and the teaching method to which Dumba introduced him corresponded exactly to that of the lesson he had received in his dream. Next Mude learned "Kariga Mombe" and "Nhemamusasa," and he was eventually taught "Mandarendare," a piece of which Dumba was a champion performer. This piece later became one of Mude's trademarks as well. After the first several lessons, it was not necessary for Dumba to teach Mude each piece one key at a time. Instead, he just played a piece continuously while Mude copied him, watching his fingers and memorizing the sound.

Mude worked for a week with Dumba and then decided to remain in Mondoro to continue his studies. At the same time he supported himself as a freelance upholsterer. So that he could practice on an instrument of his own, Mude brought his grandfather's *njari* to a blacksmith, Muchenjekwa. Using the old *njari* keys and adding a few new ones, the blacksmith rebuilt the instrument for Mude and tuned it in the fashion of the *mbira dzavadzimu*. During the next three months Mude studied and performed every day with Dumba, learning the repertory for the mbira. On weekends they went to ceremonies together and throughout the evening Mude played *kushaura* while Dumba played *kutsinhira*.

Dumba taught Mude new songs during breaks in the evening's performance at the *bira*, and on occasions when there were no rituals Mude spent the evenings at Dumba's home learning new material. After three months Mude returned to his upholstery business in Salisbury, although he continued to travel to Mondoro on weekends to perform with Dumba. Their repu- 229

tation grew in the African townships and reserves and they performed throughout Zimbabwe. At these events Mude was well
appreciated both for his singing and his mbira playing. He and
Dumba were either paid a flat rate for their services or were
paid on the basis of the number of mediums at the *bira* who had
spirits waiting to possess them. For a period of time Mude performed for a *n'anga* named Mupedzisa, who paid him in cattle.
For several years Mude and Dumba had a very fruitful musical
association. By 1961, in large part from the money and cattle he
had earned as an mbira player, Mude was able to provide the
necessary bridewealth in cattle for his first marriage.

Partly as the result of a growing conflict between them, Mude
decided to leave Dumba in 1964. Mude felt that Dumba was
not holding his own at ceremonies. Dumba used to drink too
much beer and at times would fall asleep, leaving Mude to play
alone for the remainder of the evening. Mude performed the
mbira on his own for awhile and then formed his own ensemble
with Erick and Mondrek Muchena and Ephraim Mutemasango.
During that year, Erick Mandizha of the African sector of the
Rhodesia Broadcasting Corporation invited him to perform with
his group on Mandizha's mbira program. The recordings Mude
made at the RBC studios gave him well-deserved exposure which
led to a number of prestigious engagements for Mude to perform at the National Gallery in Salisbury (for a mixed European and African audience including government cabinet
ministers), to appear on the local television network, and to
record for commercial recording companies. Between 1966 and
1971 Mude's group *Mhuri yekwaRwizi* produced over twenty
45 rpm records of their renditions of classic pieces for the mbira.

Over the years the personnel of Mude's group changed and at
different times featured such distinguished mbira players as
Erick and Mondrek Muchena, Ephat Mujuru, Justin and Cosmas Magaya, and Luken Pasipamire, and *hosho* players Ephraim
Mutemasango, Thomas Kwaramba, and Webster Pasipamire.[1]

During the years in which Mude developed as an mbira player, he was not troubled by the sickness or misfortune that had
previously been ascribed to the spirit who desired to possess him.
Mude regularly performed mbira music and attended rituals
in Mondoro, as the medium had advised. Finally, during a *bira*

---

[1] Several of these musicians perform on *Shona Mbira Music*, which
features *Mhuri yekwaRwizi*.

in 1969, Mude was possessed by the spirit. He had performed mbira music earlier that evening himself, but then he sat quietly and listened to other mbira players. Their music was very beautiful and moving to Mude, and suddenly he fell forward onto his knees, shaking. He has no memory of the events that followed, when he took on the characteristics of the spirit.

From this occasion onward, the same spirit regularly possessed Mude at *mapira* and Mude served the participants as a spirit medium. As news of Mude's possession spread, many villages invited him to attend their ceremonies and to give his professional services. People consulted Mude's spirit if there was serious illness in their families, suspicion of "bad medicine" being used by one member of a village against others, or incidents that individuals suspected were related to the spirit world. For his professional advice at ceremonies Mude received payment of cash or goods, and he gradually accumulated substantial savings. With his spirit helping him in this manner, Mude was able to build a general store in Mondoro and eventually in 1972 to provide bridewealth for a second wife.

Mude describes the spirit who possesses him as a *gombwe*, a great spirit that is not related to his own family .The "rule" or "law" of Mude's spirit requires him to arrange formal sessions (*matandaro*) at his home twice a week for the purpose of playing mbira for and honoring the spirit. While it is not always possible for Mude to follow this rule as he would like to, he does arrange *matandaro* for the spirit several times a month. Mude's own mbira ensemble performs at these sessions, and neighbors and relatives, as well as individuals who wish to consult his spirit, attend them.

Today Mude remains the outstanding singer and leader of one of the most popular mbira ensembles in Zimbabwe, *Mhuri yekwaRwizi*. Additionally, he leads an active life as an upholsterer, businessman, and spirit medium.

Mubayiwa Bandambira: born c. 1910, Njanja; virtuoso mbira player

Mubayiwa Bandambira (Plate 50) was born into a family in which there was a longstanding tradition of great mbira playing.[j] The name Bandambira first belonged to Mubayiwa's great-grandfather in recognition of his superior talent as an mbira

[j] Mubayiwa Bandambira plays on *The Soul of Mbira*, side II, band 4.   231

player. The name passed on to Mubayiwa. Bandambira's father, who was also a skilled musician, bought him an mbira when he was very young and encouraged him to learn to perform the music. When Bandambira was still a boy, his father died, but Bandambira continued to study the music with other teachers in his area, including Mukondiwa and Maichesa, who performed for important spirit mediums in Nyandoro. Bandambira used to sit next to his teachers, who would show him which keys to play for each tune. Bandambira developed a reputation as a child prodigy, surprising his teachers with his quick learning. A story goes that when he returned to his teachers the day after having been taught a new tune, they exclaimed, "Why, you're playing it better than I now. Come now and teach it back to me!"

In addition to studying the mbira directly, Bandambira reported that he also learned mbira music from dreams in which he saw the fingers of a musician playing the instrument's keys and heard new mbira pieces and their variations being performed. Upon waking, either in the middle of the night or the next morning, he was able to play the music to which he had just been exposed in his dreams. Bandambira explained that the spirits cause this; they are the ones actually playing in the dreams of mbira players, teaching the musicians to play the music the spirits most desire.

Bandambira remembers playing mbira professionally at ceremonies as a young child, when he was "barely four feet tall." At this time he formed his own mbira ensemble with other performers in the area and travelled throughout the reserves, where his music was in great demand. As he grew up he also acquired the skills of a carpenter in order to supplement his income.

Bandambira was one of the first mbira players to record for the Rhodesia Broadcasting Corporation, and his recordings have served as a source of inspiration for many young musicians. Over the years Bandambira has developed a reputation as a generous and giving teacher as well as a great performer. Young musicians report that because of Bandambira's character and high level of expertise, he was "afraid of no one" and never hid his fingers from onlookers while performing.

Bandambira expects his students to "think of the one who taught them" and to repay him with the gift of a cow, a goat, or cash. In the latter instance Bandambira requests that a student bring him one and a half dollars to initiate the lessons and

232

then the same amount for each piece that the student learns. Bandambira has also taught two of his sons to play the mbira, and they often perform together at ceremonies. His sons are in great awe of their father's expertise and work steadily toward the formidable goal of learning his vast repertory of mbira pieces. Musicians speak of the tremendous challenge of trying to imitate and to master Bandambira's style of playing. He is said to play "slow but sure," hitting all the keys evenly and never making a mistake. His music is very complex, always changing and unfolding in subtle new directions as he plays and adds new parts here and there throughout the performance of a piece.

For his great virtuosity Bandambira has become something of a legend among mbira players, who tell stories of his skill, strength, and endurance. One story goes that as a young man Bandambira could walk twenty-five miles in a day while playing his heavy mbira in a gourd resonator. His skill was so great that people would call him to their *mapira* when other mbira players had failed to bring the spirit. When Bandambira reached the spot he would "just play one song which the spirit liked and it would come right away." When a spirit was stubborn at a *bira*, Bandambira was just as stubborn. He could play for two days without stopping or repeating a song. He often sat late at night at a *bira* with his back to the wall and his eyes shut as if he were about to fall asleep. On such occasions he always surprised people who were waiting for him to drop his mbira by playing song after song and variation after variation all night long with impeccable accuracy. When I asked Bandambira if his characteristic manner of playing the mbira with his eyes closed presented the potential problem of missing the mbira keys, he remarked soberly, "It is not the eyes that play the mbira. The mbira is played by the heart." In his older years Bandambira continues as an active and well-respected member of the mbira-playing community.

Some Patterns in the Lives of Mbira Players

There are a number of common patterns that emerge in the lives of the mbira players described above. To begin with, there are similarities in the factors which originally motivated individuals to become mbira players and reinforced their aspirations toward such a goal. First, as in the cases of Pasipamire and Mujuru, many mbira players develop an interest in the mbira   233 at an early age in the ritual context of the *bira*. Drawn as children to these ceremonies by the mbira music and the excitement, musicians remember their immense fascination with the *bira*'s dramatic proceedings. Their initial curiosity and interest was enhanced by the fact that mbira were frequently both figuratively and literally out of reach to them as children; their parents often severely reprimanded them for their first attempts to examine the instruments, fearing that they would damage them. Thus many mbira players recall their first image of the mbira as an instrument that was inaccessible to them.

Second, although in some cases parents thwarted their children's first attempts to experiment with the mbira, the traditionalists of the villages, often including the prospective musician's grandparents or professionals connected with Shona religious ritual, ultimately reinforced the aspiring musicians' interest in the mbira by warm approval. In fact, these traditionalists encouraged the young musicians to perform at *mapira* themselves, as child prodigies of mbira music, and the mbira became for them a vehicle for entering the world of adults. Distinguishing themselves from other children in this respect, the young mbira players not only gained access to, but became agents of, the powerful events of the ceremonies from which they normally would have been excluded.

Third, the professional aspect of mbira playing provided an additional inducement for the young musicians. For some, mbira playing was the first skill that allowed them to earn any income. Just as the service that they performed at rituals enhanced their status in the traditionalist community at large, their ability to earn income increased their feeling of self-sufficiency and self-importance in their own villages. As in Pasipamire's and Magaya's cases, for example, they were much appreciated and respected by their parents for their ability to contribute to the family, managing or at least helping to pay for their own expenses.

While a number of performers excelled as students in secondary school, others developed such an intense commitment to mbira music that they had little interest in school and dropped out at an early age. Even when this was the case, however, the same individuals, in a manner typical of mbira players, displayed great resourcefulness with respect to their own art. Many taught themselves how to build mbira so that they could have an instrument on which to perform. They employed considerable ingenuity in developing their skills as musicians and engaged in competitive relationships with other mbira players.

As the expertise of the young musicians increased, they themselves became teachers of beginners and less experienced mbira players. This professional activity provided them with a means of supplementing the income they derived from playing at *mapira*. In some cases it enabled them to develop playing partners for their own ensembles, making it possible for them to accept a greater number of professional engagements at ceremonies. Finally, mbira players regarded the responsibility of teaching seriously because it enabled them to play a direct part in the perpetuation of the music that has been an integral part of the religious traditions passed down to them by their ancestors.

The Law of Mbira

The association of the mbira with the world of the ancestors is a strong one. In fact, I have heard musicians who are in the mainstream of mbira playing refer to this aspect of their relationship with their instruments as the "rule" or "law" of mbira. (These musicians, who perform mbira music professionally at religious ceremonies, are distinguished from others who, as amateurs, play the mbira for their own pleasure.) The "law of mbira" is not a systematized dogma. It represents a personal code of behavior that goes with the role that the mbira player assumes when he becomes a serious student or performer of *mbira dzavadzimu*. This role includes many aspects of a player's relationship to his instrument that are subject to the consideration of the ancestral spirits.

This was clearly demonstrated to me on one occasion when I travelled with several other mbira players to the village of a famous musician who played for a powerful spirit medium in Nyandoro. I had come in the hope of hearing and recording the virtuoso's music, but met with complete refusal. "I do not record for money like [so and so]," the mbira player said with scorn. "There was once another European here for three years. He stayed with the people and learned our language and our dance, but we would not teach him the mbira. [He had to find lesser musicians to teach him]. . . . If I were to record for you, I would be in trouble." His son went on to explain:

You see, we who play the mbira were chosen by the spirits to play. When we play, it is not just for music; . . . it can bring   235

rain. . . . Even these mbira themselves are not ours. They belong to the spirits and have been passed down to us. This one
was made before my father was born. This other one that is
being made for me, I will pass on to my children.

According to this traditionalist view, mbira music is the music
of the ancestral spirits, who play an active role in the lives of
musicians. For many performers, the "law of mbira" requires
musicians to remember, that is, to pay ritual tribute to, the
spirits, expressing gratitude for their support in their professional lives. For example, some musicians consider that the "law
of mbira" obliges them to recognize the ancestors formally as
owners of their instruments and to care for these instruments
with due respect: the theft of an mbira was traditionally considered in Shona culture to be a very serious crime. According
to Muchatera Mujuru, a man could have been required to offer
one of his daughters in compensation for having stolen an
mbira. Some say that even the accidental destruction of a calabash resonator bore with it the fine of as much as an ox in reparation.[1] Today such a penalty is not enforced, but, as Simon
Mashoko stressed, the owner of the gourd should inform his
ancestors of the event: "You should tell your forefathers because you know that your mbira are holy and that they belong
to them. . . . When you have found a new gourd to replace the
broken one, you should prepare beer for the spirits and say, 'We
have found another calabash, your calabash!' " Similarly, if an
mbira is damaged or sold to another person, the musician should
build or purchase a new one and present it to the spirits.

Besides appreciation of the sanctity of the instrument, the
"law of mbira" requires concern for its care. Simon Mashoko
reports that the mbira must be kept "in a special way, in a safe
place . . . like a precious book." John Kunaka said that his own
law prevented him from continually changing the tuning of his
mbira. If he kept retuning it, he said, the keys would become
loose and would eventually weaken or break. Whenever Kunaka
travelled to another part of the country to play mbira with other
musicians who used a different tuning, therefore, he borrowed
one of their mbira for the performance.

Many musicians stated that according to their law it was important not to allow anyone but a very close friend to play their
mbira. As Simon Mashoko said, the mbira is "like the girl
whom you want to marry. One would not want anyone to handle
such a personal and blessed thing." Connected with this restric-

tion is the concern for the cleanliness of a stranger who might ask to play the mbira, particularly if the person has had sexual relations that same day. "There is a big law for that," explained Mashoko. "If one day you want to play with the girls, that day, if you know that your mbira is holy, don't touch it." I heard other laws that related to sex, cleanliness, and traditional religious ceremonies. Hakurotwi Mude reported that on the day of a *bira* or a *dandaro* mbira players must avoid meeting women or having any sexual affairs. As another performer explained, mbira players must be clean before the *bira*, for they will be "next to the spirit."

John Kunaka brought up yet another consideration: musicians who loan their instruments to strangers expose themselves to a particular risk. According to him, some people are jealous of mbira players and apply "bad medicine" to the keys of the instruments, ultimately infecting the hands of the player "with pains." When an mbira player suffers from such an ailment, the musician consults either a *n'anga* or the ancestral spirits themselves for a remedy. When Kunaka himself was once inflicted with this ailment, which he called *tsinga* (*vien*), his family consulted their ancestral spirits, who instructed Kunaka to wear a copper bracelet called *ndarira* around his injured wrist (Plate 47). *Tsinga* (quite possibly tendonitis) is not uncommon among players of *mbira dzavadzimu*. Sometimes a *n'anga* offers a cure by making slight incisions on the inner side of the wrist and rubbing medicine inside the wound. Brass may be used instead of copper for the bracelet cure. If a musician does not want to wear the bracelet, he sometimes has one of the mbira keys located on the side of the mbira from which "the pain is coming" replaced by a key made of copper or brass.

The "law of mbira" also plays a role for some musicians in their development as students and in their professional association with other performers. For example, Shona traditionalists regard the spirits as being responsible for the initial interest and ability of prospective mbira players, as is apparent in the deep significance assigned to dreams. Kunaka remembers formal ceremonies in which young musicians entered the profession as performers for the ancestors and in which the village expressed its gratitude to the ancestors for their assistance in the young musician's development. Kunaka explains that on such an occasion the spirits receive ritual beer and the young musician himself abstains from performing, although other mbira players 237 can play for the spirits at the ceremony. Younger musicians, on hearing this ceremony described, remarked that their contemporaries seem no longer to observe such rituals. Some musicians reported to me that they consulted with the spirits before deciding whether or not to teach another individual to play the mbira, and when negotiating fees for giving mbira lessons, recording, and performing at a *bira*. On one occasion when I travelled with an mbira ensemble to hear a renowned virtuoso in another village, the musicians made an offering of money to the ancestral spirits of the mbira player to show their gratitude for his performance.

The Shona villagers also see the spirits as playing an active role in the music-making process itself, affecting the quality of the performances of skilled musicians. For example, during one performance at which I was present, the lack of rapport among the members of an mbira group was ascribed by Simon Mashoko to the players' failure to "inform the spirits properly of their intention to play mbira music before the performance was begun." Furthermore, it is not uncommon during a *bira* to hear individuals call out to the spirits to assist the mbira players with such statements as "Grandfathers, let the mbira sound well tonight!" At some ceremonies the participants ask "invocations of blessing" from the spirits before the music begins.[2]

Many performers, of the *mbira dzavadzimu* in particular, feel that they should maintain certain privacy concerning their association with the mbira, carrying out their roles in the traditionalist community with modesty and dignity. According to their law, performers of *mbira dzavadzimu* should not play the mbira in the street or at beer halls as do some performers of other types of mbira; they should perform only in their homes or the *bira* and the *dandaro*. Cosmas Magaya and Luken Pasipamire said vehemently that under no circumstances would they be seen carrying an *mbira dzavadzimu* in the streets. They gave three reasons: first, the musicians have an obligation to protect the mbira, a holy instrument, from the open street and crowds. Second, in a city like Salisbury people who looked down upon the mbira might make trouble for them (for example, Europeans who frowned upon the mbira as "primitive" or Africans who regard it as "old-fashioned"). Third, they wanted to avoid the pressure of being asked to perform in the streets, a practice they regard as both unprofessional and undignified.

238   Mbira players who regard the privacy of their involvement

with the instrument as important sometimes disguise the word
"mbira" by using nicknames or code names when talking in
public. For example, Pasipamire and Magaya often referred to
their mbira as "Jabav Queens," the name of an African jazz
band which once travelled through Salisbury. One of the musicians would introduce the code word "Jabav Queens" in a public conversation to signal the other that they should leave their
present company and play mbira. Pasipamire and Magaya also
sometimes used the word *nhare* (iron) to refer indirectly to the
mbira.

Finally, while musicians sometimes differ in their interpretation of the "law of mbira" and the obligations it imposes upon
them, there is general agreement regarding its most basic tenet;
mbira players should follow the "ways of the ancestors," "make
beer and call everyone together to sing and dance for their forefathers' spirits so that the old spirits can hear what their young
people are doing."[3] The relationship I observed between a group
of musicians and the medium for whom they performed epitomizes the great responsibility that mbira players feel regarding
this aspect of their profession. In this relationship the responsibility the mbira players felt toward the medium's spirit actually
exceeded that of the medium himself, and the interaction between the parties became unusually strained. The mbira players
continually pressured the medium to provide more frequent
ceremonies for his spirit than the medium felt compelled to arrange. The musicians argued that they knew the "rule" of the
medium's spirit, and that by being lax in his obligation to the
spirit the medium was inviting misfortune. The "law of mbira"
then, commits mbira players to perform in the service of the
ancestral spirits, bridging the world of the spirits and the world
of their progeny.

The Changing Status of Mbira Music
Among the Shona People

The association of the mbira with traditional Shona religion has
been strong in the lives of mbira players. At the same time that
deep appreciation for the mbira as a religious symbol reinforces
the commitment of many musicians to their art, the biographical sketches of these musicians reveal that it has also brought
them into conflict with certain segments of the European and
African community in Zimbabwe during recent history. While
mbira players have always been respected by those sympathetic 239

to traditional Shona culture, the acculturation process that has been taking place in Zimbabwe since the invasion of the Europeans in the late nineteenth century challenged their position. Among the influences most detrimental to the African arts in general and to mbira music with its strong religious connotation in particular have been European missionary movements. Missionary groups have promoted unfortunate stereotypes of traditionalists and have often caricatured mbira players as uneducated, lazy, beer-drinking heathens.

In the face of the anti-traditionalist propaganda of the churches and the mass conversions of Africans to Christianity, Shona mbira players fought to preserve their self-respect and to perpetuate their art in Zimbabwe. This struggle was evident in the lives both of older musicians like Simon Mashoko and of younger performers like Ephat Mujuru. Mashoko found himself under attack by European priests and African converts when he attempted to continue his mbira playing outside the supportive atmosphere of the traditionalist community. This basic dilemma posed by the clashing of two separate value systems appears to have been even greater for mbira players of the most recent generation such as Ephat Mujuru, whose commitment to the mbira was "tested" at an early age. These performers were originally enrolled in Christian secondary schools by their parents so that they could acquire the skills they needed to function effectively in a European-dominated country. As a consequence they sometimes found themselves subject to intense religious indoctrination as well as ridicule and abuse for being mbira players.

As a result of the hostile, anti-traditionalist pressure that followed the European invasion of Zimbabwe, mbira music suffered a decline in popularity in certain parts of the country, as the biographical sketches show. The older musicians reveal that in their respective areas of Mondoro there were few mbira players, so they were always in great demand at *mapira*. In addition, middle-aged Shona people whom I interviewed in central Zimbabwe generally had few childhood memories of young mbira players. They grew up associating the mbira with the "old men." It would appear, then, that for a period of time the older generation of mbira players had difficulty finding members of the younger generation to whom they could impart their knowledge of mbira music. Young Shona students, the products of Christian secondary school education, had had a negative image of traditional African culture instilled in them and they therefore shunned identification with the ways of the elders. Those individuals who showed musical skill gravitated toward the guitar rather than the mbira. The development of nightclubs in the townships and the cities and the influx of Western-style rock bands and African "jazz" bands, featuring electric guitars, reinforced this trend. In a sense, for a generation of Africans the guitar and the mbira came to symbolize a dichotomy of lifestyles and values. Africans associated the mbira with the poverty of the reserves and with things "unChristian" and "old-fashioned," while the guitar represented the wealth and glamor of the cities and things "modern" and "Western." Given this dichotomy, many young musicians chose to ignore the mbira as a serious musical instrument and instead constructed homemade versions of guitars and banjos.

In recent years the mbira has enjoyed a resurgence of popularity and has become a major force within the complex contemporary Shona music world. In Mondoro, for example, the same areas in which there was once a scarcity of musicians are now among the richest centers for the performance of the *mbira dzavadzimu*; a vast number of excellent young mbira players who are perpetuating the traditions of their ancestors have joined the older performers. This trend, which seems likely to continue, is the result of a number of interrelated factors, not the least of which is the growth of African nationalism and black pride in the late 1950s and 1960s. In the 1960s, before they were forced underground by the European government, the nationalist parties ZANU (Zimbabwe African National Union) and ZAPU (Zimbabwe African People's Union) placed their movement "firmly in the context of African political history," and drew inspiration from its many phases.[4] It embraced leaders representing many different segments of the African community, ranging from Christians to traditionalists. Focusing on the latter community, it brought spirit mediums, the traditional religious leaders, into the limelight again, recalling the important political role that such figures had once played in the early resistance movements against the European invaders. Furthermore, the nationalist party leaders advocated the revitalization of traditional African arts, and their political rallies were regularly accompanied by traditional music. Thus one overall effect of the rise of African nationalist parties in Zimbabwe has been to demonstrate the relevance of traditional African arts to modern African nationalism and to increase respect for traditional religious figures through their association with African political movements past and present.

By enhancing the status of traditional Shona religion and traditional Shona arts, the nationalist parties have helped to mitigate the earlier effect of the Christian European condemnation of these practices. As a result there has been renewed interest among the Shona people in traditional Shona arts and religion. Several mbira players reported to me that in their villages an increasing number of converted Christian Africans were returning to worship at the *mapira*. Disillusioned with Christianity, they continue to go to church "only as a game," waiting until later to pray to their ancestors "in private." [5] Today, *mapira* are common in the villages, and the more recent advent of *matandaro* in the townships allows Africans to keep up their traditional practices in a modern European environment. The development in the African township of numerous music associations devoted to the study and performance of traditional drums, panpipe music, and African dance is evidence of this trend in regard to Shona music. In the townships and the tribal trust lands, events of either a religious or secular nature, in which relatives and friends gather to listen to mbira music, are common.

The marked increase in the number of commercial recordings of traditional African music available in Zimbabwe also reflects a rebirth of interest in the classic arts. An executive of Gallo Records, one of the largest record companies in Zimbabwe, informed me that traditional African music, which once comprised only a fraction of the company's total record production, has in the last ten years come to comprise as much as 50 percent of Gallo's record production.

The Kwanongoma College of Music in Bulawayo, founded in 1960, provides some African students with an official institution at which they can study traditional African music and European music for the purpose of developing skills as teachers of music. Several graduates of the Kwanongoma College of Music have found teaching positions in the secondary schools of Zimbabwe, where they have been successful in encouraging other African students to pursue their interest in traditional African music.

Within the changing political and social climate of Zimbabwe, the mbira has emerged as a potent political and religious symbol for young musicians. In addition, renewed interest in the traditional religious ritual among the African public has created a greater demand for professional mbira players. This development has provided young mbira players with a means of earning an income in spite of persistent low employment for Zimbabwe's young Africans.

The European-dominated churches have also come to liberalize their former position regarding traditional Shona expressive culture. This has been the result, in part, of a more enlightened church leadership which has recognized the intrinsic value of African music.[6] Simon Mashoko's biographical sketch demonstrates the changing policy of many of the Christian churches in Zimbabwe. Although he was initially rejected by church leaders and members of the Roman Catholic Church as a perpetrator of "devil music," he has more recently been taken into the fold as a catechist, and he has the opportunity not only to compose liturgical music for the mbira but to teach the performance of mbira music to young musicians within the church.

As the churches in Zimbabwe liberalize their attitude toward the traditional African arts and the mbira achieves a position of greater respect within the African Christian community, the old stereotypes of mbira players are fading away in the population at large. The lifestyles of many contemporary mbira players who continue their training beyond secondary school and supplement their income from various vocations requiring a high level of skill challenge former stereotypes of mbira players as lacking industry and education. Certain commercial ventures reinforce the new image and status of mbira players in Zimbabwe. The African section of the Rhodesia Broadcasting Corporation provides regular programs devoted to traditional African music, including one that features mbira music exclusively. Private recording companies produce 45 rpm records of traditional African music and market them in the African community. Although Europeans enjoy most of the profits from both of these enterprises, the music media have helped to spread interest in the music throughout the country. Even in remote tribal trust lands there are radio broadcasts of traditional African music. Throughout the day at general stores, the employees play records on battery-powered record players, mbira recordings alternating with popular African jazz band records.

The reinforcement of African self-respect by commercial enterprise appropriately brings full circle the enhancement of the traditional musician in the eyes of the African citizen. It increases the status of a musician to have produced a record or to be on the radio. Such exposure also helps spread the reputation of mbira groups and brings them professional engagements to perform at *mapira* and *matandaro*. Broadcasts of mbira music on the radio and mbira records also provide young mbira players with performances by great musicians from all over Zimbabwe which they can adopt as models for the development of their own mbira-playing styles.

Finally, the increased exposure that mbira music has enjoyed in the traditionalist community, both through the mass media and in connection with the resurgence of spirit possession ceremonies, has had an impact on modern urban Shona music. In an interesting recent development in Shona "jazz bands," musicians have added to their repertories several traditional mbira pieces, reorchestrated for electric guitars and Western drums (that is, trap-sets).[k] Mbira music has come to influence contemporary Shona music in nightclubs and has made a successful comeback as a popular traditional Shona art.

It is interesting to note that mbira music appears to have had more of a "traditionalizing" influence on the contemporary Shona music than vice versa. Jazz bands reorchestrate mbira pieces, but I found no interest among the musicians with whom I worked in the performance of "jazz band" compositions on the mbira. In fact, even among those mbira players who were very interested in the music of the nightclubs, their additional ambition was one day to play the guitar with such groups rather than to adapt the nightclub music to their mbira or to play the mbira with the guitars. Players of the *mbira dzavadzimu* especially discounted the latter options because of the "law of mbira."

The degree to which musicians can be successful in compartmentalizing their involvements with traditional mbira music and the jazz band styles is reflected in John Kunaka's biographical sketch. Although he played the guitar for many years and performed professionally with the Temba Jazz Band, this in no way diluted his concept of mbira playing or hampered his development as an mbira player. In the traditionalist community

---

[k] The recorded renditions of the following traditional mbira pieces by African "jazz" bands exemplify these performances: "Taireva" (entitled "Ndozvireva" by Lipopo Jazz, Gallo Records G.B. 3868, 1974) and "Kuzanga" (entitled "Kumntongo" by M.D. Rhythm Success, Gallo Records G.B. 3185, 1973).

he is well respected as a "deep" performer of traditional music at religious ceremonies.

Rebirth of interest among the Shona in mbira music is explained as the result of a number of interrelated factors ranging from the African nationalist movements to the liberalization of the Christian churches' attitude toward the African arts. The subsequent renewal of African concern for classic Shona music has helped to mitigate the influence of those factors which, for a period of Shona history, were antithetical to the survival of the mbira, and has led to what might well be called an mbira renaissance in contemporary Zimbabwe. This renaissance is a testimony to the courage of past and present generations of mbira players who have refused to submit to the hostile colonialist pressures against their art. Because of the support that African nationalist guerrillas have received in recent years from important traditional religious figures in certain parts of Zimbabwe, some mbira players are said to have been victims of harassment for their association with these figures and for their role at Shona rituals. As early as 1973, I received unconfirmed reports of performers in northern Zimbabwe who were fined or arrested for their performance of mbira music. In spite of such harassment, the mbira players of Zimbabwe have stood fast by their conviction that they must preserve and perpetuate mbira music as an integral part of Shona expressive culture, a sacred gift from the ancestors.

Notes

Chapter 1

1. J. Roumeguère-Eberhardt, "Pensée et société Africaines," *Cahiers de l'homme* N.S. 2 (1963): 63–76. (In this article the *mbila dzamadeza* is erroneously called the *deza*.)
2. John Blacking, personal communication, 1975.

Chapter 2

1. Dumisani Maraire, University of Washington, Seattle, Washington, 1970.
2. Gerhard Kubik, "Generic Names for the Mbira," *African Music Society Journal* 3, no. 3 (1964): 25–36.
3. Percival R. Kirby, "Note on Hornbostel: The Ethnology of African Sound Instruments," *Africa* 7 (1934): 109.
4. G. T. Nurse, "Cewa Concepts of Musical Instruments," *African Music Society Journal* 4, no. 4 (1970): 35.
5. Hugh Tracey, "A Case for the Name, Mbira," *African Music Society Journal* 2, no. 4 (1961): 20.
6. J. S. Laurenty, *Les Sanza du Congo* (Tevuren, Belgium: Musée Royale de l'Afrique Central, 1962), Plates V, XVLL, XLI.
7. Ibid., Plate XXXVIII.
8. Robert Kauffman, "Multi-Part Relationships in the Shona Music of Rhodesia" (Ph.D. diss., University of California at Los Angeles, 1970), p. 69.
9. A. M. Jones, "The Kalimba of the Lala Tribe, Northern Rhodesia," *Africa* 20 (1950): 328.
10. Andrew Tracey, "The Tuning of Mbira Reeds," *African Music Society Journal* 4, no. 3 (1969): 98.
11. Andrew Tracey, "The Matepe Mbira Music of Rhodesia," *African Music Society Journal* 4, no. 4 (1970): 46.
12. Gerhard Kubik, "Recording and Studying Music in Northern Mozambique," *African Music Society Journal* 3, no. 3 (1964): 97.
13. David and Charles Livingstone, *Narrative of an Expedition to the Zambezi and Its Tributaries, 1858–1865* (London: John Murray, 1865), p. 62.
14. J. Maes, "Sculpture décorative ou symbolique des instruments de musique du Congo Belge," *Artes Africanae* (1937): 7.
15. John Blacking, "Patterns of Nsenga Kalimba Music," *African Music Society Journal* 2, no. 4 (1961): 28.

16. Margaret Trowell and K. P. Wachsmann, *Tribal Crafts in Uganda* (London: Oxford University Press, 1953), p. 327.
17. Hugo Zemp, "Musique Dan," *Cahiers de l'homme* N.S. 11 (Paris, 1971): 115–18.
18. George W. Cable, *Creoles and Cajuns* (Garden City, New York: Doubleday, 1959), pp. 369–70.
19. David Thiermann, "The Mbira in Brazil," *African Music Society Journal* 5, no. 1 (1971): 90–94; Donald Thompson, "A New World Mbira: The Caribbean Marimbula," *African Music Society Journal* 5, no. 4 (1975–76): 140–48.
20. Harold Courlander, "Musical Instruments of Cuba," *Musical Quarterly* 28 (1942): 239.
21. The description of Shona music-making activities given here is based largely on the author's field observations and on two dissertations on Shona music: Robert Kauffman, "Multi-Part Relationships"; and John Kaemmer, "The Dynamics of a Changing Music System in Rural Rhodesia" (Ph.D. diss., Indiana University, 1975).
22. Robert Kauffman, "Shona Music" (manuscript, University of California at Los Angeles, 1966).
23. J. H. Kwabena Nketia, *The Music of Africa* (New York: Norton, 1974), Section II, pp. 69–100.
24. Eric M. von Hornbostel and Curt S. Sachs, "Classification of Musical Instruments," translated from the original German by Anthony Baines and Klaus P. Wachsmann, *Galpin Society Journal* 14 (1961): 3–29.
25. A. E. Snowden, "Some Common Musical Instruments Found Among the Native Tribes of Southern Rhodesia (continued)," *Native Affairs Department Annual* 16 (1939): 72–73; idem, "Some Common Musical Instruments Found Among the Native Tribes of Southern Rhodesia," *Native Affairs Department Annual* 15 (1938): 103; Kauffman, "Multi-Part Relationships," p. 138.
26. Hugh Tracey, *Ngoma* (New York: Longmans, Green, 1948), second to last plate before p. 53.
27. Kaemmer, "Dynamics of a Changing Music System," p. 97.
28. M. L. Daneel, *Old and New in Southern Shona Independent Churches*, vol. II (1974), plates 17, 18.
29. Kaemmer, "Dynamics of a Changing Music System," p. 94.
30. Kauffman, "Multi-Part Relationships," p. 117.
31. Hornbostel, "Classification of Musical Instruments," p. 14.
32. George McCall Theal, *Records of South-Eastern Africa* (Capetown, 1901), pp. 202–203.
33. Kauffman, "Multi-Part Relationships," p. 199.
34. Kaemmer, "Dynamics of a Changing Music System," p. 82.
35. Ibid.
36. Kauffman, "Multi-Part Relationships," p. 171.
37. Ibid., pp. 113–16.
38. Carl Mauch, *The Journals of Carl Mauch, 1869–1872* (Salisbury: National Archives of Rhodesia, 1969), p. 197; J. T. Bent, *The Ruined Cities of Mashonaland*, first published 1892 (Freeport, N.Y.: Books for Libraries Press, 1971), p. 73.

39. Kaemmer, "Dynamics of a Changing Music System," pp. 98–99.
40. Ibid., p. 106.
41. Ibid., pp. 174–76.

Chapter 3

1. Roger Summers, *Inyanga* (London: Cambridge University Press, 1958), pp. 101 n1, 131, 132.
2. Basil Davidson, *The Lost Cities of Africa* (Boston: Little, Brown, 1959), p. 252.
3. T. J. Bent, *The Ruined Cities of Mashonaland*, first published 1892 (Freeport, N.Y.: Books for Libraries Press, 1971), p. 176.
4. T. N. Huffman, Keeper/Inspector of Antiquities, Queen Victoria Museum, Salisbury, Rhodesia, personal communication, 1972.
5. George McCall Theal, *Records of South-Eastern Africa* (Capetown, 1901), p. 203.
6. David and Charles Livingstone, *Narrative of an Expedition to the Zambezi and Its Tributaries, 1858–1865* (London: John Murray, 1865), pp. 62, 237.
7. J. G. Wood, *Through Matebeleland* (National Archives of Rhodesia, Hist. Mss., [WO 1/4/1: entry for July 8, 1887], 1893), p. 143. I am indebted to R. Kent Rasmussen for bringing this reference to my attention.
8. T. N. Huffman, "The Rise and Fall of Zimbabwe," *Journal of African History* 13 (1973): 353–66.
9. Andrew Tracey, "The Mbira Music of Jege A. Tapera," *African Music Society Journal* 2, no. 4 (1961): 46.
10. Idem, "The Original African Mbira?" *African Music Society Journal* 5, no. 2 (1972): 94.
11. Andrew Tracey, personal communication, 1976.
12. Tracey, "Original African Mbira?" p. 93.
13. Hakurotwi Mude, personal communication, 1972.
14. Carl Mauch, *The Journals of Carl Mauch, 1869–1872* (Salisbury: National Archives of Rhodesia, 1969), p. 194; Bent, *Ruined Cities of Mashonaland*, p. 73.
15. Phillipa Berlyn, "Some Aspects of the Material Culture of the Shona People," *Native Affairs Department Annual* 9, no. 5 (Rhodesia, 1968): 72.
16. Simon Mashoko, personal communication, 1971.
17. Theal, *Records of South-Eastern Africa*, p. 203.
18. Mauch, *Journals*, p. 194.
19. Bent, *Ruined Cities of Mashonaland*, p. 74.
20. Theal, *Records of South-Eastern Africa*, pp. 202, 203.
21. Mauch, *Journals*, pp. 194, 193.
22. A. S. J. Burbridge, "How to Become a Witch Doctor," *Native Affairs Department Annual* 8 (1930): 86.
23. F. W. T. Posselt, "Chaminuka the Wizard," *Native Affairs Department Annual* 4 (1926): 35.
24. Charles Bullock, *The Mashona* (Johannesburg: Juta, 1927), p. 24.
25. Tracey, "Jege A. Tapera," p. 45.
26. E. T. Kenny, Acting Native Commissioner at Gutu to Acting Chief Native Commissioner, at Salisbury: National Archives of Rhodesia, N3/

33/8, 5-12-1903. I am indebted to David Beach for bringing this reference to my attention.
27. Michael Gelfand, *Shona Ritual* (Capetown: Juta, 1959), p. 34.
28. Posselt, "Chaminuka the Wizard," p. 36.
29. Lazarus Kwaramba, personal communication, 1972.
30. Luken Pasipamire, personal communication, 1972.

Chapter 4

1. John Kunaka, personal communication, 1975.
2. "Nyamaropa," line 12, *The Soul of Mbira*, side I, band 3.
3. Dumisani Maraire, booklet accompanying the record *Mbira Music of Rhodesia*, University of Washington Press (1971), pp. 4, 6.
4. Robert W. Young, *A Table Relation: Frequency to Cents* (Elkhart, Ind.: C. G. Cohn, 1952).
5. Hugh Tracey, "The Mbira Class of African Instruments in Rhodesia (1932)," *African Music Society Journal* 4, no. 3 (1969): 78–95.
6. Andrew Tracey, *How to Play the Mbira (DzaVadzimu)* (Roodepoort, South Africa: International Library of African Music, 1970), p. 10.
7. Aaron Hodza, personal communication, 1972; Ephat Mujuru, personal communication, 1972; John Kunaka, personal communication, 1972; Tracey, *How to Play the Mbira*, p. 13.
8. Andrew Tracey, "The Matepe Mbira Music of Rhodesia," *African Music Society Journal* 4, no. 4 (1970): 39.
9. Gerhard Kubik, "The Phenomenon of Inherent Patterns in East and Central African Instrumental Music," *African Music Society Journal* 3, no. 1 (1962): 33.
10. Ibid., p. 42.
11. Tracey, *How to Play the Mbira*, p. 12.
12. Muchatera Mujuru, personal communication, 1972; Tracey, *How to Play the Mbira*, p. 13; John Kunaka, personal communication, 1971; John Kaemmer, "The Dynamics of a Changing Music System in Rural Rhodesia" (Ph.D. diss., Indiana University, 1975), p. 91. The definition of *madunhurirwa* is that of M. Hannan, *Standard Shona Dictionary* (Salisbury: Rhodesia Literature Bureau, 1974), p. 315.
13. Tracey, *How to Play the Mbira*, p. 12.

Chapter 5

1. A. M. Jones, "African Rhythm," *Africa* 24, no. 1 (1954): 27.
2. I am indebted to George Fortune, chairman of the department of African languages, University of Rhodesia, for providing me with the spoken patterns of these lines of poetry.
3. Dumisani Maraire, booklet accompanying the record *Mbira Music of Rhodesia*, pp. 5, 6.
4. Dumisani Maraire, personal communication, 1970.
5. Maraire, booklet accompanying *Mbira Music of Rhodesia*, p. 6. Maraire was an important early influence on my thinking about this aspect of mbira music. The points covered here are elaborated upon in his booklet.
6. Ibid., p. 3.

7. Robert Kauffman, "Shona Urban Music and the Problem of Acculturation," *1972 Yearbook of the International Folk Music Council* 4 (1973): 49.
8. Dumisani Maraire, "Nyunga-Nyunga Mbira Music" (manuscript, University of Washington, 1969), p. 16.
9. Maraire, booklet accompanying *Mbira Music of Rhodesia*, p. 5.
10. Ibid., p. 6.
11. Excerpts from performances by Manhuhwa and Pasipamire, translated by Aaron Hodza, 1972.
12. Ephat Mujuru (manuscript, Salisbury, 1972).
13. Maraire, booklet accompanying *Mbira Music of Rhodesia*, p. 5.

Chapter 6

1. Alport Mhlanga, personal communication, 1975.
2. John Kaemmer, "The Dynamics of a Changing Music System in Rural Rhodesia" (Ph.D. diss., Indiana University, 1975), p. 130.

Chapter 7

1. George Fortune, "Nhango and Ndyaringo: Two Complementary Poetic Genres" *Zambezia* 4, no. 1 (1973). See Fortune (1974) for a published version of this article.
2. Simon Mashoko, personal communication, 1972.
3. Fortune, "Nhango and Ndyaringo," pp. 28–40.
4. John Blacking, "The Role of Music in the Culture of the Venda of the Northern Transvaal," in M. Kolinsky, ed., *Studies in Ethnomusicology* (New York City: Oak Publications, 1965), p. 33.
5. Kwabena Nketia, *The Music of Africa* (New York: Norton, 1974), p. 203.
6. Luken Pasipamire, personal communication, 1972.
7. Andrew Tracey, "The Mbira Music of Jege A. Tapera," *African Music Society Journal* 2, no. 4 (1961): 55.
8. Cosmas Magaya, personal communication, 1972.
9. Dumisani Maraire, booklet accompanying the record *Mbira Music of Rhodesia* (Seattle: University of Washington Press, 1971), p. 6.
10. Ibid.
11. Ibid.

Chapter 8

1. Michael Gelfand, *Shona Religion* (Cape Town: Juta, 1962), p. 52.
2. J. F. Holleman, "Accommodating the Spirit Amongst Some North-Eastern Shona Tribes," *The Rhodes-Livingstone Papers* 22 (1953): 1–40; Michael Gelfand, "A Description of the Ceremony of Kurora Guva," *Zambezia* 2, no. 1 (December 1971): 71–74.
3. Marshall Murphree, *Christianity and the Shona* (New York: Humanities Press, 1969), p. 46.
4. John Kaemmer, "The Dynamics of a Changing Music System in Rural Rhodesia" (Ph.D. diss., Indiana University, 1975), p. 156.
5. Andrew Tracey, personal communication, 1971.
6. Cosmas Magaya, personal communication, 1972.

251

7. Kaemmer, "Dynamics of a Changing Music System," p. 123.

8. Kingsley Garbett, "Spirit Mediums as Mediators in Valley Kore-kore Society," *Spirit Mediumship and Society in Africa* (New York: Africana Publishing, 1969), p. 125.

9. Ibid.

10. Murphree, *Christianity and the Shona*, p. 58.

Chapter 9

1. Luken Pasipamire, personal communication, 1972.

2. Robert Kauffman, "Multi-Part Relationships in the Shona Music of Rhodesia" (Ph.D. diss., University of California at Los Angeles, 1970), p. 79.

3. Simon Mashoko, personal communication, 1972.

4. T. O. Ranger, *Revolt in Southern Rhodesia, 1896–97* (Evanston: Northwestern University Press, 1967), p. 383.

5. John Kunaka, personal communication, 1975.

6. Olof Axelsson, "Historical Notes on Neo-African Church Music," *Zambezia* 4, no. 1 (1974): 95–101.

Appendix I

Kudeketera *Song Texts*

Example A: "Mbiriviri," recorded 1971, performed by Simon Ma-
shoko, transcribed and translated by Aaron Hodza and George
Fortune, Department of African Languages at the University of
Rhodesia (can be heard on *The Soul of Mbira*, side II, band 1).

To assist in following the recorded performance with the text, mbira
interludes and passages of *huro* and *mahon'era* are indicated in
parentheses.

(mbira interlude and *huro*)

1. Baba, ihee ihee woihee—wosiye ngoma.

   Father, you are leaving the music (literally, song or drum) behind.

2. Wosiye ngoma ina ani, baba
Nhuka?

   With whom did you leave the
   music behind, father Nhuka?

3. Ndakanda svimbo yangu
pamhiri.

   I threw my knobkerrie [cane] to
   the other side of the river.

4. Uya uone svimbo yangu ya-
more vuchi ndafamba nabwo.

   Come and see; my knobkerrie
   has extracted some honey and I
   have taken it along with me.

5. Pandagoendawo mhiri Zvi-
Njanja

   At that time when I thought of
   going across to ZviNjanja.

(mbira interlude)

6. Mbira yangu yatandavara.

   My mbira has stretched out its
   legs wide (that is, it is so famous,
   it is known everywhere).

(*huro*)

7. Wosiye ngoma.

   You are now leaving the music
   behind.

253

(mbira interlude)

8. Ndopandagowanika zvino vakuru vanopira vadzimu vagere pasi.

Then I came across old people worshipping the ancestral spirits while the spirit medium was seated on the ground.

9. Ndoona mare.

I am seeing wonders (that is, it was surprising and shocking to see a medium in a trance sitting on the ground without a mat spread out for him).

10. Ndikati, "Zvomunogopira vadzimu vagere pasi maita zvokudiniko, nhai sakuwana?"

And then I asked, "Since you are now worshipping your ancestral spirits, while the spirit medium is seated on the ground, what are you trying to do, my good sir?"

11. Kwahi, "Tashaya rupasa rwokuwaridza."

And they said, "We have not got a mat to spread."

12. Ndikati, "Hamuruvonizve ugu guri pano ugu?"

Then I said, "Don't you see this one here?"

13. Ndopondogotarira ndione rupasa gwadamburanwa.

Afterwards (that is, having loaned it) I looked at the mat and saw that it was torn in pieces.

14. "Ko, zvamagodambura rupasa maita zvokudiniko, nhai sakuwana?"

"Since you have torn the mat, what are you trying to do, my good sir?" (that is, elderly people).

15. Kwahi, "Tati, nyarara kuchema; tokupe mombe ufambe nayo."

They said, "We say, do not cry; we are going to give you a cow instead so that you can move about with it."

16. Ndikati, "Hamuzvivone!

I said, "Oh, that's good!

17. Iyeni ndinokare nyama!"

I who like meat so much!"

18. Ndikati, "Ah! Zvandasvika mumakomo ndosesedza zuva."

I said, "Ah! since I have reached the foot hills, I keep pace with the sun."

19. Ndikati, "Ngaichimbomira."

I said, "Let it [the cow] stop here for a while."

20. Ndotarira ndoona yapinda mberi.

After that I looked at it and saw that the cow was moving ahead of me.

21. Ja ja ja ja ja . . . .

Ja ja ja ja ja . . . (onomatopoeia for the stride of the cow).

22. Iyi mombe ichandikuvadzisa iyi.

This cow will lead me into trouble (that is, people will injure him in order to take away his valuable possession).

(*huro*)

23. Baba, ihee ihee woihee—wosiye ngoma.

Father, you are leaving the music behind.

(*huro*)

24. Wakanditambira muchato, wani Muzazananda.

It is you who took the lead (literally, danced) at my marriage, Mr. Muzazananda.

(mbira interlude)

25. Ndopandagowanika zvino vakuru vanokama matatya vagere pasi.

Then I found some old people milking frogs while they were seated on the ground.

26. Ndikati, "Zvomunogokama matatya mugere pasi maita zvokudiniko, nhai sakuwana?"

I said, "Since you are milking frogs as you sit on the ground, what are you about, my good sir?"

27. Kwahi, "Tashaya mombe yokukama."

And they said, "We have no cow to milk."

28. Ndikati, "Hamuivonizve iri pano iyi?"

I said, "Don't you see this one here?"

29. Ndopondogotarira ndione mom be yangu yadamburanwa minyatso.

Then later I looked at it and found that my cow had had its teats pulled off.

(*huro*)

30. Ngore ihee ihee woihee—wosiye ngoma.

You are leaving the music behind.

(mbira interlude)

31. Chinokwegura chinosakara.

The thing that grows old wears out.

32. Kwahi, "Nyarara kuchema mwana'ngu.

And they said, "Don't cry, my child.

33. Tokupe pfuti ufambe nayo."

We will give you a gun instead so that you can move about with it."

34. Ndikati, "Hamuzvivoni izvo!

I said, "That's good!

255

35. Iyeni ndinokare nyama."

I who am so fond of meat."

36. Ndikati ndasvika kumakomo akaita saawo,

When I have reached the hills just like those there,

37. Ndocherekedza iwo aya ana manyanga akamonana.

I'll start looking for the ones with the twisted horns (that is, antelopes called kudu).

38. Ndikati ndazviziva ndogoita zionera chakapinda kunaka.

When I've found them, I'll just choose the best for myself.

39. Dzvi dzvi dzvi dzvi . . . .

Dzvi dzvi dzvi dzvi . . . . (onomatopoeia for the traveller walking with his gun)

40. Ndopandagowanika zvino vakuru vanopfura mhuka nomusvodzambudzi.

And then I found old people shooting animals with a pop-gun.

41. "Ko, maita zvokudini, nhai sakuwana?"

"Tell me, what on earth are you up to, my good sir?"

42. Kwahi, "Tashaya pfuti."

And they said, "We have no (real) gun."

43. Ndikati, "Hamuivonizve iri pano iyi?"

I said, "Don't you see this one here?"

(*huro*)

44. Kufa ndakuda wasara mwoyo.

As far as death is concerned, I'm ready. What is left is the heart.

(mbira interlude and whistle)

45. Ndakwegura ndangoti bondokoto.

I am now old and I can do no more.

46. Ndokwegura mai vachafamba. Ndokudiniko, nhai sakuwana?

I am old while my mother is still active. Isn't that unnatural, my good sir?

47. Heano matumbazuva—ndobairwe gurwe kukora!

There is an omen. I am killed for the sake of a cricket which is so fat (that is, people want to kill him to steal his cricket).

48. Ndopandagoti ndocherekedza pfuti yangu wanike vatsemura.

That is, when I looked at my gun, lo, they had split it.

49. "Ko, maita zvokudini, nhai sakuwana?"

"What is wrong with you, my good sir?"

50. Kwahi, "Nyarara kuchemazve—tokupe mukadzi ufambe naye."

And they said, "Don't cry, we'll give you a wife instead to go along with."

51. Ndikati, "Hamuvone izvo!

I said, "Oh, that's fine!

52. Iyeni ndinokare doro!

I who am so fond of beer!

53. Ndopandagoti ndasvika mu-mazimushamvi akaita saawo,

When I am about to reach those big *mushamvi* trees,

54. Ndikati, 'Ngatimbomirazve, ngatimbopedza mazuva ma-tatu uchindibikire doro.' "

I will say, 'Let's stop here for a while; let's spend three days here while you (the wife) brew beer for me.' "

55. Ndikati, "Nditarire ndione une huro yakaita seyako!

And then I said, "Let me see if I can find another with a neck as long as yours" (praising his wife for her long neck).

56. Dombotungamira mukadzi wangu."

"Just walk ahead of me, my wife."

57. Ndotarire saizvozvo ari pam-beri.

And I looked in that way while she was in front of me.

58. Ja ja ja ja ja . . . .

Ja ja ja ja ja . . . (onomatopoeia for his wife's stride).

59. Uyu mukadzi uchandikuvad-zisa pavanhu.

This wife will have me into trouble where others are (that is, his wife is so desirable people will kill him to take her away).

(laughter and *huro*)

60. Ndakwegura ndangoti bondo-koto.

I am now old and I can do no more (repetition of line 45).

61. Ndokwegura mai vachafam-ba. Ndokudiniko, nhai saku-wana?

I am old while my mother is still active. Isn't that pathetic, honored one? (repetition of line 46).

(*huro* and *mahon'era*)

62. "Mukadzi wangu, ndanyara ini.

"Oh, my wife, I am tired now.

63. Chimbondibikira doro mazu-va matatu ndiri pano."

Please brew beer for me in three days' time while we are here."

64. "Zvishomanani zvawareva murume wangu!"

"It's a small thing, my husband, that you are asking of me!"

65. Ndopaagoti abike doro wani-ke ravava.

Then she brewed the beer, but to my surprise it turned out sour.

66. Ndikati, "Zvino zvawavavi-sazve doro mukadzi wangu uchandiripira neyi?"

And so I said, "Since you have soured the beer, what are you going to give me instead?"

67. Kwahi, "Iwe uri murume zi-benzi, iwe.

And she said, "You are a big fool, my husband.

68. Ini ndakanzi namai nababa, 'musi waunowanikwa, mwana'ngu,

I was told by my mother and father, 'On the day that you get married, my child,

69. Ukaone paunosvika uchibika zvinonaka uzive kuti musha hauna kuvaka.'

when you reach your husband's village and start by cooking better things, you should know that you have not built a home'" (that is, you have not built for your future; you will not stay there for long).

70. Ini ndatotenda kuti musha ndavaka ini, chokwadi."

"But now, I am sure that I have built a home" (for myself).

71. "Asi zvaunotaura mukadzi wangu?

"But, good Lord, what are you talking about, my wife?

(laughs as he sings these lines)

72. Dombondipa hangu mbira ndimbokutambira."

Just give me my mbira, please, so that I can dance for you."

73. Tsa tsa tsa tsa tsatsa . . . .

Tsa tsa tsa tsa tsatsa . . . (onomatopoeia for his dancing while he plays the mbira).

74. "Unondibata wati ndinowa!"

"You are holding me. Did you think I was falling?"

75. "Ndaona kuti senda ndikati, 'murume wangu wava kuwa.'"

"I found you leaning over and I thought, 'Perhaps my husband is falling.'"

76. "Suduruka ndingakutsika."

"Draw back a little, otherwise I may tread on you (my wife)."

77. Povo tsa tsa tsa tsatsa . . . .

Povo tsa tsa tsa tsatsa . . . (sound of the husband continuing his dance).

(*huro*)

78. Ndooneka nyika.

I am now saying goodbye to the world.

79. Chisarai, hama vatema, zvino ndava kuoneka nyika.

Goodbye my fellow countrymen, I'm now saying goodbye to the world.

80. Kufandakuda; asare mwoyo.

Kufandakuda (is dead); his heart remains.

81. Agosare mwoyo tinorangarira.

He survives in his heart and we will remember him.

82. Chisarai, vatema; ndoona mare.

Goodbye my black comrades, I am seeing marvels.

83. Tsa tsa tsatsa . . . mai we-e.   Tst tsa tsatsa . . . mother!

Example B: "Nyamaropa," recorded 1971, Hakurotwi Mude, singer. Transcribed and translated by Aaron Hodza, Cosmas Magaya, and George Fortune (can be heard on *The Soul of Mbira*, side I, band 3).

1. Ndozvireva ndosungwa!

If I complain (say it out), I'll be arrested! (allusion to the singer's troubles).

2. Ona, ramba murume, titambe narwo waro.

Take my advice, divorce your husband so that we can go on dancing to the music (flirtation with a woman present at the musical event).

3. Ona, muzvere wembwa wasununguka.

The mother of the dogs has given birth (ridiculing a woman who previously gave birth to children who grew up to become misfits).

4. Ona, handicharugona, ndachembera wani!

Look, I can no longer manage it because of old age! (the singer is no longer able to play the mbira as he used to when he was younger).

5. Zvaita sei, mai vatombi?

What has gone wrong with you, mother of my daughter? (allusion to troubles).

6. Amai vangu, VaChimbikitori!

My mother, Chimbikitori! (singing his mother's name during the performance is a form of praise).

7. Ona, Mbudzirume namakudo tsvete.

The hill Mbudzirume is filled with baboons (reporting local news).

8. Anoda ngoma hande kwa-Rwizi waro.

Anyone who wants to hear how well the (mbira) music is played can go with us to Rwizi's place (self-praise; Chief Rwizi's area is the home of the musicians and the singer).

9. Hope dzangu nokufa jeje waro.

My dreams about death came true (the singer dreamt about death and his dreams came true).

10. Ona, mudzimu wangu ndiwo muroyi!

Look, my ancestral spirit is a witch! (the singer blames the tragedy above on his ancestral spirit).

259

11. Ona, teerera zveita mbira!

Listen to how sweetly the mbira is now playing! (commenting on the performance of mbira music).

12. Kune anorugona, dzinenge nyere.

For one who can play it, it sounds like a flute (commenting on the performance of mbira music).

13. Kana ndorutadza, kunenge kurwa.

When I fail to play [the mbira] well, it's like fighting (commenting on the performance of mbira music).

14. Ona, mubvumira waVaMa-rumbi!

Look at the *mubvumira* tree of VaMarumbi! (According to oral tradition, the mubvumira tree was once a sacred tree which provided the ancestors with food in response to a form of ritual hand-clapping. VaMurumbi is an ancestor who possesses the grandmother of the singer.)

15. Ona, ngoma yangu yoitwa yokutambwa nayo.

Look, my favorite music is now being treated like a toy (the singer complains that mbira music is no longer as respected as it was in the past).

16. Ndozvireva ndotukwa!

If I complain, I'll be sworn at! (allusion to the singer's troubles).

Example C: "Nyamaropa yeVana Vava Mushonga," recorded 1971, Muchatera Mujuru, singer, transcribed and translated by Aaron Hodza (can be heard on *The Soul of Mbira*, side II, band 3).

1. Hokuno kufa, Nhandare.

Here we face death, Nhandare. (Rozvi praise name)

2. Ho-o baba, wee, Chirongo.

Oh! my father, you, Chirongo. (Soko praise name)

3. Hokuno kufa kwauya, Nhan-dare.

Death has came to us, Nhandare.

4. Baba nepachena, Nhandare.

Father! (It comes) openly, Nhandare.

5. Ho-o kufa kwangu ndiko ku-rova.

My death means perishing for-ever.

6. Baba Mushonga, wee, Chi-rongo.

Father Mushonga, you, Chiron-go.

7. Nhamo inenge iwe iwe chi-dembo.

The trouble that is like you, pole-cat.

8. Ndiani akaite mhereka mbira Nhandare?

Who made the mbira a token of payment, Nhandare?[a]

9. Akauya nako, iwe.

He came with it (that is, the trouble that worries him), you.

10. Vana vaChigutiro vatange mbira.

The children of Mr. Chigutiro have started playing mbira.

11. Kufa kwangu ndivigei panzira.

At my death bury me by the wayside.

Example D: "Nhemamusasa," recorded 1971, Hakurotwi Mude, singer, transcribed and translated by Aaron Hodza (can be heard on *The Soul of Mbira*, side I, band 1).

1. Amai vangu vakafirei?

Why did my mother die?

2. Kudenga kuna mare.

There are wonders in heaven.

3. Seriya rakafane mombe.

Like that one [the lout] which resembles an ox.[b]

4. Meso murima dzinenge nyimo.

Eyes in the darkness are like bambara nuts.

5. Mbudzirume namakudo tsvete.

The hill Mbudzirume is filled with baboons.

6. Mune mvana ndinopinda runa.

In a house where there's a woman with one child I will go four times.[c]

7. Ndiro riye rakafane mombe.

It is still the same one [the lout] that is like an ox.

8. Mbudzirume namakudo tsvete.

The hill Mbudzirume is filled with baboons.

[a] In this line the singer refers with incredulity to the use of the mbira as a substitute for another form of compensation in a divorce suit. This line can be taken either as a challenge to the person in question or as an image meant to raise laughter because of its improbability.

[b] Line 3, which appears to be cryptic by itself, is actually the second of a pair of traditional *kudeketera* lines conveying the poetic image of a man led by his troubles like an ox pulled by a ringleader.

[c] Line 6 is the first of a pair of traditional *kudeketera* lines; the second states, "On the fifth visit I shall succeed in making love to her." These lines taken together convey the idea that a woman who has already given birth to at least one child has lost her purity and will not be as difficult to court as another who is still a virgin.

Appendix II

Absolute Tunings (c.p.s.) of Five Mbira DzaVadzimu

Mbira Keys	Ephat Mujuru	Hakurotwi Mude	Mubayiwa Bandambira	John Kunaka	John Gondo
B1	106	132	114	113	122
B2	114	146	140	147	147
B3	122	156	157	155	161
B4	133.5	184	166	175	177
B5	160	188	184	194	197
B6	170	206	201	212	215
B7	216	256	256	269	263
L1	198	232	224	234	241
L2	284	348	332	353	363
L3	244	308	310	313	325
L4	310	384	370	392	393
L5	328	416	408	431	432
L6	382	448	456	473	480
R1	234	284	276	291	293
R2	380	448	460	469	485
R3	424	512	512	525	538
R4	464	568	576	583	616
R5	504	608	648	628	660
R6	572	688	712	693	733
R7	624	760	780	778	800
R8	674	840	844	860	878
R9	772	976	976	910	981
means of measurement	T.F.	T.F.	T.F.	OSC.	OSC.

T.F.—Tuning forks
OSC.—Oscillator

Bibliography

Ankerman, Bernhard. *Die Afrikanischen Musikinstrumente.* Berlin: A. Haack, 1901.

Apthorpe, Raymond, and Blacking, John. "Field Work Co-operation in the Study of Nsenga Music and Ritual." *Africa* 32, no. 1 (1962): 72–73.

Axelsson, Olof E. "Historical Notes on Neo-African Church Music." *Zambezia* 3, no. 2 (1974): 89–102.

Bebey, Francis. *African Music: A People's Art.* Westport, Conn.: Lawrence Hill, 1975.

Bent, J. T. *The Ruined Cities of Mashonaland.* First published 1892. Freeport, N.Y.: Books for Libraries Press, 1971.

Berliner, Paul. "Music and Spirit Possession at a Shona Bira." *African Music Society Journal* 5, no. 4 (1975/6): 130–39.

————. "The Poetic Song Texts Accompanying the *Mbira DzaVadzimu.*" *Ethnomusicology* 20, no. 3 (September 1976): 451–82.

————. "Political Sentiment in Shona Song and Oral Literature." *Essays in Arts and Science* (University of New Haven, special issue: "American Ethnomusicology")6, no. 1 (March 1977): 1–29.

————. "The Soul of Mbira: An Ethnography of the Mbira Among the Shona People of Rhodesia." Ph.D. dissertation, Wesleyan University, Connecticut, 1974.

Berlyn, Phillipa. "Some Aspects of the Material Culture of the Shona People." *Native Affairs Department Annual* (Bulawayo, Rhodesia) 9, no. 5 (1968): 68–73.

Blacking, John. *How Musical Is Man?* Seattle: University of Washington Press, 1973.

————. "Patterns of Nsenga Kalimba Music." *African Music Society Journal* 2, no. 4 (1961): 26–43.

————. "Problems of Pitch, Pattern and Harmony in the Ocarina Music of the Venda." *American Music Society Journal* 2, no. 2 (1959): 15–23.

————. "Review of *Pensée et société Africaines,*" *Man* (January/February 1965): 29–30.

————. "The Role of Music in the Culture of the Venda of the Northern Transvaal." In *Studies in Ethnomusicology,* vol. 2, edited by M. Kolinsky, pp. 20–53. New York: Oak Publications, 1965.

Brisley, Thomas. "Some Notes on the Baoule Tribe." *Journal of the African Society* 8 (1969): 300.

Bullock, C. *The Mashona.* Cape Town: Juta, 1928.

Burbridge, A. "How to Become a Witch Doctor." *Native Affairs Department Annual* 8 (1930): 85–91.

263

————. "In Spirit Bound Rhodesia." *Native Affairs Department Annual* (1924): 17–29.

Cable, George W. "The Dance in the Place Congo" from the *Century Magazine*, February 1886. In *Creoles and Cajuns* edited by Arlin Turner. Garden City, New York: Doubleday, 1959.

Chitepo, H. W. *Soko Risina Musoro*. London: Oxford University Press, 1958.

Courlander, Harold. "Musical Instruments of Cuba." *Musical Quarterly* 28 (1942): 227–40.

Daneel, M. L. *The Background and Rise of Southern Shona Independent Churches*. The Hague: Mouton, 1971.

————. *Old and New in Southern Shona Independent Churches*, vol. 1. The Hague: Mouton, 1971.

————. *Old and New in Southern Shona Independent Churches*, vol. 2. The Hague: Mouton, 1974.

Davidson, Basil. *The Lost Cities of Africa*. Boston: Little, Brown, 1959.

Davidson, Marjory. "A Lunda Kalendi." *African Music Society Journal* 3, no. 2 (1963): 15–16.

————. "The Music of a Lunda Kalendi." *African Music Society Journal* 3, no. 3 (1964): 107–108.

————. "Some Music for the Lala Kankobele." *African Music Society Journal* 4, no. 4 (1970): 103–113.

Fortune, George. "Nhango and Ndyaringo." Manuscript, University of Rhodesia, 1973.

————. "Nhango and Ndyaringo: Two Complementary Poetic Genres." *Zambezia* 3, no. 2 (1974): 27–49.

————. *A Standard Guide to Shona Spelling*. Salisbury: Longman of Rhodesia, 1972.

Garbett, G. Kingsley. "Spirit Mediums as Mediators in Valley Korekore Society." In *Spirit Mediumship and Society in Africa*, edited by John Beattie and John Middleton, pp. 104–127. New York: Africana Publishing Corporation, 1969.

Gaskin, L. J. P. *A Select Bibliography of Music in Africa*. London: International African Institute, 1965.

Gelfand, Michael. "A Description of the Ceremony of Kurova Guva." *Zambezia* 2, no. 1 (December 1971): 71–74.

————. *The Medicine and Magic of the Mashona*. Cape Town: Juta, 1956.

————. *Shona Religion*. Cape Town: Juta, 1962.

————. *Shona Ritual*. Cape Town: Juta, 1959.

Hamutyinei, Mordikai A., and Plangger, Albert B. *Tsumo-Shumo (Shona Proverbial Lore and Wisdom)*. Gwelo, Rhodesia: Mambo Press, 1974.

Hannan, M. *Standard Shona Dictionary*. Salisbury: Rhodesia Literature Bureau, 1974.

Hodza, Aaron C. *Ugo Hwamadzinza AvaShona*. Salisbury: Longman of Rhodesia, 1974.

Holleman, J. F. "Accommodating the Spirit Amongst Some North-Eastern Shona Tribes." *The Rhodes-Livingstone Papers* 22 (1953): 1–40.

Hornbostel, Eric M. von, and Sachs, Curt S. "The Ethnology of African Sound Instruments." *Africa* 6, no. 2 (1933): 277–311.

————. "Systematik der Musikinstrumente." Translated by Anthony Baines and K. P. Wachsmann. *Galpin Society Journal* 14 (1961): 3–29.

Hornell, James. "Indonesian Influence on East African Culture." *Journal of Royal Anthropology Institute* 64 (1934): 305–323.

Huffman, T. N. "The Rise and Fall of Zimbabwe." *Journal of African History* 13 (1973): 353–66.

Jeffreys, M. D. W. "Negro Influences on Indonesia." *African Music Society Journal* 2, no. 4 (1961): 10–16.

Jones, A. M. *Africa and Indonesia.* First published 1964. Leiden: E. J. Brill, 1971.

————. "African Rhythm." *Africa* 24, no. 1 (1954): 26–47.

————. "Indonesia and Africa: The Xylophone as a Culture-Indicator." *African Music Society Journal* 2, no. 3 (1960): 36–47.

————. "The Kalimba of the Lala Tribe, Northern Rhodesia." *Africa* 20 (1950): 324–33.

Kaemmer, John. "The Dynamics of a Changing Music System in Rural Rhodesia." Ph.D. dissertation, Indiana University, 1975.

Kauffman, Robert. "Multi-Part Relationships in the Shona Music of Rhodesia." Ph.D. dissertation, University of California at Los Angeles, 1970.

————. "Shona Music." Manuscript, University of California at Los Angeles, 1966.

————. "Shona Urban Music and the Problem of Acculturation." *1972 Yearbook of the International Folk Music Council* 4 (1973): 47–56.

————. "Some Aspects of Aesthetics in the Shona Music of Rhodesia." *Ethnomusicology* 13, no. 3 (September 1969): 507–511.

King, Anthony. "The Construction and the Tuning of the *Kora.*" *African Language Studies* 13 (1972): 113–36.

Kirby, Percival R. *The Musical Instruments of the Native Races of South Africa.* First published in 1934. Johannesburg: Witwatersrand University Press, 1968.

————. "A Musicologist Looks at Africa." *South African Archeological Bulletin* 16, no. 64 (1961): 122–27.

————. "Note on Hornbostel's 'The Ethnology of African Sound Instruments.' " *Africa* 7 (1934): 107–109.

Kubik, Gerhard. "Carl Mauch's Mbira Musical Transcriptions of 1872." *Review of Ethnology* 3, no. 10 (1971): 73–80.

————. "Generic Names for the Mbira." *African Music Society Journal* 3, no. 3 (1964): 25–36.

————. "Generic Names for the Mbira." *African Music Society Journal* 3, no. 4 (1965): 72–73.

————. "The Phenomenon of Inherent Rhythms in East and Central African Instrumental Music." *African Music Society Journal* 3, no. 1 (1962): 33–42.

————. "Recording and Studying Music in Northern Mozambique." *African Music Society Journal* 3, no. 3 (1964): 77–100.

Kunst, Jaap. *Music in Java, Vols. I and II.* First published in 1949. The Hague: Martinus Nijhoff, 1973.

265

Kuper, Hilda. *The Shona and Ndebele of Southern Rhodesia.* London: International African Institute, 1955.

Laurenty, J. S. *Les Sanzu du Congo.* Tevuren, Belgium: Musée Royal de L'Afrique Centrale, 1962.

Liebermann, Fred. "Working with Cents: A Survey." *Ethnomusicology* 15, no. 2 (May 1971): 236–42.

Livingstone, Charles, and Livingstone, David. *Narrative of an Expedition to the Zambesi and Its Tributaries, 1858–64.* London: John Murray, 1865.

Lord, Albert B. *A Singer of Tales.* Cambridge: Harvard University Press, 1960.

MacDonald, Rev. Duff. *Africana,* vol. 1. London: Simpkin Marshall and Company, 1882.

MacIver, David Randall. *Mediaeval Rhodesia.* New York: Macmillan, 1906.

Maes, J. "Sculpture décorative ou symbolique des instruments de musique du Congo Belge." *Artes Africanae,* no. 7, (1937): 1–19.

Maraire, Dumisani. *The Mbira Music of Rhodesia.* Booklet and record. Seattle: University of Washington Press, 1971.

―――. "Nyunga-Nyunga Mbira Music." Manuscript, University of Washington, Seattle, 1969.

Mason, Philip. *The Birth of a Dilemma.* London: Oxford University Press, 1958.

Mauch, Carl. *The Journals of Carl Mauch, 1869–1872.* Translated by F. O. Bernard. Salisbury: National Archives of Rhodesia, 1969.

Mensah, Atta Annan. "The Music of Zumaile Village, Zambia." *African Music Society Journal* 4, no. 4 (1970): 96–102.

Merriam, Alan P. *African Music on LP: An Annotated Discography.* Evanston: Northwestern University Press, 1970.

―――. *The Anthropology of Music.* Evanston: Northwestern University Press, 1964.

Montandon, Dr. Georges. "La Généalogie des instruments de musique et les cycles de civilisation." *Archives Suisses d'anthropologie générale* 3, no. 1 (1919).

Murphree, Marshall W. *Christianity and the Shona.* New York: Humanities Press, 1969.

Nketia, J. H. Kwabena. *African Music in Ghana.* Evanston: Northwestern University Press, 1963.

―――. *The Music of Africa.* New York: Norton, 1974.

Nurse, G. T. "Cewa Concepts of Musical Instruments." *African Music Society Journal* 4, no. 4 (1970): 32–36.

Posselt, F. W. T. "Chaminuka the Wizard." *Native Affairs Department Annual* 4 (1926): 35–37.

Ranger, T. O. *Revolt in Southern Rhodesia, 1896–97.* Evanston: Northwestern University Press, 1967.

Roumeguère-Eberhardt, J. "Pensée et société Africaines." *Cahiers de l'homme* N.S. 2 (1963): 63–76.

Samkange, Stanlake. *Origins of Rhodesia.* London: Heinemann, 1968.

Selous, Frederick. *Travel and Adventure in South-East Africa.* First published 1893. Bulawayo: Books of Rhodesia, 1972.

Snowden, A. E. "Some Common Musical Instruments Found Among the Native Tribes of Southern Rhodesia." *Native Affairs Department Annual* 15 (1938): 99–103.

―――. "Some Common Musical Instruments Found Among the Native Tribes of Southern Rhodesia (continued)." *Native Affairs Department Annual* 16 (1939): 72–75.

Söderberg, Bertil. "Ornamentation of the Sansa." *African Arts* 5, no. 4 (Summer 1972): 28–32.

Summers, Roger. *Inyanga.* London: Cambridge University Press, 1958.

Theal, George McCall. *Records of South-Eastern Africa.* Capetown, 1901.

Thiermann, David. "The Mbira in Brazil." *African Music Society Journal* 5, no. 1 (1971): 90–94.

Thompson, Donald. "A New World Mbira: The Caribbean Marimbula." *African Music Society Journal* 5, no. 4 (1975/6): 140–48.

Tracey, Andrew. "The Family of the Mbira." *Zambezia* 3, no. 2 (1974): 1–10.

―――. *How to Play the Mbira (DzaVadzimu).* Roodepoort, South Africa: The International Library of African Music, 1970.

―――. "The Mbira Music of Jege A. Tapera." *African Music Society Journal* 2, no. 4 (1961): 44–63.

―――. "The Matepe Mbira Music of Rhodesia." *African Music Society Journal* 4, no. 4 (1970): 37–61.

―――. "The Original African Mbira?" *African Music Society Journal* 5, no. 2 (1972): 85–104.

―――. "Three Tunes for 'Mbira dza Vadzimu.' " *African Music Society Journal* 3, no. 2 (1963), 23–26.

―――. "The Tuning of Mbira Reeds." *African Music Society Journal* 4, no. 3 (1969): 96–100.

Tracey, Hugh. "A Case for the Name, Mbira." *African Music Society Journal* 2, no. 4 (1961): 17–25.

―――. *Chopi Musicians.* London: Oxford University Press, 1948.

―――. "The Mbira Class of African Instruments in Rhodesia (1932)." *African Music Society Journal* 4, no. 3 (1969): 78–95.

―――. "Measuring African Scales." *African Music Society Journal* 4, no. 3 (1969): 73–77.

―――. *Ngoma.* New York: Longmans, Green, 1948.

―――. *The Sound of Africa Series, vol. I.* Roodepoort, South Africa: International Library of African Music, 1973.

Trowell, Margaret, and Wachsmann, K. P. *Tribal Crafts of Uganda.* London: Oxford University Press, 1953.

Wachsmann, Klaus, and Kay, Russell. "The Interrelations of Music Forms, and Cultural Systems in Africa." *Technology and Culture* 12, no. 3 (1971): 399–413.

Wood, J. G. *Through Matebeleland.* National Archives of Rhodesia, 1893. Hist. Mss. WO 1/4/1: entry for 8 July 1887.

Woollacott, R. C. "Pasipamire—Spirit Medium of Chaminuka and the

267

'Wizard' of Chitungwiza." *Native Affairs Department Annual* 11, no. 2 (1975): 154–67.

Young, Robert W. *A Table Relation: Frequency to Cents.* Elkhart, Indiana: C. G. Conn, 1952.

Zemp, Hugo. "Musique Dan." *Cahiers de l'homme* N.S. 11 (1971): 115–18.

Discography: Shona Mbira Music

BERLINER, PAUL
The Soul of Mbira. Nonesuch Records (H-72054): field recordings of
   mbira dzavadzimu, njari, matepe, and *karimba*-type mbira.
Shona Mbira Music. Nonesuch Records (H-72077): field recordings
   of *mbira dzavadzimu* (featuring *Mhuri yekwaRwizi*).
TRACEY, HUGH
The Music of Africa Series. Musical Instruments 2. Reeds (Mbira)
   Kaleidophone Records (KMA-2): field recordings of *mbira
   dzavaNdau* and *njari.*
Rhodesia I. Kaleidophone Records (KMA-8): field recordings of
   mbira dzavaNdau, njari, and *kalimba.*
MARAIRE, DUMISANI
The African Mbira. Nonesuch Records (H-72043). Featuring solo
   performance on the *karimba*-type mbira.
Mbira Music of Rhodesia. University of Washington Press, Seattle.
   Featuring solo performance on the *karimba*-type mbira.
African Story Songs. University of Washington Press, Seattle. Featur-
   ing solo performance on the *karimba*-type mbira.
The Kaleidophone Records mentioned here consist of selections that
originally appeared in "The Music of Africa" series of the Inter-
national Library of African Music. Recordings of various types of
Shona mbira are on the Library's Series: "The Sound of Africa"
(albums: Tr 85, Tr 91, Tr 172, Tr 174, Tr 175, Tr 176, Tr 205,
Tr 211, Tr 212, and Tr 213) and "The Music of Africa" (albums:
16 Galp 1041, 26 Galp 1321, and 28 Galp 1323).

Films

The following series of films on Shona mbira music have been produced by Andrew Tracey of the International Library of African Music and Gei Zantzinger of the University Museum, University of Pennsylvania:
1. "Mbira: The Technique of the Mbira dza Vadzimu." Approximately 20 min.

    Introduces the musical technique and sound of the *mbira dza-Vadzimu*, performed by Ephat Mujuru.
2. "Mbira: Mbira dza Vadzimu: Religion at the Family Level." Approximately 60 min.

    Features Gwanzura Gwenzi hosting a *bira* at his village home.
3. "Mbira: Mbira dza Vadzimu: Urban and Rural Ceremonies." Approximately 45 min.

    Features Hakurotwi Mude at an urban *dandaro*.
4. "Mbira: Mbira dza Vadzimu: Dambatsoko, an Old Cult Centre." Approximately 40 min.

    Features Muchatera Mujuru and various aspects of traditional Shona religious life.
5. "Mbira: Njari: Simon Mashoko's Traditional and Church Music." Approximately 35 min.

    Features Simon Mashoko as a performer of traditional music for the *njari* and a composer of liturgical music for the Roman Catholic Church.
6. "Mbira: Matepe dza Mondoro: A Musical Healing Party." Approximately 20 min.

    This film features Saini Murira, and includes an enactment of a traditional healing party.

A more detailed description of the films appears in the *African Music Society Journal* 5, no. 4 (1975/6): 161.

These films can be obtained for rental or purchase through the Psychological Cinema Register Catalog, Audio-Visual Services, 17 Willard Building, Pennsylvania State University, University Park, PA. 16802.

Index

Accentuation: in interaction between *kushaura* and *kutsinhira*, 91, 94; in creating variations, 108, 144; in distinguishing musicians' styles, 153

Acculturation: adoption of guitars and banjos, 21, 219–220; adoption of Western music concepts, 24, 219; adoption of English terms, 61, 94; challenge to mbira players, 146, 209–210, 217, 225, 226, 238, 239–240; adoption of European dress, 200; adoption of Western drums, 244. *See also* Christianity

Acoustic properties: of mbira, 129; of house where *bira* held, 195

Aerophones, 21–22

Ambira, 9n, 28

Ancestor worship: among Lemba, 2, 34n; among Shona, 186–187. See also *Bira*; Religion and mbira music

Ancestors: role in learning mbira, 86–87, 136–138; role in relationship of mbira player to mbira, 235–239

Angola, mbira in, 9–10, 14

Archeological finds of mbira, 28

Audience: perception of mbira music, 73, 78, 90, 110, 111, 163; participation at *bira*, 113, 130, 160, 190, 195, 197; response to mbira music, 115, 133–134, 158; response to *kudeketera*, 160–161, 166, 169–172, 176, 177, 179, 180

Baines, Thomas: paintings of 19th century mbira, 15, 29, 38, 135, 153n

Bandambira, Mubayiwa: field research with, 3–7; on various musical matters, 33–34, 56–59, 78, 94, 135n; model for mbira players, 139; as child prodigy, 151; reputation at *bira*, 199, 221; biographical sketch, 231, 231n, 232–233

Bandambira, nickname, 44, 152–153, 216, 231–232

"Bangiza", 222

Banibus, Pasipamire's teacher, 213

Bantu-speaking peoples, 18

Banya, 188, 189; acoustics of, 195

Baroque music, 88

"Baya wabaya", 82, 84

Beatrice, 30, 219, 220, 221

Beer: parties, 115; for ritual use, 188, 190, 196, 197–198; halls, 220, 238

Bent, Theodore, 41

Benzi, 58

Bindura, 30–31

Biographical sketches of mbira players, 207–233

Bira: background and function, 23, 187–190, 198, 205, 228–229, 230–231; performance of mbira players, 95, 108, 145, 149, 150, 152, 233, 238; *kudeketera* performance, 115, 160, 173, 179, 182, 184, 185, 192; interaction among participants, 187, 195–199; dance, 192–194; consultation with medium, 202–205; in biographical sketches of mbira players, 208, 209, 211, 212–213, 214, 215–216, 217, 218, 222, 223, 226, 228–229, 230, 231; music of, 190–191, 191n, 192–194, 194n, 195–200; former attendance restrictions, 226–227, 228; professional opportunities for mbira players, 235, 244; sex taboos, 237; rebirth of interest in, 242. *See also* Medicine and mbira music; Religion and mbira music; Spirit mediums; Spirit possession

Blacksmith, 28, 29, 41, 45, 59, 59n, 69, 71–72, 140, 229

Boers, 20

Bohera, 214

Bows, musical, 21, 25

Brazil, mbira in, 17

Bridewealth, 230, 231

British Commonwealth, 20

Bula, mbira player, 17n

Bulawayo, 23, 30, 210–211, 242

Buzzing mechanisms of mbira, 10, 11– 271

273

278

090248